Herman Amberg Preus (1825–1894), about 1867.
(Courtesy of Herman and Florence Preus.)

Vivacious Daughter

Seven Lectures on the
Religious Situation Among
Norwegians in America

by

Herman Amberg Preus

Edited and translated with an Introduction

by

Todd W. Nichol

1990

The Norwegian-American Historical Association

NORTHFIELD • MINNESOTA

This volume is dedicated to

HERMAN AMBERG PREUS (b. 1896)

DAVID WALTER PREUS (b. 1922)

MICHAEL ROGNESS (b. 1935)

grandson, great-grandson, and great-great-grandson of the author;
ministers of the Evangelical Lutheran Church in America;
colleagues in the faculty of Luther Northwestern
Theological Seminary.

FOREWORD

In 1973 the Association published as volume eight in its Travel and Description Series the narrative of travels among Norwegian immigrants and the Koshkonong parish journal of J. W. C. Dietrichson, a pioneer Norwegian Lutheran pastor in Wisconsin in 1844–1850. Dietrichson returned to Norway before the founding in 1853 of the immigrant church, generally known as the Norwegian Synod, which Herman Amberg Preus spoke for in his "Seven Lectures on the Religious Situation Among Norwegians in America" delivered in Norway in 1867. The two men, however, shared a Lutheran orthodox faith and social and educational background, and in the documents they produced illustrated the process of transfer and adjustment of a religious tradition, though at a more advanced stage when Preus directed the attention of his Norwegian audience to the religious situation among their compatriots in America. The demands of the American environment—the crudeness of life in the West and the unique religious and political circumstances, all of which encouraged a sense of unbridled freedom and independence—as well as conflicting Lutheran positions, distanced the immigrant church Preus represented from the theological thought and church practices of the state church of the homeland, as under difficult conditions it sought a viable and distinct Lutheran identity in America based on biblical and confessional orthodoxy.

The Association is pleased to publish *Vivacious Daughter* as volume eleven in this series; it is a skillful and well annotated translation of Preus's "Seven Lectures." In addition to presenting the rather ponderous nineteenth-century Dano-Norwegian style used by Preus in a readable and accurate English rendering, Todd W. Nichol provides a thoroughgoing introductory essay that places the lectures in the context of theological controversy in the Norwegian-American community and within the religious traditions of America. With a fresh and insightful approach Nichol documents a persistent influence of Norwegian-American Lutheran orthodoxy and piety on American Lutheranism from the pioneer days until the present time and thereby demonstrates the vigor of the Lutheran tradition Preus and his fellow believers sustained and advocated as the only pure doctrine of their faith. By inference the situation described in the present volume becomes a commentary on the process of the transfer of immigrant cultures in general.

Todd Nichol is Assistant Professor of Church History at Luther Northwestern Theological Seminary in St. Paul, Minnesota, specializing in the history of American Christianity and American Lutheranism. He has published many articles and two books in his field and is currently engaged in a study of the theological training of Norwegian-American Lutheran pastors.

Finally, I wish to acknowlege with much appreciation the dedicated and competent assistance of Mary R. Hove, my resourceful and friendly helper in the editorial work for the past ten years, in preparing the manuscript for publication. As in past volumes, she is also responsible for the index.

ODD S. LOVOLL
St. Olaf College

ACKNOWLEDGMENTS

I owe many people thanks for help in editing and translating Preus's "Seven Lectures." As always, the community at Luther Northwestern Theological Seminary has provided an atmosphere congenial to historical research. Chief librarian Norman Wente spares nothing to meet the needs of the seminary faculty, and reference librarian Ray A. Olson is equally generous with his skill and his time. Faculty secretary Bobbi Smith produced an immaculate typed draft of the translation in an early form as well as the original rendering of the charts appearing in the present volume. Emeritus professors Eugene L. Fevold, Herman A. Preus, and Paul G. Sonnack provided important suggestions along the way. Colleagues Roy A. Harrisville and Walter C. Sundberg read and commented at length on the introductory essay. Professor Gracia Grindal introduced me to the sketches of Linka Preus, two of which appear among the illustrations of the present volume. The archivist of Luther Northwestern Theological Seminary and of Region III of the Evangelical Lutheran Church in America, Paul A. Daniels, answered numerous questions about the material in his care. From photographs in their personal possession, emeritus professor Herman A. Preus and Florence Preus kindly provided other illustrations. I thank these colleagues and friends, as I do President David L. Tiede and Dean Daniel J. Simundson for their encouragement of scholarship.

In addition to the editor of the Norwegian-American Historical Association, two other members of the faculty of Saint Olaf College lent their erudition to this project. Emeritus professors

Howard V. Hong and E. Clifford Nelson answered questions about translation and the historical background respectively. August Suelflow, director of the Concordia Historical Institute in St. Louis, Missouri, lent his expertise on matters related to the history of the Missouri Synod, as did Roy A. Ledbetter of the Institute staff. Archivist Duane Fensterman of Luther College in Decorah, Iowa, kindly provided illustrative material touching on the early history of that school. Archivists Chester Johnson and Edi Thorstensson of the Lutheran Church Collection and the archives of Gustavus Adolphus College were hospitable and knowledgeable guides to the collections in their care and provided access to important materials on the early history of the Augustana Synod. I thank all of them.

It is also a privilege to thank the government of Norway for a grant from the Emigration Fund of 1975 which made research in that country possible during the early summer of 1984. The Royal Ministry of Foreign Affairs did everything in its power to make that stay pleasant and fruitful. Johanna Barstad of the University Library in Oslo was a splendid guide to the resources at her command and members of the staff of the same institution courteously answered several queries by mail, as did Niels Kr. Høimyr of Det norske Misjonsselskap.

Finally, thanks are due to Odd Lovoll, editor of the Norwegian-American Historical Association, and to his assistant, Mary Hove. No one could ask for more encouraging, demanding, capable, and friendly editors. Professor Lovoll urged translation of the "Seven Lectures" and, as they took shape in English, has consistently offered wise and learned advice. I am very grateful to him.

TODD W. NICHOL
Luther Northwestern Theological Seminary
Saint Paul, Minnesota
Ash Wednesday, 1990

NOTE ON THE TRANSLATION

Herman Amberg Preus published *Syv Foredrag over de kirkelige Forholde blandt de Norske i Amerika* in two forms. The lectures appeared serially in Gisle Johnson's *Luthersk Kirketidende* in the summer and fall of 1867 (Vol. 9, numbers 1–10, 12–13, 16–17) and in the form of a small book printed on commission with Jac. Dybwad of Christiania in the same year. The present translation is based on the latter text.

Other than the challenge to construe and translate into contemporary English Preus's lengthy nineteenth-century sentences, the text presents no unusual difficulties. While usually clear and direct, Preus was not an elegant stylist, and I have tried to resist the temptation to make him write smoother English than he did Norwegian.

Only one technical term invites comment: *kirkesamfund*, literally "church association" or "church body." Preus, like other Norwegian Americans of the day, used an often colorless vocabulary. They sometimes, for example, called Luther College their *universitet* or "university," but more often referred to it as their *læreanstalt* ("teaching institution"). They showed the same preference for a bland terminology with respect to the church and its structures. Yet in the instance of the words they chose to describe their church, they also displayed their theological convictions. It is, for example, revealing that Preus does not customarily use the term *sogn*, or "parish," reflecting the life of the established, territorial church in Norway. He prefers the term *menighed*, or "congregation," emphasizing the gathering of Christians in their local assemblies rather than a geographical or hierarchical identity. Preus is similarly reluctant to use the term *church*, heavily freighted with theology and European history as it was for him, to describe the Norwegian Synod. He generally prefers to speak of *synoden*, "the synod," or *kirkesamfund*, "church association," instead of "the church." Since the rendering of *kirkesamfund* as "church association" neither bears enough of the meaning Preus assigns to the Norwegian term nor lends itself to idiomatic English, I have usually used "church body" instead. In certain respects the term "denomination" would communicate the theological reserve implicit in Preus's choice of words, but I have avoided it on the ground that it would be anachronistic regularly to put this word into his mouth.

I have omitted several passages from Preus's Norwegian text in the translation. These include series of prooftexts from Luther, classical Lutheran writers, and the Lutheran confessions; appended material from other sources; and brief references to matters of only ephemeral interest. In every case, these omissions are mentioned in notes at the appropriate place in the text. In one instance I have transposed a passage to an appendix. Preus printed the entire constitution of the Norwegian Synod in the text of the first lecture. In the present volume a translated version of this document appears in Appendix I.

CONTENTS

———————

Vivacious Daughter

INTRODUCTION

B y the time of the American Civil War relations between the
Church of Norway and Norwegian Lutherans in the United
States were sorely strained. Rejecting the age-old pattern of
establishment obtaining in the Lutheran lands of Europe, many immigrant pastors considered the Norwegian church lax in doctrine
and practice, while ecclesiastics in Norway often regarded the
several Norwegian Lutheran bodies in the United States as frac-
tious and doctrinaire. This conflict was aggravated by the desperate need for pastors in the pioneer settlements and the failure of the
authorities in Norway to send the needed supply of clergymen. It
is unlikely that anyone felt the tension between the old and the new
churches more acutely than the immigrant pastor and church president, Herman Amberg Preus.

Late in 1866 Preus returned to Norway for a stay of several
months. He took this visit as an opportunity to portray the situation of the immigrant church to those who had remained behind.
Although Preus had much to say of competing denominations
among the Lutherans of North America, he felt it most important
to explain the history of his own church body, the Norwegian Synod. In view of the desperate need for pastors to work among the
Norwegian immigrants then flooding into North America, Preus
thought his mission urgent. At the same time, he faced a formidable
apologetic task, since it was already apparent that this lively
offspring of the Church of Norway in the American Midwest was
of a different spirit than its sedate parent.

In order to explain circumstances in America to the Norwegian

3

audience and to recruit pastors for the church across the sea, Preus delivered a series of seven lectures in the Norwegian capital during the spring of 1867. Those who heard him may well have been startled by his sketch of church life in the United States, already so different from what they knew in Norway. Knowing how dramatic the comparison between the two churches would be, Preus began his remarks with a plea for sympathy toward the immigrant church: "Forget that, like a more vivacious daughter, she may not be as demure and considerate as her mother, and that—clad in weakness as the bride of Christ always is on earth—she also has some bad habits because she feels so free and is not yet used to her freedom. My friends! She is still the inwardly beautiful bride of Christ whose life is hidden with Christ in God. That you, too, may hold her dear I intend in these lectures to show you this bride of Christ in her true light." A telling remark, it spoke volumes about the situation among Norwegian-American Lutherans in America and reflected the direct, vigorous character of the young pastor who stood before them.

Herman Amberg Preus (1825–1894)

Herman Amberg Preus was born in Kristiansand, Norway, on June 16, 1825, and grew to maturity there in the family of his mother and father, Anne Rosine Preus (née Keyser) and Paul Arctander Preus.[1] Grandson of a bishop of Kristiansand and nephew of distinguished Norwegian clergymen, the young Preus was from his earliest years shaped by the Lutheran piety of his forebears. He was at the same time imbued with a respect for learning; his father was a schoolmaster and through his mother he was related to several of Norway's leading academics. It was therefore natural that as a boy he was enrolled in Kristiansand's cathedral school. His godfather, Herman Amberg, was rector of that institution, and among its faculty was Ole Christian Thistedahl, who inculcated into his students a strenuous biblical literalism, a strict Lutheran orthodoxy, and a severe pietism.

Preus began his studies at Royal Frederik's University in Christiania (now Oslo) in 1843. There he studied with his uncle, Christian Keyser, and his colleagues of the theological faculty, Jacob F.

Dietrichson and Jens M.P. Kaurin. In his last year at the university he attended the lectures of Carl Paul Caspari, who had brought a conservative German Lutheran confessionalism to this moderate Norwegian faculty. Preus also heard lectures on the philosophy of religion by M.J. Monrad and took courses in dogmatics and ethics from Gisle Johnson, not yet a professor in the university, but already lecturing in the capacity of a *stipendiat*. The revival of church life associated with the name of Gisle Johnson, however, still lay some years in the future when Herman Preus sat among his students.[2]

In December of 1848 Preus took his final examination at the university and graduated *laudabilis*. For three years thereafter he taught at both the royal military school and Nissen's Latin school in Christiania. In the spring of 1851 the young schoolteacher accepted a call from three immigrant congregations in Wisconsin and was ordained to the Lutheran ministry by Bishop J.L. Arup. Along with his wife "Linka," his cousin Caroline Dorothea Margrethe Keyser, whom he married the same spring, Herman Amberg Preus left Norway for the United States on May 24, 1851. After a strenuous journey of more than two months the young couple arrived at their new home in Spring Prairie, Wisconsin, in August of 1851.[3]

Preus threw himself into the work of a pastor with abandon, eventually taking as many as ten congregations into his care and regularly traveling thirty-five hundred miles a year on visits to Norwegian congregations throughout the Upper Midwest and elsewhere.[4] He did not, however, confine his labors to work in these congregations. Even before leaving Norway in 1851, he had read of the formation in the United States of the Norwegian Evangelical Lutheran Church, and, when this body convened in 1853, Preus took the lead in calling for its dissolution and the framing of a new constitution. Regarding certain features of the first constitution as inconsistent with a true Lutheran understanding of the nature of Scripture, Preus persuaded the assembly to adopt a document reflecting his own increasingly rigorous Lutheran confessionalism. On the basis of this new constitution, the Norwegian Evangelical Lutheran Church in America (Den norsk-evangelisk-lutherske Kirke i Amerika) came into being in October of 1853. Later known as the Synod for the Norwegian Evangelical Lutheran Church in America, or more simply as the Norwegian Synod or the Old Synod, this body reflected the spirit and convictions and personality of

Linka Preus (1829–1880), about 1867. (Courtesy of Herman and Florence Preus.)

Herman Amberg Preus, who served as a member of its church council from 1853 until 1894; as editor of its church periodical from 1861 to 1868; and as its president from 1862 to 1894. Like its pioneer leader, the Norwegian Synod was conservative in doctrine, effective at organization, and aggressive in its mission to Norwegian-American Lutherans.[5]

Contemporaries recalled Herman Preus as an able administrator skilled at adapting European patterns to the American context. Yet he did not lead the Norwegian Synod in the interests of expediency alone. A biblical literalist and a confessional purist, Preus was unbending in defense of what he took to be the dictates of Scripture and confession. He was, as one historian said, "orthodox to his very fingertips."[6] A forceful personality and his commitment to what he conceived of as Lutheran orthodoxy made him sharp and uncompromising in debate, and friend and foe alike often winced under his cutting rhetoric.[7] It is, indeed, as president of the Synod and controversialist that he is most often remembered by encomiasts and critics alike. While hagiographical, a description by one contemporary, who belonged to another Norwegian Lutheran synod often scored by Preus for false doctrine, has the ring of authenticity to it: "His noble and symmetrical physique, his fine abilities, and varied acquisitions will always secure for him the high respect of every intelligent mind. In disposition he combines gentleness with a certain resoluteness and inflexibility, characteristic of his nationality, which rarely fails to influence those who approach him. He is strictly conscientious even in apparently minute matters, and as a pastor he has ever been rigid toward himself, full of sympathy for the poor, the sick, and the suffering, and totally forgetful of himself, when he heard the voice of his duty."[8]

Well educated and an able debater, Preus was not primarily a man of letters. When he put pen to paper it was generally to prosecute the business of the Synod or to enter into theological polemics. The pages of the Synod's journals and its regular reports were filled year after year with official communications, controversial articles, responses to opponents, reviews, and commentary written in his often hasty, sometimes ponderous style. Characteristically, the most extensive theological treatise he published, *Professorerne Oftedals og Weenaas's "Wisconsinisme" betragtet i Sandhedens Lys* ("Wisconsinism" by Professors Oftedal and Weenaas reviewed in the light of truth) is a cut-and-thrust response to a polemical attack on the Norwegian Synod by theologian August Weenaas.[9] This piece, like his earlier "Seven Lectures on the Religious Situation Among Norwegians in America," reflects Preus's immersion in the affairs of the immigrant synod to which he devoted his life. Although a man of parts, he had neither the leisure nor the bent to pursue more substantial works in theology or history.

It is not surprising that Herman Amberg Preus was away from home on the business of the Norwegian Synod when he died on July 2, 1894. "I have devoted to it the best days of my youth," he had said of his struggling immigrant church almost thirty years earlier in his addresses of 1867, "and, so long as the Lord preserves me, I will consecrate to it the energies of my manhood." That vow kept, his thoughts turned to the Norwegian Synod as he lay dying. "Greet my congregations!" and "Greet the brethren!" were among his last words.[10]

The "Seven Lectures"

In its early years the Norwegian Synod repeatedly sent appeals to the Church of Norway for pastors to work among the burgeoning immigrant population in the United States. One such request was, for example, issued in 1860 over the signatures of all the clergy of the Synod.[11] In desperate straits, the tiny church resolved in the same year to send one of its pastors, Laur. Larsen, to make their appeal in person. Larsen traveled to Norway that year, but his efforts met with little success. During the course of his visit, however, he delivered lectures on Norwegian-American Lutheranism in the form later adopted by his childhood friend and ministerial colleague, Herman Amberg Preus. Larsen's lectures strike several themes upon which Preus and other Norwegian Americans would later play variations: the sacrificial spirit of the pioneers, the virtues of the free church, purity of doctrine, and the challenge of the frontier for young ministerial candidates.[12]

Although Larsen's work in Norway brought only a few candidates for the ministry to American shores, several other ministers from the immigrant church made similar attempts only to meet the same disappointment. It may, then, have been in a pessimistic frame of mind that Herman Preus conceived his "Seven Lectures" in 1867. Caustic passages in these addresses and elsewhere indicate plainly the bitterness of the young Norwegian-American pastors at the neglect of the mother church toward the immigrant diaspora in the United States.[13]

Herman Preus had not, however, traveled to Norway only to recruit pastors for the Synod. Troubled by lingering illness in 1866, Preus had been urged by the Church Council of the Norwegian Synod to travel to Norway for the sake of his health. With the permission of his congregations, he left Wisconsin on August 14, 1866.[14] The family traveled first to Cleveland, Ohio, where Preus took part in a district meeting of a German-American Lutheran body, the Missouri Synod, with which the Norwegian Synod had closely allied itself. Following this meeting, he took his family by way of Buffalo and Niagara Falls to New York City, arriving on August 26th. An account of his work there appears in the "Seven Lectures." From New York, the Preus family sailed for Bremen on November 8 and arrived in Christiania, after traveling through Hamburg, Copenhagen, and Sweden, on December 17th. Shortly thereafter, the family

8

Kirkelig
Maanedstidende
for den norsk-evangelisk-lutherske Kirke i Amerika.

| Mai 1866. | Redigeret af Pastorerne H. A. Preus og J. A. Ottesen. | 11te Aarg. No. 9-10. |

Uddrag af Reiseberetning til Kirkeraadet fra H. A. Preus.

Efter Opfordring af vor almindelige Präste-Konferents forlod jeg den 14de Aug. mine Dyrebares Menigheder for over Cleveland at begive mig til New York. I Cleveland, hvor jeg nöd vor kjäre Architekt, H. Grieses, Gjestevenskab, önskede jeg nemlig at bivaane Missourisynodens midtre Distriktssynodes Forhandlinger. Efter en lykkelig Fart over Buffalo og Niagara ankom jeg ved Guds Beskjärmelse i god Behold til New York Löverdagen den 26de Aug. Her blev jeg med megen Kjärlighed modtaget af Hr. Danckel og Familie, i hvis Huus jeg havde min Bolig, og hvis opofrende Gjestevenskab jeg nöd under mit ganske Ophold i New York. Samtidig med min Ankomst til denne Stad holdt Missourisynodens östlige Distriktssynode sit Möde; det blev mig saaledes forundt at höste Nytten af Deltagelsen ogsaa i dets Forhandlinger. Her er ikke Stedet videre at indgaa paa disse; de vare tidssvarende og saare lärerige; de dreiede sig fornemmelig om, hvorvidt Skriften med dens Vidnesbyrd kan väre os et tilforladeligt og fuldständigt Bevis for Kristendommens Sandhed. Svaret löd naturligvis bejaende. Jeg maa dog ved denne Leilighed udtale min hjertelige Tak for den Kjärlighed og Velvilje, hvormed jeg ogsaa denne Gang blev mödt af de kjäre Missouribrödre saavel ved Synodemöderne, som ved flere andre Leiligheder under denne min Reise.

Förend jeg nu begynder at skildre den religiöse Tilstand saaledes, som jeg fandt den blandt Skandinaverne i New York, maa jeg gaa lidt tilbage i Tiden, og omtale, hvad der har väret gjort for at opbygge et luthersk Zion blandt vore Landsmänd der. Ligesiden de kirkelige Forhold begyndte at ordne sig i Vesten, har

Title page of Kirkelig Maanedstidende, 11 (May, 1866). "An Extract of a Report on his Travels to the Church Council from H. A. Preus," this article gives an account of the family's journey to New York and of the situation there.

set out again to go to Frederikshald to celebrate Christmas with his father and an aged aunt, both in ill health. After arriving in Frederikshald, Herman Preus became seriously ill himself, recovering just enough to talk with his eighty-eight-year-old father only a few days before he died and to deliver a funeral sermon to the household. It was not until the end of January that the physician attending the younger Preus would allow him out of bed. When he was able to travel again, he planned to visit Christiania, and perhaps did so, at the time of the annual market fair in February to visit with prospective candidates for the ministry in America.

By spring Preus had recovered his health sufficiently to deliver a series of public addresses in Christiania, the "Seven Lectures on the Religious Situation Among Norwegians in America." He may also have delivered some or all of these essays elsewhere in Norway.[15] His aim in preparing these lectures, presented in Christiania over the course of nearly a month, from the end of May through the third week of June, was twofold. He intended, first, to give an account of the Norwegian-American church to a Norwegian audience. Some Norwegian ecclesiastics had by this time come to think of the Norwegian Synod as brittle and contentious in its orthodoxy, and many Norwegians had no informed conception at all of the situation of the church in the United States. Preus's second purpose was to recruit candidates for the ministry of the Norwegian Synod. To this end he took the biblical summons of the Macedonian to Paul the apostle as the theme of his lectures: "Come over and help us!"[16] In the effort to recruit candidates for the ministry of the Synod he seems, however, to have met no more success than had his colleague, Laur. Larsen.[17]

Who may have assisted Preus in sponsoring the lectures is not known. It is possible that Sven Bruun, pastor of Trinity Church and a prominent minister in the city, and Professor Gisle Johnson may have had a hand in making these arrangements. They are known certainly to have been advocates of the Synod in its effort to obtain pastors from Norway.[18] Reports in the Christiania press indicate that the lectures were delivered in the mission house of the Norwegian Mission Society (Det norske Misjonsselskap) at number 72 Akersgaten.[19] This may indicate that the society itself sponsored the lectures, although no mention of them has been uncovered in its records.[20]

When the lectures were completed, Gisle Johnson published

10

Syv Foredrag

over

de kirkelige Forholde blandt de Norske

i

Amerika.

Af

H. A. Preus,

Pastor.

———— ⟶⟵ ————

Christiania.
I Kommission hos Jac. Dybwad.
Trykt hos H. J. Jensen.
1867.

Original title page of the "Seven Lectures."

them in his journal, *Lutbersk Kirketidende*, and the Norwegian publisher Jacob Dybwad also made them available in the form of a small book sold on commission.[21] The present translation is based on the latter text. In addition to several polemical pieces, Preus later published two sequels to the "Seven Lectures" in *Lutbersk Kirketidende*.[22]

The "Seven Lectures" evoked relatively little comment in Christiania's newspapers, but Preus's presence in the country did arouse renewed criticism of the Norwegian Synod.[23] Preus personally occasioned a minor controversy when he attacked a Norwegian pastor, Ole Larsen Domaas, for false doctrine. In response to two sermons by Domaas, one a Sunday address in Our Savior's Church (Vor Frelsers Kirke) in Christiania and the other at the funeral of a well-known clergyman, Preus accused Domaas of holding a semi-pelagian theological position and for teaching that the dead in heaven intercede for the living on earth.[24] As important to Preus as his criticism of the substance of Domaas's teaching, however, was his insistence that the Norwegian cleric had introduced theological innovations without basis in Scripture. These charges occasioned a polemical exchange in the pages of *Lutbersk Kirketidende* that began with an article by Preus appearing on September 15, 1867, the day he left Norway to return to the United States.[25] The debate continued for some time across the Atlantic, with the last word coming from Preus in 1870.[26] In his own summation of this controversy, Preus identified what he took to be the "shibboleth of true Lutherans": an insistence that "the Holy Scripture is the only and highest rule and norm for faith and doctrine."[27]

The exchange with Domaas aptly illustrates the paramount importance attached by the founders of the Norwegian Synod to their doctrine of Scripture. Profoundly influenced by the grammatical literalism of Christian Thistedahl, all of them left Norway before the historical-critical study of the Bible had been introduced into the Royal Frederik's University in Christiania. They were, therefore, deeply committed to an understanding of the Scripture worked out in the seventeenth century by the Lutheran scholastics and repristinated in the nineteenth century by confessional conservatives opposed to modern innovations in Christian theology. Life on the American frontier, in turn, only confirmed these pastors in a passionate commitment to the doctrine of the verbal inspiration of Scripture and its literal inerrancy.[28] On the basis of these fundamental convictions about the Bible, and influenced by a pietism that pervaded even the most confessional circles in the Church of Norway, the immigrant leaders of the Norwegian Synod recreated the Lutheran tradition in a new situation. Free of European precedent, they took as their motto a single Greek phrase: *Gegraptai*, "It is written." The conviction that Scripture, verbally inspired and literally inerrant, was the touchstone of Christian life and practice lent a consistent integrity to the life of their church. It was on the basis of this belief and the collateral conviction that the Lutheran confessional documents are a true interpretation of Scripture that the pioneer pastors of the Norwegian Synod worked out a sense of denominational identity in the United States. As they did this, they reckoned as well with their Norwegian inheritance, the American social context, other Scandinavian-American Lutherans, and Lutherans of different ethnic traditions.

The Norwegian Inheritance

In the fourteen years which had elapsed between the Synod's founding in 1853 and Preus's lectures in 1867, the immigrant church had differentiated itself from the Church of Norway to a startling degree. Indeed, as the "Seven Lectures" allows us to see, the pastors and people of the Norwegian Synod were remarkably innovative in their approach to church life. They were, in fact, so effective in the work of establishing a new order on the other side of the Atlantic that strained relations quickly developed between the American church and its European parent. It was not until well into the twentieth century, after the Norwegian Synod had merged with two other bodies to form the Norwegian Lutheran Church of America (Den norske lutherske Kirke i Amerika) in 1917, that entirely cordial relations were established between the Church of Norway and the Norwegian Lutheran Church of America.

Distance, the passing of time, vastly altered circumstances, and the inevitable transition to the English language created predictable differences between Norwegian Lutherans in Norway and in the United States, but the evolution of the Norwegian Synod cannot be explained by reference to these factors alone. From their earliest years in the United States, the architects of the Synod aimed to create in the United States a Lutheranism purified of errors they ascribed to the influence of the territorial patterns of state control pertaining in the Lutheran churches of Europe. They were, in short, foes of the "state church" polity characteristic of Lutheranism in Europe and ardent advocates of the "free church" arrangement obtaining in the United States.

Although hostile to the principle of establishment favored by Puritan divines, the immigrant leaders of the Norwegian Synod resembled the early New Englanders in their determination to renew and complete a Reformation they thought had been aborted by the accidents of European history. To this end, like the Puritans, the founders of the Norwegian Synod practiced a rigorous intolerance of anything they conceived of as backsliding error, whether in theology or in practice. They recognized in the American civil regime an opportunity to build a church authentically Lutheran in doctrine and polity and immune to meddling by civil authorities. America, to put it another way, offered them an occasion to reform and renew the Lutheran tradition as they could not in Europe. It is not, then, surprising that like their Puritan predecessors they often spoke of their church in biblical accents as a city set on a hill. What have we done here in the Midwest, H.G. Stub, who later became the last president of the Norwegian Synod, asked his hearers in an address celebrating the four-hundredth anniversary of Luther's birth? We have, he answered, built a "Lutheran Zion."[29]

The opportunity to build a church on the American frontier allowed the founders of the Norwegian Synod to resolve a centuries-old problem at once distinctively Lutheran and European: how to contain the revolutionary theology proposed by the Lutheran Reformers in the traditional forms of piety, polity, and practice favored by Lutherans. America offered these young Lutherans an opportunity to resolve this dilemma, by permitting them to be at once conservative and innovative. They were conservative in that they referred their questions, without necessarily consulting European precedent, to the formal norms of Lutheran theology: Scripture and confession. They were innovators when they applied their findings to the task of building a church without unreflective deference to European tradition. The result of this new venture was a church at once strongly traditional and surprisingly novel in form.

The conservatism of the founders of the Norwegian Synod is plainly evident in their approach to worship. One cannot think of them without seeing in the mind's eye the long black gown and the starched white ruff of the Norwegian pastor, often carried across the prairies in saddlebags and worn rumpled from packing and unpacking. While they might easily have abandoned the elaborate usage of the parent church, they were scrupulous in the preservation of most Norwegian liturgical customs. Yet even in these things, the founders of the Synod were self-consciously reformatory, as Preus's discussion of confessional practices in the "Seven Lectures" clearly indicates. Here, as in much else, the pastors of the Norwegian Synod took America as an opportunity to restore what they thought of as proper Lutheran practice over against Norwegian latitude. Their preference for older as opposed to newer Lutheran rites and customs is crucial to understanding their convictions in these matters. In the synodical constitution of 1867, for example, they recommended liturgical texts from the seventeenth century, the *Ritual* of 1685 and the *Alterbog* of 1688, rather than more recent liturgical formularies influenced by the rationalism of the eighteenth and early nineteenth centuries.[30] This tendency is also reflected in their prescriptions for pentitential practice. At the same time, however, in their ways of worship as in so much else they displayed a considerable capacity for adaptation to American circumstances. Their devotion to catechesis for adults as well as children is an instance of their intention to elaborate a church order appropriate to a new situation, and with passing time the inheritors of this tradition adjusted their liturgical practices even more dramatically to the new context.[31]

It is perhaps in the area of church polity that the innovative spirit of the founders of the Norwegian Synod is most immediately apparent. In this matter they found precedent in both the Bible and the Lutheran confessional tradition for a quick adjustment of their inheritance to the demands of the American context. Indeed, they swiftly became expert denominationalists. In this effort a renewed study of the Lutheran theological tradition, the precedent set by the Missouri Synod, whose German founders had arrived on the scene considerably before the Norwegians, exposure to American religious pluralism, experimental common sense, and pietist impulses united to produce a polity strictly Lutheran in its theological rationale and, in practical terms, well suited to the American scene.

In devising a polity for their synod, the founders of the Norwegian Synod placed both authority and power to determine their membership in the hands of the congregations. Where baptism

15

alone had been sufficient for membership in the Church of Norway, the pioneer pastors provided for a rigorous examination of the faith and life of applicants for membership in their congregations and required the congregations or congregational councils to vote on the admission of prospective members. In these things the congregations of the Norwegian Synod, at least in the ideal, resembled the gathered churches of Lutheran pietism and the American Reformed tradition rather than the territorial parishes of European Lutheranism. Preus's marked preference, when speaking of the Norwegian Synod, for the terms *menighed* ("congregation") as opposed to *sogn* ("parish") and *kirkesamfund* (literally "church association" or "church body") rather than *kirken* ("the church") are in this instance revealing. His modest vocabulary is a matter of theology rather than accident. It reflects an ecclesiology cautious about identifying the hidden church of God with the visible historical structures of particular Christian churches.

In other matters as well, considerable authority and power were vested in the local congregations. Consistently with Lutheran theology, which teaches that the church fully exists where the Word of God is preached and where the sacraments are administered, the Synod's first pastors recognized the local congregations as complete and authentic expressions of the life of the church. At the same time, however, they provided for a synodical organization in which the congregations could cooperate in a variety of matters they could not undertake alone. Among the functions assigned to the larger body and its president was the oversight of the congregations, but like their Norwegian and Swedish counterparts in other synods the founders of the Norwegian Synod, after careful and repeated consideration, rejected the episcopate with which they were familiar, providing instead for the regular election of a presiding officer for their new synod. In practice, both the synod and the clergy exercised considerable power in the life of this immigrant church, but its strongly congregational, democratic polity assured that its active laity would make its weight felt as well. The polity created by the immigrant pastors who might have ordered their common life otherwise was, in the last analysis, strongly democratic and relied on the active participation of the laity for its success.

Examples of both conservatism and innovation in the life of the Norwegian Synod might be multiplied. They would, however, only reinforce the perception of an immigrant church at once conservative and innovative in its elaboration of a new way of life.[32] In light of the experience and convictions of the pioneer pastors of the Norwegian Synod, it is not surprising that relations between the Church of Norway and its American offspring, which coveted the good will of the ancestral church less than it did its freedom to embody a pure Lutheranism in the United States, were difficult in the early years and never entirely easy.

The American Context

The "Seven Lectures" are remarkable for their lack of emphasis on Norwegian ethnicity. While the immigrant pastors of the Norwegian Synod pursued their work almost entirely among Norwegian immigrants and usually in the Norwegian language, they did not finally count their ethnic identity as essential to the preservation of their religious tradition. Because the needs of the immigrant population were so great, these pastors simply assumed that their work would be largely confined to their own people. They generally understood the need for the immigrants to assimilate into the American culture and for an eventual transition to the English language. Perhaps even more important, they were almost immediately ready to cross ethnic lines in search of ecclesiastical alliances with other like-minded Lutherans, and their history records that they found their best friends not among other Scandinavians but among the German Americans of the Missouri Synod.

Preus was unabashed in identifying himself as an American citizen to the Norwegian audiences that first heard the "Seven Lectures" and he gave evidence of a keen understanding of the society he had adopted as his own. The American culture may, in fact, have had a stronger grip on his spirit than he himself knew. While he is blunt in criticizing American materialism and the frenetic speculation characteristic of life on the frontier, he cannot himself resist describing in detail the college building recently raised by the Synod in Decorah, Iowa, in characteristically American terms, devoting special attention to the dimensions of the intentionally grand, thoroughly modern building of which the people of the immigrant church were immensely proud.

On a deeper level, however, Preus displays a nuanced under-

17

standing of the place of religion and the Christian churches in the American context. While the version of Lutheranism that he had embraced even before leaving Norway disposed him to a preference for the free church, he had also quickly discovered both the possibilities offered to the Christian churches on the American scene and the nature of the restrictions placed upon them. He had discovered, for example, that the price exacted of the churches in America for their freedom is their support of the civil regime guaranteeing this privilege as well as an endorsement of the moral consensus undergirding the political order. He had also, as already mentioned, learned the advantages of an ecclesiastical polity corresponding in some measure to the civil polity of the nation and that of its local jurisdictions.

Preus and his colleagues had, further, entered into the most enduring problem of American nationality: the coexistence of various races under one civil regime which favored the racial majority. Preus says little about Native Americans in the "Seven Lectures," although he was much aware of them as were all white settlers in the Upper Midwest in the middle of the nineteenth century. Passing remarks elsewhere indicate that he was not easy in conscience about the treatment meted out to the natives of the land by white pioneers and that he considered missionary work among them as inadequate recompense for their treatment at the hands of the settlers.[33] In spite of these considerations, he did not dwell on the fundamental question of the morality of the white settlement of North America.

He had, however, pondered the implications of black slavery at length. Along with other leaders of the Norwegian Synod, Preus took the stand that slavery in and of itself was not sinful. In this he displays the disposition of the Synod's pastors to pursue the study of theology and the articulation of doctrine in abstract terms. Like the other pastors who stood with him, Preus was appalled by the historical institution of chattel slavery as it existed in the United States and favored its legal abolition. In spite of this he continued to maintain that the Bible does not condemn but rather endorses the institution of slavery in and of itself. Fully aware that this would arouse controversy among the constituents of the Synod, united in their aversion to slavery as it had been practiced in the United States, varying in their political opinions, and inclined in traditional Lutheran fashion to obedience to civil authority, the pastors of the

18

Synod (with the exception of Claus Lauritz Clausen, whose role in this matter Preus discusses at length in his "Seven Lectures") considered themselves obliged to take this position in virtue of their commitment to the inspiration of Scripture. In this instance, the leaders of the Synod chose what they conceived of as theological integrity over adaptation to the milieu of the northern states in which nearly all of their people had settled. Not surprisingly, controversy over this question dogged them for years after the peace at Appomattox.

The young captains of the Norwegian Synod selectively put themselves at a distance from the American culture in less dramatic ways as well. In the name of Lutheran doctrine, for example, they objected to the theology and practice of Anglo-American sabbatarianism, insisting that the observance of Sunday was not a matter of divine institution but a freely chosen Christian ordinance for the sake of proper worship of God. Similarly, they objected to American public schools for their children. They understood immediately that the public schools of the United States were the temples of its culture and, in the nineteenth century, centers for the unofficial propagation of the tenets of a generic Anglo-American Reformed Protestantism. In view of this, the pastors of the Norwegian Synod proposed the creation of a system of Lutheran schools for their young people. While they were concerned for the preservation of the Norwegian culture and language, their most fundamental commitment in this cause was the propagation of pure Lutheran doctrine among the children of their church. The vision of an enclosed, independent system of schools for the children of the Synod was never, however, fully realized. The constituency of the Synod was in the end unwilling to support both public and private schools and generally favored public education for its children. In this as in a multitude of other matters, the pioneer leaders of the Norwegian Synod took a considered position based on their identity as confessional Lutherans rather than on Norwegian ethnicity, their cultural inheritance from Europe, the will of their constituency, or an inclination toward outright approval or disapproval of the American culture.[34] That is not certainly to suggest that these factors were insignificant to the founders of the Norwegian Synod. These things were, however, strictly subordinated to their effort to establish in the United States a Lutheranism pure in doctrine and practice.

North American Lutheranism

The "Seven Lectures" are an invaluable historical resource not least for the glimpse they offer into the formation of several Norwegian-American Lutheran denominations. The volatile pluralism characteristic of the Church of Norway in the middle of the nineteenth century quickly expressed itself among the Norwegian Lutherans who came to the United States, producing a number of competing denominations among the settlers. With its sharply articulated doctrinal position, its cadre of able and dedicated clergy trained in Norway, and its steady growth, the Norwegian Synod seemed for a time destined to outstrip them all in its ability to gather the immigrants into its fold. Given to theological polemic and for that reason prone to division, however, the Synod was from its earliest years a cynosure of controversy and eventually suffered a schism which deprived it of its preeminent position in the immigrant community. That event, however, was still some years in the future when Herman Amberg Preus delivered these lectures in Christiania in 1867.

In its early years the Norwegian Synod was more inclined to controversy with Lutherans of other bodies than to internal debate. On one flank stood a group of Norwegian-American pietists under the leadership of Elling Sunve Eielsen who organized the Evangelical Lutheran Church in North America (Den evangelisk-lutherske Kirke i Amerika), or the Eielsen Synod as it was usually called, in 1846.[35] This synod represented in the United States the ardent, moralistic piety springing from the revival in Norwegian church life associated with Hans Nielsen Hauge. In controversy with the so-called "Ellingians," the Norwegian Synod defended the need for an orderly church life, the prerogatives of the ordained ministry, Norwegian liturgical usages, the study of theology, and orthodox doctrine. The Eielsen Synod, on the other hand, advocated a highly selective approach to church membership, lay activity, and the need for repentance and conversion among nominal Christians. Although devoted to Luther's Small Catechism and the *Explanation* of the catechism by Erik Pontoppidan, Eielsen was little interested in doctrinal theology.[36] A running conflict between the two synods contributed to the sharp articulation of denominational identity in both groups and in the end probably contributed to the widening and deepening of differences among Norwegian-American Luthe-

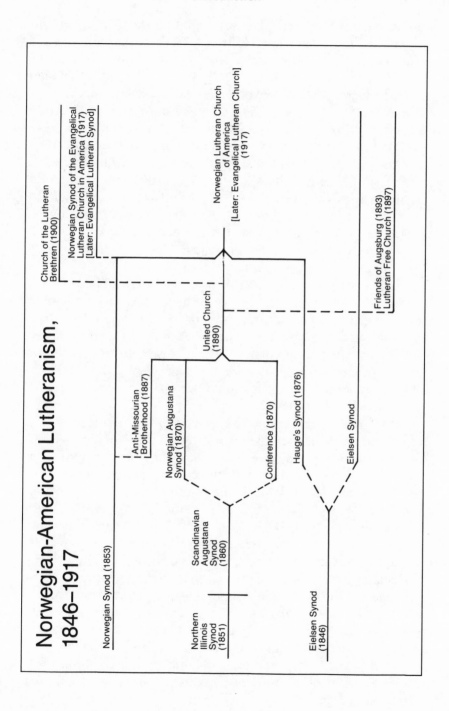

Norwegian-American Lutheranism, 1846–1917

Norwegian Synod (1853)

Church of the Lutheran Brethren (1900)

Norwegian Synod of the Evangelical Lutheran Church in America (1917)
[Later: Evangelical Lutheran Synod]

Anti-Missourian Brotherhood (1887)

Norwegian Augustana Synod (1870)

Northern Illinois Synod (1851)

Scandinavian Augustana Synod (1860)

Conference (1870)

United Church (1890)

Norwegian Lutheran Church of America (1917)
[Later: Evangelical Lutheran Church]

Hauge's Synod (1876)

Eielsen Synod

Friends of Augsburg (1893)
Lutheran Free Church (1897)

Eielsen Synod (1846)

rans, some of which were never resolved. Like the Norwegian Synod, the Eielsen Synod later suffered a serious schism, with the majority of its members leaving Eielsen's side to form the Hauge's Synod (Hauges norsk evangelisk lutherske Synode) in 1876 and another small group continuing on under the synod's original name.[37]

On the flank opposite the Ellingians stood the Scandinavian Augustana Synod (Den skandinaviska Augustana evangelisklutherska Synoden), a group originating in the connection of several Scandinavian pastors and congregations with an American body, the Synod of Northern Illinois. Organized in 1860, the Scandinavian Augustana Synod included Swedes, Norwegians, and Danes.[38] It was primarily, although not solely, with the Norwegian contingent in this synod that Preus was concerned in the "Seven Lectures." It was only later, when the Norwegians and Danes of this body amicably parted company with the Swedes in 1870, that the Augustana Synod became a primarily Swedish-American body. While the Swedes formed one homogeneous church after this separation, the Norwegians who withdrew from the Scandinavian Augustana Synod formed two separate bodies, the small Norwegian-Danish Augustana Synod (Den norsk-danske Augustana Synode) and the larger Conference for the Norwegian-Danish Evangelical Lutheran Church in America (Konferentsen for den norsk-danske evangelisklutherske Kirke i Amerika).[39]

At the time Preus delivered his lectures in Christiania, then, the Scandinavian Augustana Synod included both Norwegians and Swedes as well as a small number of Danes. In controversy with the Augustana Synod, however, the ethnic factor played only a small role. In the heat of this strife, Preus argued in the pages of *Kirkelig Maanedstidende* that the Norwegian pastors of the body were more unorthodox than its Swedish clergymen.[40] The concern of the Norwegian Synod in this controversy was with polity and theology rather than nationality. Of the several topics controverted between the Augustana and Norwegian Synods, the most significant issues to the leaders of the Norwegian Synod were questions of church order and the doctrine of absolution.[41] To Preus and the other theologians of the Norwegian Synod, as the "Seven Lectures" indicates, the constitution of the Augustana Synod displayed alarmingly hierarchical tendencies inappropriate to a Lutheran church. At the same time, the pastors of the Norwegian Synod criticized the Augustana Synod for laxity in doctrine. In an extended controversy over the meaning of absolution, the theologians of the Norwegian Synod were particularly concerned to emphasize and defend the objective reality (*væsen*) of the Scriptural word of forgiveness as distinct from its effect (*virkning*) in the heart of the believer. The Augustanans, they believed, were unclear about this and had thus compromised not only the objective reality of the Word of God, but the doctrine of grace as well.[42]

This conflict, acrimonious and not without an overtone of denominational competition, nevertheless clearly illustrates the emergence of definite identities on the part of the contesting parties. The Augustana Synod, on the one hand, embodied the mild confessionalism and heartfelt piety of the Scandinavian revivals of the nineteenth century as well as a church polity that placed considerable power and authority in the hands of the clergy and the synod. The Norwegian Synod, on the other hand, took this controversy as an occasion to emphasize again its concern for the objectivity of Christian truth and to defend its strongly congregational, democratic approach to church polity. As in the case of the conflict with the Ellingians, this controversy hardened and deepened divisions within the immigrant community, producing as it did a heightened sense of denominational identity in the contending synods.

Probably more important to the Norwegian Synod's development than its controversies with other Scandinavian synods was its friendship with the Missouri Synod, a German-American body formed in 1847, strictly conservative in doctrine, congregational in polity, and observant in practice.[43] As the "Seven Lectures" makes clear, the bond between the Missouri Synod and the Norwegian Synod was warm and affectionate. C. F. W. Walther, Missouri's leading theologian, is rightly listed among the fathers of the Norwegian Synod, and he returned the affection of those whom he called "my dear Norwegians."[44] An oral tradition records that Walther had a special liking for Herman Amberg Preus, whom on first meeting he is said to have called "ein determinerter Kerl"—"a determined fellow."[45] The association with the Missouri Synod demonstrates once again that doctrinal convictions proved stronger than the ethnic factor in the development of the Norwegian Synod's sense of Lutheran identity. The continuing history of the Norwegian body indicates that in both theology and practice the Norwegians learned much from Missouri, although this alliance also

23

cost them dearly in the eyes of the Norwegian laity, who were often profoundly suspicious of the German-American Lutheran synod. It was the Norwegian Synod's decision to educate its clergy at the Missouri Synod's Concordia Seminary in St. Louis that was indirectly responsible for the slavery controversy among the Norwegians, some of whom suspected the Missourians of southern sympathies. Pressure from the constituency of the Norwegian Synod to end this cooperative arrangement with Missouri eventually led to the decision on the part of the Norwegians to establish Luther College in Decorah, Iowa, and its own seminary, first located in Madison, Wisconsin, and finally moved to St. Paul, Minnesota. The "Seven Lectures" gives us a glimpse of some of these events as they were occurring.

The connection with Missouri was also responsible for drawing the Norwegian Synod into an extended controversy in the 1880s over the arcane mysteries of the doctrine of predestination.[46] While the principal contestants in this controversy were two German-American bodies, the Missouri Synod and the Ohio Synod, the Norwegian Synod eventually found itself divided between those who favored Missouri's position in the debate and those who took a different position, based on Erik Pontoppidan's *Explanation* of Luther's Small Catechism, a book familiar to generations of Norwegian Lutherans.[47] When reconciliation among the Norwegians appeared impossible, about one third of the pastors and congregations of the Norwegian Synod separated from it to form the Anti-Missourian Brotherhood (Det antimissouriske broderskab) in 1887. This body eventually united with the Norwegian Augustana Synod and the Conference for the Norwegian-Danish Evangelical Lutheran Church in America to form the so-called United Norwegian Lutheran Church in America (Den forenede norsk lutherske kirke i Amerika) in 1890.[48] Another result of the controversy over predestination was the Norwegian Synod's eventual withdrawal from the Evangelical Lutheran Synodical Conference, a federation of conservative Lutheran synods organized at the prompting of the Missouri Synod in 1872. The Norwegian Synod nevertheless retained its affection for Missouri until 1912 when the several Norwegian-American synods settled their controversy over the doctrine of election and permanently forfeited the friendship of the Missouri Synod which did not endorse this settlement, or *Opgjør*.[49]

George Henry Gerberding, an English-speaking Lutheran belonging to the largely eastern General Council of the Evangelical Lutheran Church in America founded in 1867, was likely right when he remarked that "the Missouri straight jacket never did and never could fit the free Norwegian back," but the long friendship between the Missouri and the Norwegian synods nevertheless played an important role in the course of Norwegian-American Lutheran history.[50] In its association with Missouri, the Norwegian Synod was reinforced in its inflexible biblical literalism, its confessional rigor, its predilection for doctrinal controversy, and its congregational polity. Through the influence of the Norwegian Synod, in turn, these traits were conveyed to and corroborated throughout the whole of Norwegian-American Lutheranism. When the three largest Norwegian-American churches—the United Church, the Conference, and the Norwegian Synod—united in 1917, Hans Gerhard Stub of the Norwegian Synod was elected first president of the new Norwegian Lutheran Church of America (Den norsk lutherske Kirke i Amerika), and inheritors of the Synod's traditions played a prominent role in the life of that church through its history of fifty-three years. A group of congregations and pastors of the Norwegian Synod which refused to enter the union of 1917 separated to form the "Norwegian Evangelical Lutheran Church in America" in 1918. Claiming the heritage of the Norwegian Synod as its own, this small group, sometimes referred to as the Little Norwegian Synod, later changed its official name to become the Evangelical Lutheran Synod and continues to the present its effort to represent faithfully the traditions of its parent body.[51]

In 1960–1963 the Norwegian Lutheran Church of America (renamed the Evangelical Lutheran Church in 1946) merged with several other bodies to form the American Lutheran Church and once again the heritage of the Norwegian Synod played an important role. The events and attitudes that produced this development were anticipated almost one hundred years earlier in the "Seven Lectures" of 1867. In his addresses, Preus is sharply critical of the Lutherans belonging to the largely eastern General Synod of the Evangelical Lutheran Church in the United States of America, formed in 1820, and the General Council of the Evangelical Lutheran Church in America, then in process of formation. This latter Lutheran body merged with two other groups, the General Synod and the United Synod of the Evangelical Lutheran Church in the South founded in 1863, to form the United Lutheran Church in America

Forming the American Lutheran Church

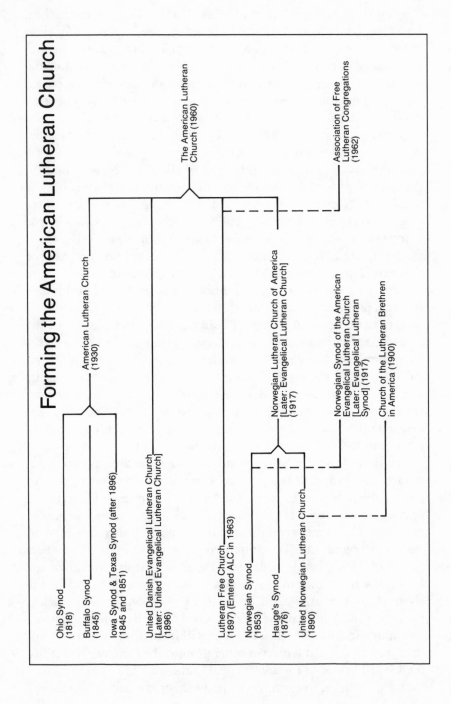

Ohio Synod
(1818)

Buffalo Synod
(1845)

Iowa Synod & Texas Synod (after 1896)
(1845 and 1851)

American Lutheran Church
(1930)

United Danish Evangelical Lutheran Church
[Later: United Evangelical Lutheran Church]
(1896)

The American Lutheran
Church (1960)

Lutheran Free Church
(1897) (Entered ALC in 1963)

Norwegian Synod
(1853)

Hauge's Synod
(1876)

United Norwegian Lutheran Church
(1890)

Norwegian Lutheran Church of America
[Later: Evangelical Lutheran Church]
(1917)

Norwegian Synod of the American
Evangelical Lutheran Church
[Later: Evangelical Lutheran
Synod] (1917)

Church of the Lutheran Brethren
in America (1900)

Association of Free
Lutheran Congregations
(1962)

in 1918.[52] Due in part to the historical position of the Norwegian Synod already evident in the "Seven Lectures" and even more apparent in the sequel to it published in 1868, relations between the United Lutheran Church in America and the Norwegian Lutheran Church of America were always marked by caution and often strained by antagonism.

Severe toward the General Synod and the General Council, Preus is more moderate in his attitude toward other groups including the Evangelical Lutheran Joint Synod of Ohio and Other States constituted in 1818; the Synod of the Lutheran Church Emigrated from Prussia (more often known as the Buffalo Synod) organized in 1845; and the Evangelical Lutheran Synod of Iowa and Other States founded in 1854.[53] Of these primarily German-American synods Preus is at once approving and critical, noting a generally conservative tendency among them but raising significant questions about their theology and polity as well. It was, however, with these groups that Norwegian-American Lutherans would eventually ally themselves. When the Norwegians broke with Missouri over the doctrine of predestination, they turned away intentionally from the primarily eastern bodies and toward the cultivation of better relations with these German-American synods that had also been embattled with Missouri and were preparing to enter into a merger of their own. In 1930 the Buffalo, Iowa, and Ohio synods merged along with the very small Texas Synod organized in 1851 to form the American Lutheran Church of 1930, often called the "Old" American Lutheran Church to distinguish it from its namesake, the American Lutheran Church formed in 1960–1963.[54] Shortly after the formation of the "Old" American Lutheran Church, the Norwegian Lutheran Church of America and three other synods, including the Lutheran Free Church, a Norwegian-American body organized in 1897 which stood outside of the Norwegian union of 1917, joined it in forming a federative organization, the American Lutheran Conference.[55]

During the negotiations that led to the emergence of the American Lutheran Conference, Hans Gerhard Stub, last president of the Norwegian Synod and first president of the Norwegian Lutheran Church of America, played a key role. Stub had been instrumental in turning the attention of the Norwegian Synod away from a preoccupation with predestination in the 1890s and in focusing it on the doctrine of the inspiration of Scripture, and it was at Stub's insistence that a statement on the verbal inspiration of Scripture was written into the theological statement adopted by the bodies forming the American Lutheran Conference as their common confession of faith.[56] During the thirty-four year history of the Conference, T.F. Gullixson, another inheritor of the traditions of the Norwegian Synod and a protegé of Stub's, emerged as a leading figure in its deliberations on theological questions and denominational politics.[57]

When four of the churches of the American Lutheran Conference united to form the American Lutheran Church in 1960–1963, Gullixson played a key role in preparing its confession of faith and creating its polity.[58] It was at the instance of Gullixson and likeminded colleagues, for example, that the American Lutheran Church included in its constitution a statement first written by H.G. Stub in 1925: "The American Lutheran Church accepts all the canonical books of the Old and New Testaments as a whole and in all their parts as the divinely inspired, revealed, and inerrant Word of God, and submits to this as the only infallible authority in all matters of faith and life."[59] Similarly the influence of the Norwegian Synod is apparent in the polity provided for the new body, perhaps most obviously in its designation of the national church as a "union of congregations."[60]

For a century and more Lutherans of the synods that formed the American Lutheran Church repeated arguments advanced in the "Seven Lectures" and its sequels against the bodies — including the United Lutheran Church, the Augustana Evangelical Lutheran Church, and two smaller denominations — which united to form the Lutheran Church in America in 1962, charging these groups with hierarchical tendencies in polity, laxity in doctrine, and unwarranted latitude in practice. Conflict over these matters among American Lutherans continues to the present. Open debate, latent tension, and regional diversity within the Evangelical Lutheran Church in America formed in 1988 as a result of the merger of the American Lutheran Church, the Lutheran Church in America, and the Association of Evangelical Lutheran Churches can be explained in part as consequences of historical factors mentioned in the "Seven Lectures." While Herman Amberg Preus and the Norwegian Synod were by no means alone in creating the distinct variant of the American Lutheran tradition reflected in these addresses to a Norwegian audience, the "Seven Lectures" are striking early evidence of the formation of a strongly midwestern tradition that continues to influence the unfolding history of American Lutheranism.

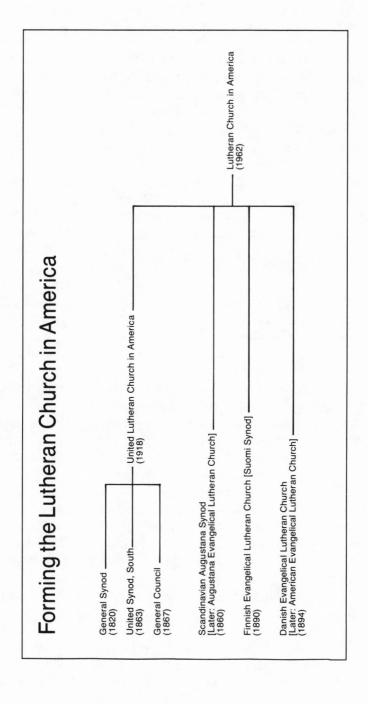

Forming the Lutheran Church in America

General Synod
(1820)

United Synod, South
(1863)

General Council
(1867)

United Lutheran Church in America
(1918)

Scandinavian Augustana Synod
[Later: Augustana Evangelical Lutheran Church]
(1860)

Finnish Evangelical Lutheran Church [Suomi Synod]
(1890)

Danish Evangelical Lutheran Church
[Later: American Evangelical Lutheran Church]
(1894)

Lutheran Church in America
(1962)

A unique element in a welter of synods and churches, the Norwegian Synod exercised an influence out of proportion to its size on the history of American Lutheranism. Even in the present its traditions animate the Lutheran churches of North America. The Evangelical Lutheran Synod; a multitude of congregations of the Evangelical Lutheran Church in America; Luther College in Decorah, Iowa; and Luther Northwestern Theological Seminary in St. Paul, Minnesota, all bear its legacy in the present. When the question of Lutheran identity is essayed in these quarters today, echoes from the history of the Norwegian Synod can still be heard plainly.[61] Although their approach to theology has usually been tempered and shaped by the advent of historical criticism of Scripture and a new appreciation for the historical nature of all religious tradition, a lively passion for the objectivity of the truth and a participatory, democratic approach to church life remain characteristic of those who consciously or unconsciously inherit the traditions of the Norwegian Synod.

The "Seven Lectures on the Religious Situation Among Norwegians in America" offers modern readers a revealing look at the formative years of a denomination that played a distinct role in the history of an immigrant community and in the larger history of American religion as well. While much in these lectures is today of only historical interest, they reveal more that is important to the interpretation of Norwegian-American life and the continuing history of American Lutheranism. Among other things, they show us a religious tradition in a formative moment defining itself with scrupulous care over against an inherited European tradition, the American context, and denominational counterparts.

Orthodox and pietist, European and American, adaptive and confrontative, conservative and innovative, the Norwegian Synod was in many ways a puzzling study in contrasts. The "Seven Lectures" suggests, however, that its pioneer leaders built their church on the basis of theological convictions more important to them than any other factor in their efforts. It was the consistent integrity of their theology—however one may evaluate it from the perspective of the present—that made the often controversial Norwegian Synod so vibrant a presence in the Norwegian-American community. Whatever else the Norwegian Synod may have been, it surely was, as Herman Amberg Preus said to his Norwegian audience in 1867, a "vivacious daughter" of the Church of Norway in the United States.

Seven Lectures

on

The Religious Situation Among

Norwegians

in

America

by

H. A. Preus

Pastor

Christiania

On commission with Jac. Dybwad

Printed by H. J. Jensen

1867

LECTURE I[*]

M y esteemed audience! Before beginning these lectures I would like to express my regret that on this occasion our Norwegian Lutheran church body could not have had another more capable and talented spokesman to portray our body, its characteristics, and the conditions under which it works. If I venture to make the attempt myself it is because I deeply love this body. I have devoted to it the best days of my youth and, so long as the Lord preserves me, I will consecrate to it the energies of my manhood. I would gladly wish this fellowship to be an object of your fraternal love and sympathy here in this country. I cannot tell you how it has saddened me to witness so much here that convinces me we are instead an object of complete indifference, misunderstanding, even severe judgment. And yet it is your countrymen who settle and build, who labor and struggle far away in America's distant West. To be sure, they have departed from you and the land of their fathers, but does that deprive them of every right to fraternal sympathy? Is their very departure a crime over which any one

---

*Preus introduced the published version of his lectures with these words. "At the request of several people, I hand these lectures over to the printer knowing full well how much they leave to be desired in several respects. I do so, nevertheless, because I am convinced that they are not only faithful and truthful, but also a more complete and comprehensive presentation of our religious situation than any hitherto produced. I nourish the hope that, despite their deficiencies, they may be of use to those intending to make America their future home just as, I daresay, they will not be without interest to those of my countrymen who desire a closer acquaintance with our situation."

of you dares to set himself up as judge, a lapse which gives you the right to exclude them from participation in the communion of faith and its love? Most of your countrymen have brought the Word of Life to distant regions trodden before only by the feet of wild Indians. Now, by the grace of God, they are working there to build the Lord's temple. The more they feel alone in their work, the more they comfort themselves that in the old homeland there are many whom they may call brethren in faith. They, in turn, wish to be considered and regarded as such and to be united in the bond of faith and love though separated in the flesh. They wish also to find here brethren who will genuinely sympathize with them and, as much as possible, help them in their labor for the salvation of souls and the glory of God.

This is Jesus' bride whom he purchased with his blood, whom he still cares for and looks upon with deep love and mercy. Forget that, like a more vivacious daughter, she may not be as demure and considerate as her mother and that—clad in weakness as the bride of Christ always is on earth—she also has some bad habits because she feels so free and is not yet used to her freedom. My friends! She is still the inwardly beautiful bride of Christ whose life is hidden with Christ in God. That you, too, may hold her dear I intend in these lectures to show you this bride of Christ in her true light. At the same time, unfortunately, since the material is diffuse and diverse, I have often lacked the necessary documents and preparatory materials, and I have also been constantly interrupted. The lectures do not, therefore, appear in the form I might have wished and are sometimes no more than suggestive. I beg your friendly indulgence, and I hope that these deficiencies will not influence your judgment of our church body or hinder the achievement of my purpose in these lectures.

In order to do my part in winning capable, faithful collaborators in the Lord's vineyard across the sea, I would like to present a rather detailed picture of our situation. For a good many years the cry of our distress in the Norwegian Lutheran church body in America has been heard here, urging Norway's many unemployed theological students to come over and help supply our pulpits and take up the care of our spiritual needs.[1] We have, to be sure, extended ourselves to train the teachers we require, and our work to this end has not been without blessing. But those prepared for the ministry of the Word in our schools have not been enough to meet the great need. Partly because we are in arrears from earlier days and partly because emigration in recent years has been on so large a scale, we have not been able to hold our own. The need actually waxes rather than wanes. We have therefore continued to make public and private requests for Norwegian theological students to come over and help us. But it appears that fewer and fewer candidates have taken our cry and that of our congregations to heart and had pity on the thousands of souls in need. Fewer and fewer have heeded that cry and the pastoral call to preach the gospel of the Kingdom of God among their forsaken countrymen in the American West.

For the moment, I shall not allow myself a closer consideration of the reasons for this apparent indifference and insensitivity to the cries of brethren in faith by those equipped by God and called to meet the need where it is greatest and most obvious. One can imagine different reasons among different people. Naturally, I concede at the outset that some are excluded from consideration. There are some whose reasons are of such a kind that they are fully justified in not heeding the cry, but there are others whose reasons are just empty excuses, only rendering it clearer and more obvious that they lack or are greatly deficient in what is essential for theological students taught by God: a recognition of souls in need and an enthusiasm and a zeal to work, in spite of any kind of affliction and privation, for the salvation of souls and the glory of God. As I said, I shall not go into this or argue with the many excuses I hear. I want in all charity to reckon with only one cause and that is the total ignorance of the Norwegian-American situation—religious, geographical, and social—that I have so often met among Norway's theological students. It can hardly be denied that this ignorance has not infrequently been linked to misinformation on several counts and to one-sided judgments of our church body. Certainly I have met individuals who seemed to be right at home in our situation, but as a rule they are the ones who have already taken our cry of distress to heart and seized the opportunity always available to acquire the necessary information. Most are really as good as completely ignorant of our circumstances. In order to eliminate this excuse it has seemed advisable to me to convey as much information as I can about our situation. In this I comply with the many written and oral requests for this kind of report which I have received since my arrival.

Colonization

In order to help you, my listeners, better to orient yourselves to our situation I will first say a little something about the process of settlement.

As you know, the emigration had its real beginning in the year 1836, but it did not assume substantial dimensions until last year, during which it has been reckoned that more than 16,000 emigrants left for America. Certainly this year an equal if not greater number will depart. The number of registered emigrants, this year's included, can safely be estimated to be as high as 120,000. To this count must be added an uncertain number, mostly from the cities, who came over alone and who have planted themselves especially in America's larger cities. To recognize that their number is by no means insignificant, one need only consider that the number of Norwegians and Swedes in New York City alone amounts to 30,000. The total number of Norwegians who have emigrated to America can safely be estimated at 150,000. How large the number of Norwegians in America actually is at present cannot be precisely determined. Noting these things: 1) that the thirty- to forty-year-old age group has contributed most to the immigration, and 2) that easier employment allows the young to marry early in America, one would not be putting the count too high to estimate it at 300,000 souls.[2]

The first Norwegian colonies of the modern era were near Rochester, New York, and in Texas. Later the emigration went west, first around Fox River, Illinois, and the southern part of Wisconsin; then northward through Wisconsin up to Green Bay, Stevens Point, and the area north of St. Paul, Minnesota; after this through the northern and a bit of the central section of Iowa and over all of Minnesota, from Alexandria in Douglas county and St. Croix county in the north to Jackson county in the west.[3] Most recently—besides small settlements in Kansas, Missouri, Nebraska, and California—a goodly number of Norwegians have settled in the Dakota Territory, 500 to 600 English miles west of the Mississippi. It is very probable that the emigrant stream will flow in a westerly and southwesterly direction from Minnesota.[4]

The planting of a colony or settlement takes place as follows. The majority of our emigrants, chiefly composed of cotters (*husmænd*) or poorer farmers (*gaardbrugere*), land in Quebec or

New York. From there they go by railroad to Chicago, Illinois, or to Milwaukee, Wisconsin. Then they set out by various railroads or by steamship to go to family or friends living in the older settlements in Illinois, Wisconsin, Iowa, and particularly Minnesota. The newcomers stay with their families or friends three or four and as many as five years, some as hired hands, some as tenants. Some join whatever Norwegian congregations they find right after they arrive, but often they procrastinate for some years, a course from which they ought urgently to be dissuaded. When, by dint of hard work and the Lord's blessing, they have obtained a team of horses or oxen, a wagon, some cows, and enough money to get through the first year, they start to think about looking for their own homes in the Far West, up until now the haunt of Indians alone. Either a few men go out to find a new area fit for planting a Norwegian settlement, or they accept the direction and invitation of friends who in preceding years may have found a place and now want more people in order to make the settlement big enough to support both church and school. In both instances five or ten families get together to make a caravan, which, with its wagon covered in white canvas and filled with children and household paraphernalia, sets out in a long line on the "emigrants' trail" to the Far West.

The faster these Norwegian "pioneers" who begin planting new settlements succeed in getting friends and countrymen to follow them, and the larger the Norwegian settlements grow, the easier it is for them to acquire the spiritual benefits which they require as Norwegian Lutheran emigrants. It cannot be avoided that here and there a Yankee, a German, or an Irishman settles down among the Norwegians, and sometimes it happens that only a rather small settlement of Norwegians remains. Consequently there is sometimes spiritual trouble to contend with unless they are fortunate enough to have in the vicinity larger or smaller Norwegian settlements with which they can unite in establishing a parish.

As a rule, the Norwegians are known for their clever choice of good, usable land. They like to choose places where they can handily cultivate the fertile, woodless prairie and yet have sufficient timber and easy access to good water. Our countrymen also have a good reputation for industry, frugality, and honesty. Many of the emigrants, especially those who have left the cities of Norway in recent years, settle in New York or in one of the larger cities of the West. Thus it happens that besides those in New York and

Chicago—the New York of the West, counting perhaps 20,000 Scandinavians among its population—there are Scandinavian populations of over 1,000 in cities like Milwaukee, Madison, LaCrosse, Decorah, Red Wing, and St. Paul.[5] On the whole, though, relatively few of our common country folk choose the city.

So it is that our Scandinavians make their home in the western region of the New World. The Lord has blessed these orderly, industrious laborers in the harvest of America's rich earth.

Greater prosperity, neighborly contact, and intercourse with more refined families of other nationalities gradually have their effect on our countrymen, who might before have lived in the humblest circumstances and whose way of life may have been utterly wretched. Not only can he build a house of wood or stone in place of his first sod or log hut; not only can he live more amply, with his domestic affairs in better order; but he also feels an increasing need for more knowledge, for more cultural refinement, a need his greater prosperity and his free way of life open to him and make it possible for him to satisfy.

And yet, all these temporal advantages and benefits cannot meet his deepest needs and longings. Still less can this happen because these are Norwegians who from childhood on have had the opportunity to learn and know God's grace in the gospel and to enjoy the benefits and blessings of a proper church body. Granted that there is widespread ignorance and spiritual indifference among our common folk, but they have not yet—thank God!—been prey to stark infidelity, as unfortunately has been the case in many parts of Germany. On the other hand, among common Norwegians there is, alongside great spiritual indifference and apathy, only intensified by the ineffectiveness and immaturity of the congregations, an external respect for what is holy, a piety, and a tenuous adherence to the faith and doctrine inherited from their fathers. As a rule, the Norwegian immigrant in his new home in the American West wishes to have church, pastor, and school, as he is accustomed to them. But, wherever and whenever he lands and plants a new settlement, none of this is to be found. He can quite often be sure of finding himself next to or closely surrounded by some Yankees or Germans who feel the same religious need he does or who have already organized a church body. Partly because of linguistic differences, but even more because of doctrinal differences, there can be no talk of the Norwegian joining or cooperating in ecclesiastical matters with his neighbors. He

A coffee party at the Spring Prairie parsonage, early 1870s. With Linka and Herman Preus are their children, from left to right: Johan Wilhelm Keyser, Paul, Agnes Wilhelmine Rudolpha, Christian Keyser, Rosine Pauline Keyser. (Courtesy of Herman and Florence Preus.)

often has to live among Americans who have never been baptized and do not show the least interest in the church or the Word of God. On top of that, on arrival in his new home he sometimes discovers an American district school already underway, or he will soon get one started. But, principally because Christian instruction and discipline are excluded from these schools, he will not find in them the help he needs with the religious nurture of his children. Finally, there is a third element for us to consider. As a consequence of American civil polity, church and state are entirely separated. The state promises protection to all religious societies that do not violate the common moral code, but gives no support to any religious society whatsoever. The state leaves it to its citizens to see to their own religious responsibilities just as it leaves it to them to make their own arrangements and defray the costs.

If he is going to remain in the faith of his fathers, the Norwegian emigrant to the American West has to consider how, with God's help, he can organize a Norwegian Lutheran church body in his new home. To preserve the faith of their fathers for themselves and those who come after them, the Norwegian emigrants have had to take things into their own hands, dispose themselves into congregations, secure pastors, and build churches. In a word, they have had to take steps to meet all the exigencies of establishing and maintaining Norwegian Lutheran congregations in the Norwegian settlements.

The Norwegian emigrants took the business in hand. They arranged themselves into Lutheran congregations, they called pastors, they got religious schools underway, and the congregations united into a church body that bears the name "The Synod for the Norwegian Evangelical Lutheran Church in America" (Synoden for den norsk-evangelisk-lutherske Kirke i Amerika). This Synod, to which most of the Norwegians in America belong, will be the first topic for our consideration.

The Norwegian Lutheran Synod

The men who first took up the evangelist's task in America and founded the first congregations to make up the Synod were pastors Wilhelm Dietrichson and C. L. Clausen.[6] The latter, a Dane who received a call from the congregation in Muskego, Wisconsin, was examined and ordained by the German Lutheran Pastor [L. F. E.] Krause in Milwaukee.[7] The other, now parish pastor in Østre Moland, was, chiefly through the efforts of the late dyer [Peter] Sørenson, sent to America around 1843 by Christian friends to assist in ordering religious affairs among our countrymen.[8]

No one can deny that these men, whose efforts involved them in great trouble and adversity during this early period, deserve credit for their work and that God has granted his blessing to it. But we cannot deny that the blessing on their work would have been far greater had both of them not at that time been adherents of the Grundtvigian (the so-called "churchly") view.*[9] This circumstance, and especially Pastor Dietrichson's zeal for implanting in the con-

---

*Pastor Clausen later confessed before the Synod and recanted his Grundtvigian errors. [Preus's note].

gregations this view and other contemporary errors, gave Elling Eielsen and his faction nourishment and support.[10] It also awakened in many places a dislike and mistrust of the clergy, the aftereffects of which not only we teachers but our whole church body continue to suffer under in many ways up to the present time.

Although Pastor Dietrichson returned to Norway in 1850, the number of Norwegian pastors still increased that year with the arrival of pastors [H.A.] Stub and A. C. Preus.[11] The following year a first attempt was made at creating a Norwegian Lutheran Synod. Since the second paragraph [of the synodical constitution] containing the statement of the Synod's doctrine and confession was formulated to express Grundtvigian views, the synodical bond had to be dissolved in 1852 and a new draft for a synodical constitution prepared.[12] This was placed before the congregations for their approval and again revised at a meeting in Koshkonong the following year. Thus, in the year 1853 the Norwegian Synod was organized by the seven pastors and the score of congregations who accepted this synodical constitution.

It was, however, not long before we were convinced that this constitution needed significant improvement and, in several points, essential revision. When the constitution was drawn up we were all, pastors and lay folk, fresh from Norway and we were ignorant of how to organize congregations or a church body entirely independent of the state. It was natural for us to have some false and confused ideas of, for example, the relation of the individual congregation to the church, church governance, and church discipline. Accustomed as we were to the extensive blending of church and state, it was reasonable to expect that our ideas would be mixed up, too. So, for example, we granted a power and authority to the government of the church warranted only if it could have been backed by the exercise of civil authority! Since we were in practice following sounder principles than those laid down in our old constitution, we wished to undertake its revision as soon as it was feasible, but also to do as good a job as we could. After it was drafted by two committees, by the clergy in conference, and finally by the church council, an attempt at a new synodical constitution was placed before the Synod in 1865 and accepted. This constitution is now being examined by all of our congregations. After being again accepted by the Synod, which meets in June of this year, it will be in force among the congregations belonging to the Synod.[13]

Before I go into more specifics about the main features and characteristics of our synodical constitution, we will look in a little more detail at the external side of our church body's life.

The Size and Extent of the Church

When the Synod was founded in 1853, seven pastors served about forty congregations, of which only around a score belonged to the Synod. Our synodical association now numbers thirty-eight pastors with about 200 congregations, of which 160–170 have affiliated with the Synod. (A pastor who belongs to the Synod can also serve an orthodox congregation not belonging to the Synod.) These 200 congregations count about 35,000 confirmed members and an aggregate of souls probably reaching 70,000. Some pastors—[B. J.] Muus and [Thomas] Johnson in northwest Minnesota, for example—actually serve as many as thirteen to sixteen congregations.[14] These congregations can be up to 300 English or 40 Norwegian miles from each other; they can be reached only by horse and wagon.[15] These many congregations are dispersed through the following states: Wisconsin, Iowa, Minnesota, Illinois, Kansas, Dakota, New York, and Texas. The congregations in Kansas and Dakota have up until now been served by a pastor who lives in Chicago, 600 English miles away. The congregations in Texas, like the congregation in New York, are more than 1,000 English miles from Chicago and are visited by one of our pastors during the winter. One should note here that most of these congregations have just been organized, that everything has to be started from the ground up, that they have to learn to understand and use the power granted by God to congregations, and that often two of them are large enough to require the undivided attention and service of one pastor. Add to this the considerable work necessary on behalf of the entire church body devolving on a small number of the clergy. If you add all this up, it is easy to see that the Norwegian pastors in America are greatly overburdened with work, even though they are able to stretch themselves by doing only what is absolutely necessary for the edification, preservation, and growth of the congregations. That in consequence a number of our congregations are at present in great spiritual poverty ought to be obvious. Nor should one forget

42

Bernt Julius Muus (1832–1900), pastor of the Norwegian Synod, later to become founder of Saint Olaf College and a leader of the defecting Anti-Missourian Brotherhood in the 1880s.

that sizeable growth in congregations and souls alike is due to the exceedingly large emigration now taking place.

A good share of the work of our pastors is like that of missionaries. This is especially true of the pastors stationed on the frontier where the emigration is in full swing. Try to imagine it. One is called to the pastorate of six or seven congregations, all a good distance from one another. He begins work among them and thinks he has his hands full and can hardly cope with the burden on his shoulders. Then one fine day there arrives a letter or a deputation from a new settlement—it happens day after day. They explain to him that somewhere out there is a group of his countrymen without a pastor or spiritual care. They ask him if he would be so kind as to come out and visit them. He answers that he cannot handle the work of the congregations already in his charge and that he hardly knows how he could take them on too. Then they begin to describe their need to him. They have been there two, three, four, sometimes as many as seven years without a visit from a Norwegian Lutheran pastor. It may be that someone from one of the sects has visited them, but they do not wish to abandon the church in which they have been raised. In all these years they have not partaken of the Lord's Supper and many of them have children, some of them large, who are not baptized. With no one to preach to them and thus to teach, advise, and admonish them, a good many of our people have already grown indifferent to the Word of God and the church. Many of our young people who have grown up without proper Christian instruction are leading a life of idle dissipation. Indeed it can be heartrending to hear of it and even worse to see spiritual conditions in these places. They truly are sheep without a shepherd. It makes one thank God that there is someone left who knows how bad things are and calls for help.

My listeners! You may want to say that these are exceptions and no longer the rule. Well, let me tell you what I myself experienced not more than three or four years ago in Wisconsin. I had then, in addition to the president's office and the editorship of *Maanedstidende*, ten congregations to serve.[16] I was asked to visit a congregation fifty miles from my home. There were fourteen families who had lived there six or seven years without any spiritual ministration. For eight families I baptized thirteen children who were up to seven years old. Two of the women had not been confirmed, and the children were terribly neglected.

Congregational Organization

In those places the first task is to organize a congregation and put it in order. Procedures vary depending on whether time is plentiful or scarce and on the state of affairs among the people. Sometimes it happens as it did in New York: the pastor preaches a few times, administers baptism, and then gathers those individuals interested in the Kingdom of God and in whom he has reason to believe there is Christian earnestness. In association with them he works out the basic provisions for a Lutheran congregation; then he calls these men to a meeting in which they unite into a congregation and assent and bind themselves to general congregational rules. One of these rules will certainly contain provision for admission of members, according to which the concerned person communicates with the pastor, who tests his knowledge of Christianity, talks with him, and examines his religious witness. If the pastor finds nothing to hinder admission, he commends the candidate to the congregation and requests that any in that body who may have legitimate grounds for objecting to the admission inform the pastor before the next service of worship. There being no objection, the applicant is received during divine service or at a parish meeting during which the pastor addresses him and bespeaks God's blessing on him. If objection is made and found legitimate, the matter is put before a congregational meeting for decision.

When the congregation is first organized, the pastor does not as a rule have time for this sort of procedure. He may have only one or two days in which, if possible, to hold a congregational meeting, organize the congregation, preach, catechize the children, hear confession, baptize, administer the Lord's Supper, conduct burials, and perhaps consecrate the cemetery. It may be as much as three to six months before he can come again. Sometimes he simply has to do things in short order. He takes down the names of those wishing to join the congregation, examines their testimonials, addresses a few words to the gathering about what is required of an upright member of a Christian assembly, inquires if any of the applicants is such that his life or conduct does not fit him for membership in a Christian congregation, and receives all against whom no objection or complaint is raised. He then reviews the structure of the congregation and, with the consent of all and with no changes being proposed by those who will belong to it, the congregation is founded. But what a congregation! You must understand that the state of affairs is sometimes deplorable. Indeed, the longer this crowd of our countrymen has been without the public ministry, the more evident it is that, unfortunately, the pastor has come not to a people spiritually languishing but to a people almost dead. There is great dullness and ignorance among the mature and even more among the young. Many of them walk in the vain and sensual ways of the world. Many of the adults are caught up in drunkenness and extravagance or in an avaricious concern for their substance that shows itself in all kinds of sharp dealing in business, in usury, in sinful speculation and other ventures which, rooted as they are in unbelief, extinguish charity and hinder its exercise. And this the pastor has to deal with from 50 to 100 English miles away in only a few visits a year.

Congregations like this cannot simply be indoctrinated, disciplined, admonished — in a word, built up — but must rather be instructed and trained to take care of themselves and to undertake the responsibilities of the church, the purely spiritual as well as the more practical. They must be led to self-government and in concert with their pastors to exercise the authority of the church, the "Office of the Keys" given by God to the congregations to keep and freely to exercise.[17] It is true, is it not, that this is a herculean task. It is a task so gigantic and important that had he not a faith supported by the rich promises of the Lord who in his Word has promised to strengthen the faint and who perfects his power in weakness, the servant of the Lord, sensing his unworthiness, could be tempted to despair and give up the work.[18]

You will perhaps say: Is it comprehensible, is it at all possible that congregations like this can possess and exercise the authority of the church and ecclesiastical government? Is not the reason a synod is formed to exercise authority in the leadership and governance of the congregations?

Answer: Because of the way the shortage of pastors has initially required us to organize congregations, it is certainly true that many are received as members whom it would be desirable to exclude. These people do make congregational self-government difficult, so much so that before the congregations mature they are exposed to internal dissension and quarreling which easily lead to division. And sometimes a close sifting is, in fact, necessary to separate those who are plainly of different spirits.[19] If congregations could come into existence along the lines I sketched earlier, everything would be easier and in the future many dangerous battles could be avoided. But, as we see it, even under conditions as they are, there can be no talk of anything other than placing the real governance of the church in the hands of the congregation; this excludes talk of a transfer of any essential authority to the synod. If, especially in the beginning, the existence of the congregation is precarious, the cause is not to be found in the polity but in the congregation itself and in its spiritual condition. It would not improve the situation and dangers would not be avoided but only temporarily evaded were ecclesiastical authority and the governance of the congregations transferred to the synod. Not only would we depart from the simple exposition of God's Word which entrusts the office of the keys to the individual congregations, not only would we multiply difficulties in

46

church order across the board, but were we to do this we would thereby set up an ecclesiastical authority and place a power in its hands which would undoubtedly, as ancient and modern church history teaches us, come to play pope among us as surely as does the one who sits in Rome. At the same time, presuming that they would allow the power to be taken from them, the congregations would be fettered and deprived, I feel sure, of one of the chief and most powerful incentives toward awakening and developing the life of the church as well as an interest in ecclesiastical responsibilities and an enthusiasm for working toward the good of the church and the extension of God's kingdom as a whole.

But what then is the synod for if not to exercise real ecclesiastical governance and authority over the congregations? Why do not the congregations do without any connection and each undertake its own work? I hear this question being asked.

I will answer in the words I used on an earlier occasion to explain the reasons why in America our Lutheran congregations of the same faith and language have reason to gather themselves into a synod.

Relationship of the Congregations to the Synod

While it must be acknowledged that the formation of congregations is God's ordinance and God's work and that affiliation with an orthodox congregation is the absolute duty of every individual, God's Word, on the contrary, nowhere unconditionally ordains or requires the association of individual congregations into a synod or larger church body. It is not therefore sinful, where circumstances or the interests of the concerned congregations warrant it, for individual congregations to do without this association. Even less will this result in their exclusion from the Lutheran Church. On the contrary, each such congregation possesses of itself and can properly exercise the ecclesiastical authority Christ has granted to his whole church.

But while, on one hand, over against a false conception of the church we must emphasize the rights and power Christ has given the individual congregation, on the other hand, we must also beware of a false sense of independence putting all the emphasis on the autonomy of the individual congregation and of considering the as-

47

sociation of individual congregations at any time and in any form if not precisely sinful, then very dangerous and harmful, and in any case unnecessary and unhelpful. An association like this is certainly within the sphere of the freedom of each congregation, and the congregation must consider its situation with an eye to judging where the affiliation would be helpful and serviceable to itself and other congregations. If under the given circumstances this is found to be the case, then association is a duty for the congregation. Just as little as are individual Christians, congregations are not supposed to use the freedom granted them at whim or by fancy but for what is profitable. If congregations do not associate, they sin against charity, cause offense and schism, and impede in manifold ways the building up of Christ's kingdom among themselves and beyond their own circle.

That an association like this is beneficial, indeed relatively necessary, and therefore a duty of individual congregations is demonstrable for the following reasons:

1) Our congregations of the Lutheran faith are often located far from each other and surrounded by all kinds of sects and those who spread false doctrine. To strengthen the orthodox faith, to preserve unity in a pure confession with respect both to defense against false teachers and to protection against separatism and sectarianism—to achieve all this—an external union and association is very serviceable and a relative necessity according to God's Word (Ephesians 4:3–6; I Corinthians 1:10; Romans 16:17).

2) According to God's Word it is our duty to extend the gospel and the kingdom of God as far as possible by all means available for its promotion. Individually the congregations, especially the small ones, can accomplish nothing or next to nothing toward this goal in comparison to what, with God's blessing, they can accomplish by joining forces and collaborating in the establishment of schools; in the publishing of Bibles, hymnals, confessional writings, school books, and devotional books; and in home and foreign missionary endeavors.

3) For the healthy growth of the congregation it is of the utmost importance that the ordinance of the Lord with respect to the office of the ministry be preserved and that the public servants of the Word not be restricted in the prerogatives and duties granted them by the Lord. It is equally important that they not encroach upon or interfere with those prerogatives and duties with which the congregation

is endowed. By virtue of human weakness it is easy enough for the congregation and its pastor to become isolated. In contrast, a connection with other congregations of the same faith and confession will secure and protect the prerogatives and duties of the congregation as well as the pastor.

4) Just as they often require advice, encouragement, and correction, congregations as well as pastors as a rule require supervision to see that everything is done according to God's rule. This happens only rarely and with difficulty when congregations do not unite to render each other such assistance. If they do, they can establish a supervisory office among themselves if it is found necessary and the requisite gifts are at hand.

5) Sometimes particular gifts are found and put to use in one congregation that are lacking in another. It is the Lord's will that the diversity of gifts be demonstrated as far as possible for the common good and the edification of all (I Corinthians 12:4–31). This is best and sometimes only done when the congregations walk together with each other in external unity.

6) Uniformity in ceremonies and liturgical customs is not, to be sure, necessary to preserve unity in faith, but it is indeed edifying, while diversity in ceremonies often fosters deplorable antagonisms and the cooling of love. On the other hand, the inward bond and collaboration between congregations can be promoted by the greatest possible uniformity in liturgical customs and church order.

7) Finally, we would add that even the apostolic church gives us an example and prototype of a connection and collaboration between individual congregations (Acts 15:1–31). We therefore conclude that only wrong thinking or obstinacy would abstain from this kind of association where not only the dispersion of congregations in so great a space prompts it but where the congregation's freedom relative to the state, so far from hindering it, favors and even encourages it, and—a reason that bespeaks it all the more—prevents the great measure of freedom granted it from being abused and converted into false independence, indeed, total chaos.[20]

Synodical Polity

The real significance of the Synod for the church body depends on the diligence and zeal with which its members undertake and carry out their responsibilities to the church body in conjunction with their fidelity to God's Word and their love of the congregations.

It might perhaps seem incomprehensible to many a person not acquainted with our situation that a church body could cohere and reap blessings when the congregations retain so much freedom and independence and are without any external authority to coerce obedience from the unruly and the unwilling. We are, however, completely convinced that only this kind of church body has a future, if it otherwise abides by the Word of the Lord. Nor are we entirely without experience in this matter. While the Missouri Synod, guided by these basic principles, has shown an amazing vitality in its external and internal development, other synods built on more strictly hierarchical lines but with looser confessional moorings are already on the path to dissolution. What binds us together is God's Word, the common faith expressed in these words: "unity of spirit in the bond of peace."[21] This is what is essential and it is sufficient. We consider a church body held together in what seems to be the bond of peace but without unity of spirit, without a common faith, to be a nonentity, a falsehood, a Babel bearing within it the germ of its own disintegration and fostering not the edification but the destruction of God's congregation and the Christian faith.[22]

The Synod manifests itself and executes its work chiefly during the synodical meetings held every year or every other year. Even disregarding the specific actions taken by these meetings and the directives drawn up at them aiming at the benefit of the whole church body, it is difficult to overestimate the blessings attendant upon these meetings. Representatives elected by the congregations—generally from among their finest, most devout, best informed men—gather here from the farthest reaches of the church body. During fourteen days together they learn to know and love one another as brethren in faith; they tell each other of their experiences, struggles, sorrows, and joys; they are instructed and strengthened in the faith they share; they are cheered on and strengthened to zeal in a shared task, to courage in a shared struggle, to patience in shared suffering. That is why pastors and laity alike meet with tears of joy at these assemblies of the Synod and part with pain, although they give thanks to God and to the brethren for encouragement, strengthening, and fortification in the truth. The Synod does not do all its work in the meetings of the Synod; it has its own functionaries through whom to carry on its tasks. Chapter III of the synodical constitution names the president and the church council among the officers of the Synod.

The church council, in which the president occupies the chair, is charged with seeing to the execution of the decisions of the Synod. In the interims between meetings it works to promote the Synod's goals and the interests of the church body. To this end it stands watch over purity of doctrine and the development of the Christian life, it examines candidates, it mediates disputes, and as necessary it provisionally suspends pastors from the privileges of membership in the Synod. The Synod's president, whose office is in essence that of a bishop, is charged with carrying out annual visitations, ordaining pastors, presiding at meetings of the Synod, looking after matters prepared for deposition at these meetings, reporting to the Synod on his own activities and those of the Synod as well as on the state of the church body as a whole. Since as a rule the church council assembles only a few times a year, he must in many instances act on behalf of the church council, exercising supervision over the church body as a whole and seeking its welfare in every respect.

Although ecclesiastical government so-called in our church body is substantially different from that here in Norway, there is a resemblance in the way it specifically distributes authority and offices. A comparison of this distribution in the two church bodies will perhaps put the contrast between the forms of governance in its proper light.

In the state church ecclesiastical government in its most extended sense is divided between the Storting [parliament], the king and his ministers, the bishops, and to some degree the supreme court. As you know, the Storting possesses legislative and decision-making authority even in ecclesiastical matters. It is charged with promulgating laws of all sorts with regard to the external organization of the church, establishing seminaries and faculty posts, and providing for their maintenance. It can, indeed, alter the confession of the church through constitutional amendment, and, by virtue of the Fourth Commandment, all members of the state church would in this case have either to obey or to depart. And yet the members of this parliament to which is entrusted such extraordinary power over the church do not, in fact, have to belong to the Lutheran Church. Among us, the synodical assembly corresponds most closely to the Storting, although it does not ultimately possess any legislative authority. It can propose liturgical changes and make arrangements for our schools and their faculties, but everything depends on the congregations and whether they accept the proposals offered and the arrangements made. Actually, there can be no talk of obedience by the congregations to the Synod on the basis of the Fourth Commandment, but only of humble and charitable service.[23] The question of whether the congregations find proper and beneficial the proposals offered and the provisions and arrangements made is decided by their acceptance and implementation. Even when the majority of the congregations have agreed to proposals or arrangements by the Synod one can — except in cases when something is indicated in God's Word — speak only of an obligation of the minority to follow along with the majority for the sake of charity and love alone. The Synod possesses absolutely no authority to impose assessments; this is left entirely in the hands of the congregations.

Here in the state church the king's government possesses the executive authority. It is responsible for seeing that laws promulgated by legislative authority are followed, that arrangements made are executed, and in general it exercises oversight over the whole church body and prepares such proposals for parliamentary action as the church's interest requires. Further, it can establish liturgical ordinances, change the *Ritual*, and introduce new textbooks; it possesses the right of call; it can partition congregations, fill pastoral charges, and conduct examinations for the ministry.[24] Among us, the duties of the church council most closely answer to this description. It prepares matters for the attention of the Synod, attends to the execution of approved recommendations, exercises oversight, makes recommendations to the congregations concerning changes in the *Ritual*. In contrast, the congregation retains the right of call; it alone decides on the partition of pastoral charges and on the introduction of new textbooks and liturgical usages.

The office of oversight is essentially entrusted to the president of our synod, just as here in the state church it is to the bishops. He conducts ordinations, visitations, and other such functions. Indeed in some respects the president exercises the leadership which in the state church is in the hands of the government. In contrast, the president, unlike the bishops of the state church, has nothing to do with the exercise of church discipline. This is the responsibility of the congregation, and he only gives advice on request. Nor can we speak of any obedience due him by virtue of synodical law. While the bishops of the state church rule according to the stipulations of the law and the canons and require obedience according to the Fourth Commandment, the president of our synod—and the pastors of individual congregations—rule by the Word of God. It is thus this Word and not the president who rules, it is the Word and not the person that commands obedience.

Finally, in the state church the supreme court possesses judicial authority in church affairs. In the final instance it must decide what is the proper interpretation of the law and also what is the right understanding of God's Word and the confessions. The supreme court also has the power to judge pastors and dismiss them from office. Among ourselves we say: "Scripture interprets Scripture," and according to that same principle the appropriate authority—synod, church council, or congregation itself—can construe the authentic interpretation of its own ordinances.[25] The right to dismiss a pastor belongs only to the congregation having the right of call.

The essential differences between the two ecclesiastical polities should be apparent from the foregoing. The state church is governed by laws of human devising, and all the officials among whom ecclesiastical power is distributed command unconditional obedience according to the Fourth Commandment. Here in Norway one always hears "Thou shalt!" In our church body, in contrast, Christ alone is acknowledged as Lord and King. He governs through his Word. This is the only law to which the members of the church owe unconditional obedience. Those who hold office or positions of authority in the Synod govern with the Word alone and without coercion or force. Those who will not obey the Word without external force or power do not belong to Christ's congregation. He himself says: "My sheep hear my voice and follow it."[26] In America one hears: "For God's sake you are obligated because God's Word bids it," or "For the sake of peace and love you ought to conform to the desire and opinion of your brethren, insofar as you cannot show it to be sinful or harmful." Naturally, I will not here permit myself an evaluation or rationale for the advantages of one polity over the other. For the unprejudiced I hardly think it necessary.[27]

It is obvious that what binds and sustains our church body are not ordinances of human devising and still less external power or temporal advantages or privileges under civil law, but only, as I have said above, God's Word. It is only the common faith in this Word that preserves "unity of spirit in the bond of faith."[28] This is what is essential and what is needful. It is sure and certain: blessing is secured only by adhering to the truth of the Word of the Lord. It is for this reason that God's Word is the essential substance of our discussions at meetings of the Synod. Usually a presentation is prepared beforehand of one or another point of doctrine which either in itself or in light of circumstances seems to us especially important. With this presentation as a basis, we then seek as thoroughly and comprehensively as possible to clarify and state the doctrine at issue, to prove it from Scripture, and to elucidate it with the symbols of the church and the writings of the Lutheran fathers.

In this fashion we have discussed the following points of doctrine: lay preaching, or the fourteenth article of the Augsburg Confession, along with points of doctrine related to the ministry of the Word, the call, and the spiritual priesthood. Further, we have discussed the doctrines of confession and absolution, of Sunday and the Third Commandment, and of church discipline, something about slavery, and in our treatment of synodical polity the doctrine of church order and related issues. God's Word has also been used and applied in many ways in our treatment of other issues such as, for example, the seminary, the preparatory school, and the congregational school in its relation to the district school, as well as in other deliberations of the Synod prompted by congregations or individual members.

To be sure, the Synod's handling of various doctrinal issues has occasioned a good deal of controversy not only with other church bodies but even within our own church body. Discussion in the Synod, however, has not so much been the occasion of controversy as it has been the result of controversy, even if this means that for a time discussion in the Synod gets to be widespread and vehement. It is also true that some of the Synod's doctrinal discussions — of absolution and church discipline, for example — have not been accompanied by controversy, just as other discussions in the Synod — of lay preaching and the Third Commandment, for example — have been just the essential element in ending controversy and uniting the controversialists.

Since our opponents fault us for a rigid orthodoxy and some people here in Norway seek to attach the same judgment to us, it is necessary that I go a little more deeply into the confession of our synod on these controversial issues. For the moment, however, I will postpone this until I come to speak of the various Norwegian churches with which we have been in controversy over these doctrinal points. Before I discuss and elucidate in more detail things that need to be straightened out pertaining to other matters to which the Synod has devoted special attention — church discipline, confession, educational institutions, for example — it will be helpful, I think, to take a glance back at the individual congregations and their order, arrangement, and activity, because it is only through the collaboration of the congregations with the Synod that real results are accomplished.

LECTURE II

Congregational Polity

W e paused earlier to discuss the initial organization of congregations. As I explained, a congregational order is
drawn up and accepted on that occasion. As a rule, this
is very brief and contains only the absolutely necessary provisions.
They are as follows:

1) *Concerning the doctrine, confession, and liturgical practices*
of the congregation to which all agree and which are in accordance
with the constitution of the Synod.

2) *Concerning the administration of the public ministry*, the
procedures for electing a pastor, the qualifications he must possess,
and the proceedings for the dismissal of an unfaithful servant. To
this end it is provided that no one shall serve in office without having been properly examined, regularly called, and ecclesiastically
ordained, and without having been called by the congregation either directly through the congregation or indirectly through a pastor, the church council, or the president. Pastors do not, as is the
case in the state church, seek to move from one call to another, although they may be so called by the congregations. Such transfers
very rarely occur among us.

3) *Concerning other officers*, trustees, assessors, deacons. Of
these, the trustees are charged with the responsibility for financial
affairs, managing and maintaining the property of the congregation, and securing the necessary means to defray the congregation's
expenses.[1] The congregation itself decides whether this shall be
done by means of free-will offerings or by assessment of the adult

members of the congregation. By the act of incorporation, the congregation assumes the status of a legal body under the civil law, and the trustees retain the same power as public tax collectors to assess contributions. It has, however, been very seldom that a pastor and congregation have thought it prudent to press the provisions of the law to their full extent in the collection of funds. In this respect, too, we have tried through enticement, admonition, and the discipline of God's Word to achieve the desired results, and as a rule the Word shows itself to be a powerful agent when properly applied. The deacons serve a different purpose among us than in Norway, according to the prescription of the *Ritual*.[2] We have found in practice that the usual provisions which apply to this office are to some degree out of accord with the Word of God and, in fact, hamper and constrain the growth of the Christian life in the congregation. More about this under the heading of church discipline. The deacons serve us as counselors to the pastor and especially as almoners. They supervise the school, solicit the free-will offering for the purposes of the whole church body, maintain order during divine service, and in the absence of the pastor conduct public worship. When the pastor is unable to preach, it is a fairly common practice in our church body for the congregation to assemble in the church on Sundays for a public reading service. In these cases a sermon by Luther or another orthodox teacher is read, the prescribed prayers are offered, and hymns are sung.

4) Provision for *congregational meetings*. As a rule, voting members in these meetings include every male member of the congregation who is twenty-one years old and not under church discipline. In congregations regularly served by a pastor, meetings customarily include both ordinary monthly sessions and extraordinary ones scheduled and announced by the pastor as necessary. These meetings cover doctrinal topics and issues as well as the financial affairs of the congregation and the church body. Synodical actions are reviewed, church discipline is exercised, and decisions are made about the call and dismissal of pastors as well as about congregational polity and other miscellaneous matters. Next to the public preaching of the Word of God there is hardly any ordinance in our church body I consider more important than the congregational meetings. It is hard to overestimate their importance. Their fruits are: instruction, especially in matters which cannot be handled well in the pulpit; discipline; encouragement; stir-

ring of the congregational conscience; and awakening of interest in the affairs of the congregation and of the church body. Here anyone can broach any issue he wishes. Here he can lodge complaints against shortcomings and abuses. All this, taken together with the fact that the congregation itself exercises the right of call and can appoint as many teachers as it chooses to support, means in essence that there is in the regularly served congregations of our church body only as much lay preaching as necessity requires. There is full opportunity in the congregational meetings for everyone to express himself publicly before the entire congregation. In the meetings of the congregation and in private conduct in the pursuit of a temporal vocation, each person has more than sufficient opportunity to exercise his gifts.[3]

5) Provision for church *discipline*. By church discipline we mean the definite procedures prescribed for the church by our Lord for dealing with those members who have succumbed to one or another sin.[4] These procedures consist of progressively more severe warnings and have as their aim either to win the erring or to free the congregation from an accomplice's role in sin and purify itself of unrepentant sinners. In the earliest period our synod followed the provisions for church discipline which still obtain here in the state church.[5] The deacons first spoke with the pastor who then privately admonished the party concerned. If, however, the admonition was to no avail, the person was summoned before the church council, consisting of pastor and deacons, for rebuke and admonition. If this discipline failed to produce repentance, the affair was passed in appeal to the church council or, as a last resort, to the president.

We were quickly convinced of the need to formulate different provisions, more in accord with the Word of God, for church discipline. For it to be practicable and for us to expect it to yield blessing, it had to be done quite differently and according to different principles. This came about partly because we lacked a scriptural basis for our accustomed mode of procedure and partly because it had evil consequences. It became evident to us that: 1) the first step in church discipline, the private admonition, and certainly the second step, a step which Christ imposed in equal measure and under all conditions on every member of the congregation, had been laid upon pastor and deacons as obligatory, without and indeed contrary to Christ's orders; 2) their consciences were unjustifiably burdened by this obligation; 3) the exercise of this duty was an offense against the Eighth Commandment involving berating a sinner and telling others of the sin which should have been kept for the sinner himself in private, thereby offending and embittering him and impeding the beneficial effects of discipline; 4) the deacons not only were considered to be but actually were informants on their brethren and exposed themselves to general mistrust and dislike; 5) consciousness of the general obligation of every member of the congregation to undertake the first step in church discipline was weakened, while the opinion gained currency that the admonition and rebuke of sinners was something for the pastor and of no concern to others, thus rendering this exercise by others a token of arrogance and even an intrusion into the official prerogatives of the pastor and deacons; 6) the final degree of church discipline came to take place not only by the authority of the congregation, as Christ decreed, but also involved persons who did not even belong to the congregation, discipline thus suffering a diminution of its power and significance. We considered all of this to do irreparable harm to the congregation and it caused us to alter our whole method of administering church discipline.

The basis of our new order for the exercise of church discipline is Matthew 18:15–17: "If thy brother shall trespass against thee, go and tell him his fault, between thee and him alone; if he shall hear thee, thou has gained thy brother. But if he will not hear thee, then take with thee one or two more, that in the mouth of two or three witnesses every word may be established. And if he shall neglect to hear them, tell it to the church; but if he neglect to hear the church, let him be to thee as an heathen and a publican." There are certainly other places in Holy Scripture speaking of the same thing, but they are really only explanations and examples. Matthew 18 is the principal passage and, as we call it, the *sedes doctrinae* of church discipline.[6] We therefore obligate every member of the congregation to admonish and rebuke in private the Christian brother whom he has seen sinning. We take note of the following with respect to this first step in church discipline: 1) the one who is to be subjected to church discipline is a member of the congregation; 2) since church discipline is occasioned by certain specific sins, the person concerned must in fact have done the deed, and for the deed to be sinful a divine commandment must have been transgressed; 3) the brother who sees the sin or who has been sinned against and consequently offended shall administer the rebuke. 4) We know how inclined human beings are to enlarge upon the faults of their neighbors and to tell others about their neighbors' sins. When this happens we ask such a person whether he has first admonished his brother, and if he has not we bid him recall the Eighth Commandment and note that Christ does not say that we should go to others, not even to the pastor, and tell them all about it, but to the sinner and rebuke him.[7] Christ thereby shows us that we are not to make the sin any more public than it already is. If you hear, "I am telling you about it so that you can rebuke him. It does no good for me to do it," the answer is: Christ knows best what instrument to use. No one, not even the pastor himself, can do it better than the brother whom Christ commands to do it when it is done in his name. 5) In the end you must actually rebuke the brother, but "between thee and him alone," says Christ, because he will thus speak more easily than in the presence of others.

After this step in admonition, one of two things happens. Either he listens, obeys the admonition, and repents, and the discipline is finished because you have "gained thy brother." Or he does not listen. Then occurs the second step in admonition: "take with thee one or two more." Then in the presence of the witnesses make the admonition to which they shall bear witness: 1) against the sinner to rebuke him; and 2) on behalf of the congregation, if it is necessary and called for, to warn the sinner if he will not heed the warning of his brethren. There shall be one or two witnesses, but no more, preferably neighbors and friends who one may hope will accomplish the most. The pastor is not necessarily among them, because it is not certain whether he could accomplish more than anyone else. At the same time, however, the pastor can administer an admonition if he knows about the sin.

If the sinner does not then listen, it is time for the third and final step in the admonition. If it has not been done earlier, the matter is brought to the pastor's attention and laid before a meeting of the voting members of the congregation either by those who have earlier administered the fruitless admonitions or by the pastor. At this point the congregation is permitted to hear how the sinner has been admonished, rebuked, pleaded with, and prayed for by one person after another. Then everyone, as he is compelled by Christ's love and as God gives it to him, shall admonish, rebuke, pray, and plead. Then all—man for man of them—shall rise and tell of it to the brethren. If anyone cannot say much, let the testimony be brief but powerful. The Lord God has given gifts to all his faithful, and no one—if he has faith and a heart that beats—is so ill-equipped as not to be able to utter a few fitting words. Truly this step depends on everyone exerting all his strength to disentangle the brother from the devil's snare. No one who has not experienced it can believe the irresistible power of this persuasion, intercession, and fervent entreating when it takes place properly. It takes a heart harder than steel and diamond to resist the collective power of a united congregation. Individuals who have come into these gatherings filled with the most spiteful malice and who have scorned the most heartfelt admonitions are not infrequently, and sometimes in spite of what they will, softened and converted.

Congregations that have anxiously and uneasily assembled for such meetings often depart with loud doxologies to the great God who helped them in ways they could not have prayed for and understood. Therefore, a congregation must not neglect what has been entrusted into its hands. When the third step is taken, it is rarely in vain. As a rule, such an admonition can and must occur not once but several times. If the sinner heeds the congregation, then the congregation must absolve him. How this takes place— whether, for example, it is to be during public worship or at some other time— depends on the particular circumstances and the gravity of the offense. It may also happen, in cases, for example, of repeated backsliding in the same sin or where there is suspicion of a hypocritical repentance, that a congregation may need to impose a probational period before pronouncing absolution. During this period, the penitent is naturally suspended from admission to the sacrament and other privileges of congregational membership. If the person concerned does not listen, but demonstrates open lack of repentance by refusing to hear the congregation, then by unanimous decision of the congregation he is publicly excluded from the congregation and thus allowed to be "a heathen and a publican," as Christ says. In the meantime, the church council along with other pastors and congregations are kept advised.

Unfortunately our practice of church discipline still leaves a great deal to be desired. This is especially true with respect to the third step, in part because of a disinclination to undertake discipline and in part through misunderstanding of the procedure. On top of this, if this discipline is to be effected correctly it requires a good deal of time both to instruct the congregation properly and to admonish the sinner. The pastors hardly have the necessary time for this, and it must thus often be neglected where it is needed and where a sufficient supply of pastors could provide it. Yet it goes apace, and an awareness of its necessity penetrates farther and farther. Where the first step is properly applied, offenses will tend to be less common. Indeed, where the discipline of the first step takes root in hearts, the other disciplinary steps do not require application. In addition, public penitence, or *open confession*, as it is called in the *Ritual*, is here and there used in the congregations.[8] But this calls for great care and consideration of whether both sinner and congregation are mature enough for this, so that it does not serve to punish and coerce but rather out of consideration and love to remove an offense. When it is done properly, it often bears the fruit of great blessing.

6) Provision for the *religious school*. It is said that the public, English schools are *religionless*. This is due to the multiplicity of confessions that exist in America. The congregations themselves must therefore provide for instruction in religion. It cannot thus be considered as exclusively a parental duty but also as a congregational one to provide what is necessary to rear the children as Christians and see that they receive the necessary instruction in Christianity. This religious instruction is provided both in the home and in the congregational schools supported by the congregations themselves.[9] The English district schools, on the other hand, are free and open to all, although no one is forced to use them. In the congregational schools, some of which are permanent while others are itinerant, instruction is provided in Norwegian, reading, religion, a little penmanship, and ciphering. It is our endeavor to arrange things with our congregational schools in such a way as to render the public, English schools superfluous on the part of the members of our congregations. Naturally this will happen only if we in the congregational schools pick up the subjects taught in the English schools, first and foremost the English language, then arithmetic, geography, and a bit of history. This is certain to create difficulties, because there are not many who care, by means of their taxes, to maintain the English schools without having any use for them while at the same time supporting a congregational school to teach in part the same things that are taught in the public schools. But we must still work toward this end. The reason is not so much

the drawbacks associated with having two schools, which often meet at the same time and one of which may be neglected only to the detriment of the children. Both are important, indeed the one more for this life and the other both for this life and for the one to come. Nor is the cause of this that the schools are so bad that the children learn nothing. If they learn nothing else — and I do not say that this is the case — they do learn to read and speak well. No, the cardinal reason is that the school is religionless and that on principle neither Christian instruction nor Christian discipline can find a place in it. As Christian parents we do not think that with good consciences we can make use of these schools that neither adopt nor confess any religion, whatever else there may be to commend and support such schools. We Lutherans cannot abandon our children to the discipline of teachers who are Roman Catholics, Methodists, or atheists. This is not merely because they will miss in school the blessings of Christian discipline, but because the effects of an unchristian or a spurious, weak discipline cannot fail to appear when a child is exposed to it through so many years of childhood and youth. Because the American school system has been praised here in this country and our stance toward it in America has been the object of harsh attack by our opponents, I shall express myself more fully on this matter.

While I want at the same time to give it the honor due it for the service it renders the great masses of the unreligious in America, I must also point out a few of its questionable aspects. One is that the teachers in the school are always changing. During the summertime when the youngest children are in school, the teacher is most often a young girl. On the other hand, during the wintertime when the older youth are in school, it is as a rule a man. Another problem is the glaring lack of external discipline, obedience, and order. As a consequence, of course, the principles of a false freedom and independence are inculcated in the children, a practice that in time cannot but bear its tragic fruits in domestic relations with parents and masters and in civil relations with the authorities. Finally, the public school system is patently less appropriate for conscientious Christian citizens because the unreligious are favored at their expense. There ought to be certain requirements with respect to what is taught in the schools and every school that fulfills these requirements — even if additional subjects are taught — ought to have equal access to public support proportionate to the number of children in attendance. Our position on the English schools is best understood from the following theses which were the basis for our treatment of the issue as it came up at our last synod meeting in 1866. The most important of the theses (1–5 and 18–20) were considered carefully and adopted.[10]

1) It must be considered only natural for Christians to employ Christian schools for the instruction of their children.

2) Here in America it must, therefore, normally be considered desirable that Christians establish such congregational schools and that in these there also be taught what is taught in the so-called "common schools," so that they need not be used.

3) We are obligated as citizens to support the common schools, even if we do not employ them for our own children.

4) The chief purpose of these state-supported schools is to serve that portion of the people which does not receive Christian instruction.

5) The lack of religious instruction in these schools is a necessary consequence of the religious freedom which we count ourselves fortunate to enjoy under the civil polity here obtaining, but it is also a sorrowful testimony to the current defection from Christianity and the sectarian divisions among Christians.

6) The financial cost of extending the congregational schools mentioned in thesis number 2 ought not to prevent a Christian from doing what the spiritual well-being of his children requires and what he can do to protect the child from worldliness.

7) We set our fellow citizens the most excellent example when, for religious reasons, we do not use the public schools, but do everything in our power to promote them.

8) We work best to promote unity and solidarity among our people when we obtain the finest Christian instruction for our people.

9) Everything asserted above pertains to its fullest extent to our Norwegian Lutherans in the United States.

10) We do not thereby wish to set aside the English language, which it is especially important for all of our youth to learn as they grow. Yet this, along with every other earthly good, ranks behind the well-being of the soul.

11) We shall gladly acquaint ourselves with American education and borrow from it everything serviceable to our own schools.

12) We must at all costs protect our schools from the false spirit

of freedom now current. If the common schools are nurseries of such, it is all the more reason for us not to employ them for our children.

13) Everything said above — even if the common schools were what they ought to be — is not only valid but all the more significant because for the most part their condition is unfortunately really worse than this, partly because they have incompetent teachers, partly because the teachers display patent infidelity or coarse morality, partly because discipline is bad, and partly because in every instance the children are corrupted by a faith other than our own.

14) The American common schools take the best time away from the religious schools and make it difficult for them to extend regular calls to teachers.

15) Since other Christians and others who speak foreign tongues have done it before, it ought to be possible for us to foster congregational schools that would render the American common schools superfluous.

16) It should be easier for us to procure teachers for schools such as those proposed here than it has been for congregational schools like the majority of those we now have.

17) Christian young people who possess the gifts for it should gladly and for God's sake be willing to offer themselves to the calling of the Christian schoolteacher, and Christian congregations should likewise be willing to support them in their preparation.

18) Where the kind of program proposed above cannot quickly or in every instance be introduced, the members of our congregations must in every way seek as much influence as possible over the district school, partly through the employment of teachers and partly through determination of their tenure.

19) Where this is not possible and the district school is conducted in such a way that there is prevalent danger to the Christian faith or morality, it is the explicit duty of Christian parents to keep their children out and work all the more zealously to develop congregational schools.

20) Where it cannot well be otherwise, sufficient acquaintance with English may be obtained by attending English schools only after confirmation.

21) A good Norwegian reader suitable for grammar schools ought to be published as soon as possible.

22) Where it is necessary the congregations must build their own schoolhouses for their schools.

23) Parents do not have leave to excuse themselves, saying they cannot spare the time and work to send their children to Christian schools.

24) Children can well learn two languages, but this ought not to occur as it now does by beginning with two at once. The natural order is to allow them to read Norwegian with some degree of competence before beginning English.

25) We ought to seek to awaken zeal for fulfilling our bounden duty to obtain Christian instruction for our children through preaching, admonition, discussion, and meetings, as well as through diligent attention to this by the pastor and thorough preparation for confirmation.

26) Christian Sunday schools are recommended for all congregations, but as Lutherans we must shun the Sunday schools of the sects.

27) According to the law as it stands, a satisfactory association between the district schools and the congregational schools could hardly occur.

Our congregational education is far from the level at which it ought to be. The cause is in part the lack of fit teachers and in part that the congregations are new and thus have many things to do and for the most part must learn to estimate properly the importance of a good Christian school and to sacrifice willingly for it. Yet progress is made. In many parts of our church body attempts have been made to meet the need with *Sunday schools*. These must not, however, be confused with the vaunted American Sunday schools.[11] These on occasion might indeed be rigorously confessional and serve as worthwhile expedients in place of weekday congregational schools, but in fact they are most often unconfessional. In them a Methodist or a Baptist may instruct children of different confessions in the basic religious truths, simplified to what all church bodies hold in common. This as a rule amounts either to propaganda for one or another sect or to instruction for the children in an out-and-out spiritually destructive morality. Our Sunday schools are strictly Lutheran and confessional. They are conducted partly in place of and partly alongside of the weekday congregational schools, often by assistants considered most fit by the pastor and appointed by him and the congregation. Reading and religion are the sole subjects. Both types of religious school are under the supervision of the pastor and men elected by the congregation.

7) In several congregations constitutional provision is made for confession. I have already explained in my discussion of how congregations are established that want of time has sometimes forced our pastors to receive members without a very close examination. The same condition has applied and still does, especially in many of the annexed congregations, in the case of confession. In America, as here in this country, one often has to be satisfied with a confessional address before the Lord's Supper and the granting of absolution with the laying on of hands, always unconditionally.[12] This loose handling of confession must in general be excused only if it is absolutely necessary. In this respect, private confession in the form prescribed by the *Ritual* of the church is to be considered the goal toward which we must strive.[13] Not only do we think it utterly natural that a person intending to go to the altar make confession with the lips, as the church itself shows in its contemporary practice by requiring this of communion guests, but we also believe that the congregation as well as the pastor, as its servant to whom the public administration of the benefits of the church is entrusted, are obligated insofar as possible to take care and stand guard so that the plainly unfit and unrepentant do not go to the altar and profane what is holy while bringing judgment upon themselves. We know that ignorance is often unbelievably great. Indeed I myself have seen examples of people who, just as here in Norway, have been at the altar many times and yet do not know what is conveyed to them in the Lord's Supper, who do not even have a notion of who Christ was, what he suffered, and what he has provided for us.

We therefore believe that both congregation and pastor are obligated to establish an examination which guests at the Lord's Supper are obligated to undertake. As Christ says, "Give not that which is holy unto the dogs, neither cast ye your pearls before swine."[14] The form of this examination, however, is left to the congregation's own free choice. In many congregations private confession has already been introduced by congregational decision. In other places there is a transition to its introduction. In some places the guests at the Lord's Supper kneel at the conclusion of the confessional address and with an audible "Yes" respond to some questions concerning their repentance, their faith, their will to amendment of life, and their desire for absolution. This, in customary fashion, is granted with the laying on of hands. Sometimes on Saturday or Sunday a so-called confessional service is held. In it the pastor deals in special cases with individuals, but as a rule with several people, sometimes as many as ten to twelve at once, speaking of the conditions for a worthy reception of the sacrament, briefly reviewing the most important truths of the faith, and ascertaining whether they have the knowledge of Christianity necessary to receive the sacrament. To be sure, this way of doing things has its drawbacks. Time is short on Sunday mornings, divine service is often disturbed, and the pastor tires. It also has a way of stirring up a sensation when the pastor needs to speak to someone individually, who is then without reason made the object of suspicion and talk. Finally, doing it this way means separating confession from absolution, which customarily takes place in the church during the confessional address. Many of our congregations as well as pastors have thus found that the prescriptions of the *Ritual* pertaining to private confession comprise the best and most desirable arrangement. In spite of the difficulties with respect to time and place standing in the way of the introduction of private confession, in spite of the great trouble and time it costs the pastor, in spite of the ignorance and misunderstanding and ill will the common people show toward this ordinance, it has made its way into many of the congregations. There it has been demonstrated that though the difficulties have been considerable they are not insurmountable, while the blessings attendant upon its use cannot be denied where confession is practiced in a properly evangelical spirit.

Things usually happen this way. The communion is held with confession, with catechization variously every other or on occasion every Sunday.[15] Saturday, or Sunday morning for the old and infirm, is appointed for holding confession. This takes place in the sacristy of the church or in private houses and in the latter case now here and now there in the parish. This is done in part so that distances can be somewhat equalized for members of the congregation and in part to prevent too many penitents coming at one time. As a rule they seek to come to the Lord's Table when confession is held in the district where they reside. When, at confirmation, for example, it is feared that the time will be too short to take care of them all, then the confessional service alone or both the confessional service and communion are held in the different districts, and generally only for the confirmands and their close relatives. In this way it is possible to introduce private confession even in the larger congregations, although naturally with considerable effort on the part of the pastor.

The service begins with prayers and hymns, after which confessions follow straightaway. In recent years, I have allowed a half or a full hour's catechization to precede this. We go through the five parts of the catechism and the section on absolution, partly by question and answer and partly discursively.[16] As a result of this, the people are prodded to more reading of their catechisms and more time is saved for the many people who have come to confession. When the catechization is over, each individual comes to the pastor in the sacristy or in a room set apart. Confession takes place either as the penitent himself makes confession or as he answers certain questions directed to him by the pastor. The pastor pronounces absolution when the confession is finished, if there is no evidence of impenitence. While private confessions are in progress, the rest of the congregation sings hymns or someone reads to them from the Bible or a book of communion devotions. On the following Sunday there will not be a confessional service, but rather a communion address will usually be given immediately before the Lord's Supper.

We are not, of course, blind to the abuse to which private confession can lead when it is administered by an arrogant, domineering pastor or in an unevangelical manner, but we believe that the blessings attending upon a proper evangelical administration of private confession are so great that we ought not to preclude or abolish its usage. Private confession gives the pastor an excellent opportunity to learn about his penitents' understanding of Christianity and not infrequently it puts him in a position to search out and unveil unconscious self-deception as well as patent hypocrisy. This also makes it possible for him to fulfill the duty obligatory both for him and for the congregation, that is, to take care that no one who is openly unfit or unworthy partakes of the Lord's sacrament. Through the proper administration of private confession the shepherd of souls also enters into a more intimate and confidential relation to his parishioners, teaching them to understand their weaknesses better so that he may minister to them with instruction, comfort and encouragement, exhortation and warning. In a word: through a conscientious, evangelical use of private confession, the pastor can develop an acquaintance with his parishioners and exercise an influence on them that he could hardly achieve in any other way. For this to be understood, I need only mention the significance it can have for his general effectiveness as a pastor, particularly with reference to church discipline. But, as has been said, it is necessary for both pastor and congregation to be on guard against abuse. We try to stop this, which like any other abuse of position is a matter for discipline and punishment, by assiduous discussion and instruction on the topic both among the pastors themselves and in the congregations as well.

In order to get a better idea of our synodical doctrine and practice with respect to confession, I shall cite a few of the theses agreed upon by the Synod in 1861:[17]

1) Absolution does not mean that the confessor sits as a judge giving a verdict on the inner state of the penitent.

2) In close connection with private absolution stands private confession, which latter is nothing other than a request for absolution. It also has the advantage of giving the confessor an opportunity to examine his parishioners, to apply sermon and catechism, to admonish against unworthy use of the sacrament, and to give all sorts of advice in difficult cases of conscience. Finally it is an exercise in self-humiliation. *Summa*: it is an exercise in the law and the gospel.

3) Confession is not commanded by God, but is nevertheless very useful. It thus ought not to be required of any man as a necessary act, but where it exists it ought to be maintained and where it has fallen into disuse it ought to be restored by recommending and praising its usefulness.[18]

These are the essential elements of the special provisions of our congregational polity. As explained above, the use of the Norwegian *Altar Book* and *Ritual* is observed in our congregations. As a consequence of this, divine service and churchly acts among us are, for the most part, carried out as in Norway. Here I will only draw your attention to a few individual points.

1) *Holy Days.* Besides the festival and holy days now observed in Norway, our church body has adopted Epiphany, on which we generally have a mission festival, and All Saints' Day, as a Reformation festival. We also usually celebrate the regular three days of the high festivals, as well as Michaelmas and the day set aside each autumn as "Thanksgiving Day" by the governor of the state, to-

gether with the days of general humiliation and prayer established from time to time by the national government.[19]

2) *Confirmation* is practiced among us as in Norway.[20] Because it is a matter of completely free choice in the eyes of the civil authority, because the state neither requires it of anyone by law nor entices or tempts anyone to it with secular advantage, our pastors are naturally free of much that makes this act so oppressive to the pastors of the state church. But then among us there are other circumstances that make this act difficult and weight it with responsibility.[21] On the one hand, because the children are often very deficient in knowledge, especially in places where there is no religious school, there can be difficulties in providing the necessary instruction in Christianity. On the other hand, when they leave home our youth are tempted much more than in Norway, because most of them enter the service of those who believe other than we do and are thus exposed to the seduction of apostasy, to the many kinds of sects, or to outright unbelief. Though, as I have said, no legal compulsion obtains in America in favor of confirmation, our people, even the more indifferent, follow this beneficial custom, if only because of the mistaken belief that this is what really makes "Christians" of the children. The requirements they place upon the pastor are, therefore, often immeasurable, and he is as often in danger of requiring too much as too little. In the first case, he makes it so that the children do not return to confirmation instruction, but rather stay away; they are often thus lost not just to the Lutheran Church but for eternity. In the other instance, he runs the danger of allowing the confirmands too easily to become prey to all sorts of spiritual error and — if they remain in the Lutheran Church — of never becoming properly fit for effective participation in the affairs of the congregation, a requirement of every mature member of a free church.

3) *Marriage*, according to the laws of the state of Wisconsin, is fully valid when entered into before either a judge or a pastor; in other states a license from the secular authorities must be presented to the pastor before he can conduct the ceremony. Those to be married must swear on oath that there are no impediments, as stipulated by the laws of the state, to their marriage. Among the impediments are: kinship nearer than cousinage; that either of the partners is bound by an earlier marriage vow; that they have not reached majority, being eighteen and twenty-one years old. If this

latter is the case, written permission from parents or guardians is required. Naturally we consider the giving of the church's blessing through the pastor's consecration of the marriage a good Christian usage which members of the church upon entering marriage ought not to despise, and as such it is therefore in general use. Yet we do not regard this as a necessary condition for the membership of married people in the church. Sometimes, when a marriage has already been contracted before the secular authorities and thus possesses civil validity, the blessing from the minister of the congregation is given later. This is not, however, required as something absolutely necessary, nor is a marriage considered unchristian on the ground that it lacks a pastor's blessing.[22] Often the church's blessing cannot be procured without great difficulty, and even when it is omitted because of poor judgment, embarrassment, or other causes born of the frailty of the individuals, it does not mean that those concerned ought to be put under church discipline, but rather that they should be admonished and taught. It is, of course, another matter when a general indifference and contempt for God's Word and the congregation reveal themselves as the reasons for the omission.

4) The banns of marriage are not published in most congregations.[23] This is partly because compliance with this injunction would often be difficult, if not impossible, in the places where there is such a long interval between divine services and partly because all the moving around among our people would make it of little use.

5) When a congregation is first formed, divine service usually takes place in the largest house or in a public schoolhouse. These are sometimes too small to hold more than half the crowd; in that case baptism and communion are held in the house and the sermon in the open air under some trees. There you will see the pastor perched up on a high wagon, used for the occasion as a pulpit, with his listening flock standing, sitting, or reclining on the grass around him. If a large barn with a roof is available, one counts himself very fortunate. It is, after all, of secondary importance where the sermon is preached. The main thing is that the Word is preached plainly and purely. Still, the congregation tries as quickly as possible to get a proper church erected. Usually the faster they go, the more modest the church is, most often a simple structure built of "logs," that is, undressed timbers. The congregation, of course, is

The first church at Spring Prairie, built in 1853.
A larger church was built in 1886.

still small and without great means at its disposal. But usually after a half-score years the church is found to be too small. By this time the congregation has grown larger and stronger and it builds a roomier church of stone or wood with siding on the outside and plaster on the interior, provided with a steeple and quite nicely furnished. Sometimes a congregation waits some years before building in order to be in a better position to build all at once a worthy house of the Lord.

LECTURE III

Topics Discussed at Meetings of the Synod

We have now briefly considered the congregational polity, ordinances, and public worship of individual congregations. Before glancing at their spiritual state as well as at relations between pastor and congregation, we will return to a more detailed examination of some matters coming up for consideration by the Synod but depending for their execution on the approval and cooperation of the congregations. In our review of congregational affairs we have already considered church discipline and confession. We will therefore move right along to a discussion of the matter more than any other under constant deliberation by the Synod and a subject of concern and effort for the whole church body. I have in mind our institutions of higher learning and their relation to the formation of our pastors and schoolteachers.

The more the count of Norwegians in the country increased, the more the number and size of the congregations grew, the greater was the spiritual need among our people and the more the lack of pastors was felt. Cry after cry for help was sent to the homeland, where we thought there must always be some in positions and circumstances permitting them to come over and help us if they would. But either the young theologians did not hear our cry or the need of their brethren in faith did not touch their hearts. To be sure, there were some who saw their plight, took pity on them, and came and helped with the labor in the Lord's vineyard, but they were few. From 1848 to 1858, fourteen theological candidates came over and accepted calls to the pastorate. Of these, three have forsaken us and returned home. From 1858 until this year no more than six candidates have heeded our call, so that there are now in all seventeen pastors trained at the University in Norway.[1] The Lord be praised, indeed, that in the long course of twenty years not a single one has been taken away by death, although the heavy burden has seriously weakened, if not broken, the health of several of them.

In the meantime, our need has increased and our hope of seeing it met from the fatherland has diminished more and more. We have had, therefore, to direct our efforts to procuring properly competent teachers from within our own church body to see to ministerial training. Of course, even had there been more pastors from Norway, we would have had to consider this step for the sake of the future, when our congregations will become more Americanized and when pastors from Norway will be less suited for our circumstances, if not entirely unsuited because of the difference in language. Thus the issue was considered early. Indeed, the greater our need grew, the more earnestly it was tackled and the more vigorously it was pursued. But how to carry it off with our narrow financial means and with the even more limited number of teachers available to us? This was not an easy question to answer.

Our first thought was to establish a Norwegian Lutheran seminary and operate it in connection with the American state university in Madison, Wisconsin. The plan ran aground on difficulties raised by the university. We now see that it was well for us that nothing came of this plan. The Synod then decided in 1855 to allow pastors [Nils O.] Brandt and [J.A.] Ottesen to visit several German and English Lutheran synods in America to see if their theological positions were such as to allow us to work in connection with them.[2] The Lord in his grace consequently led the brethren to the German Lutheran Missouri Synod, in which they found brothers of the faith who had both the means and the will to help us.[3] This synod, in existence for some time, already possessed in full operation in St. Louis, Missouri, a college (Latin school), and a theological seminary where pious youths could get both the necessary academic preparation and the complete theological course required for service in the office of the ministry.[4] In our circumstances as they then were, nothing could have been more fortunate than for our young men to have the opportunity to take their training under the guidance of the competent teachers employed there. Even the cir-

cumstance that made it necessary for our Norwegian students to receive their instruction in the German language was nothing compared to the difficulties we would have had to overcome had we at
that moment been forced to start work on establishing the necessary schools on our own. The Missouri Synod met us with great
love and opened its schools to us. They have continued until the
present hour to show us the same love and sacrificial spirit.

When our students were about to start at the college in St.
Louis, we considered it both necessary for them and equitable with
respect to the Missouri Synod that we appoint and pay an instructor there. Thus in 1859 Pastor L[aur.] Larsen was appointed
professor in St. Louis and as such taught in the college as well as
in the seminary.[5] The number of Norwegian students the first year
was three and it increased the next year by four. Because of the tur-
bulence of wartime, the connection between the theoretical seminary and the college was dissolved in 1861. The latter was moved
to Fort Wayne, Indiana. The practical-theological seminary, on the
other hand, which until then had been in Fort Wayne, was moved
to St. Louis and joined to the theoretical seminary already there.[6]
These changes, in conjunction with other circumstances, made our
synod decide to strive immediately to establish our own college or
Latin school; this took place in the autumn of the same year under
Professor Larsen's direction in the vacant parsonage of the La-
Crosse congregation.[7] Professor [F. A.] Schmidt was called as an
associate instructor; he was trained at the theological seminary in
St. Louis and subsequently served as pastor of the English Lutheran
congregation in Baltimore.[8] It was a great gift of grace that the
Lord supplied us with this competent Christian teacher, because in
addition to his thorough knowledge of theology he is equally at
home in the English and German languages, and in the course of
a few years he has also acquired for himself considerable competence in Norwegian.

The school remained in LaCrosse no more than a year, since
the parsonage was needed for the congregation's pastor, Pastor [J.
B.] Frich, who arrived that year from Norway.[9] By 1861, the Synod had decided to purchase a parcel of land close to the town of
Decorah in Winneshiek county in Iowa to be dedicated to the erection of a building for our college. Because some time was expected
to transpire before this could be completed, the Synod decided in
1862 to purchase a building in Decorah to do temporary duty for

the school and another as a house for Professor Schmidt. As the stream of students poured in from year to year, it quickly became apparent that our temporary schoolhouse, which besides the necessary classrooms had to accommodate the living quarters required for all of the school's students as well as its director, Professor Larsen, was too small. An attempt was made to meet the need by erecting an addition, but it, too, was quickly outgrown. In 1863, therefore, the Synod decided to undertake the necessary preparations for a new college building, and in the following year the Synod decided that the work should be pursued as vigorously as incoming contributions would permit, in the hope that the building might be put under a roof by autumn. The cornerstone was laid with great solemnity in June, 1864, but the early winter hindered us from getting a roof on the building that year. Yet God allowed the building work to go forward so that as early as October, 1865, we were able with great ceremony—about which one could read in the newspapers here in Norway at the time—to dedicate a large, handsome, solid, well-appointed school building under the name "The Norwegian Luther College" and at the same time to take it into use.

In 1863 the university candidate [Lyder] Siewers was appointed assistant director, but since the school's enrollment was increasing, more faculty were required, especially since a seminary for training schoolteachers had been established in connection with the college.[10] Pastor Brandt was, therefore, called in 1865 as the fourth teacher to work at the school, especially in the schoolteachers' seminary.[11] Along with this he also had the office of parish pastor in the Decorah and Madison congregations. Since that time, the school has operated with a student body of sixty to eighty under the care of four teachers in five classes. We are now in need of another teacher and desire one with real competence in Greek and Latin philology.

The Norwegian Luther College in Decorah

Our college was established and is maintained in its entirety by freewill contributions from the Synod's congregations. It is most specifically a preparatory school for future theologians, although there is no obligation for the students to go on to the study of theology and the school is also used by many students who after a few years' instruction either return home to continue with farming or move on to other occupations. Although we naturally wish that as many as possible of our youth receive a more extensive general education than they can get through the congregational and district schools, we specifically desire that through a few years' residence at the school they can be subjected to the Christian discipline enforced there and acquire a clearer and more thorough knowledge of Christian truths. They can be fitted not only to be good citizens, but also to take a fruitful and blessed part in the responsibilities of our church body, which, just as it bestows great privileges on its members, makes great demands on their aptitudes and efforts.

Our college corresponds closely to the Latin school, but with two differences.[12] First, it is a boarding institution where all the students live together as a family in the college building under the fatherly supervision and Christian discipline of the teachers. Second, quite otherwise than in the Latin school, emphasis is placed here on the coming of the students to a clear, thorough, and correct knowledge of God's Word according to the Lutheran confessions. This, in tandem with the earnest Christian discipline, mild and strict at once and exercised from the top to the bottom of the school, gives it quite a different Christian aspect and character from that of the Latin school here in Norway. Furthermore, all of the school's teachers are considered servants of the church. Over and beyond their positions at the school, they offer all of their abilities, to the extent to which God has endowed them, to the general use of the church body insofar as this can be done without hindering their proper work. Beyond this, the subjects taught are essentially the same as here in Norway, although along with instruction in the ancient languages special emphasis is placed on acquiring competence in English and German. The school is divided into six classes with a six-year course. As a rule students do not begin before age fourteen, so the higher classes, usually composed only of those who have chosen to study theology, are as a rule mature, earnest Christian youths who through their conduct exercise a strong and beneficial influence on the younger students. Tuition was at first only $40 per year. The war and the times have required that this be increased to $60. But if you consider that for this students have free instruction, board, room, and heat, and that the congregations through their free gifts not only support the school's teachers and maintain the school buildings, but also contribute to the household

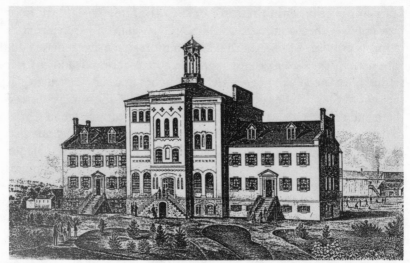

The Missouri Synod's Concordia Seminary in St. Louis in the 1860s. (Courtesy of Concordia Historical Institute.)

expenses and supply whatever is lacking, everyone will concede that it is worth it. Over and beyond this, a number of poor students are supported at the school by freewill contributions to the so-called scholarship fund. Teachers' salaries presently range from $650 to $950 per year in addition to free housing. Salaries are determined mostly on the basis of need.

The Theological Seminaries in St. Louis

The students who wish to study theology go from our college to one of the two German theological seminaries in St. Louis. Students who have been through all six classes in our college are accepted at the theological seminary. There are usually also some individual students of older years who, although they have not completed a full course in school and have not acquired the necessary mastery of the ancient languages, have, on the other hand, demonstrated themselves to be mature, earnest Christians driven by an inner desire, once they have become servants of the Word, to preach the gospel to their fellowmen. These we usually send over to the practical seminary.

The difference between these two seminaries is as follows. In the *theoretical* seminary those with the necessary academic prerequisites are, during a three-year course, given complete instruction for the pastoral office in theoretical as well as practical theology. Indeed, the confessional writings of the Lutheran Church are thoroughly reviewed, while the students are also made closely acquainted with the great theologians of the Lutheran Church from the period of the Reformation and the *Book of Concord*.[13] This theoretical seminary has three to four theology professors, among whom Professor [C. F. W.] Walther, instructor in dogmatics and pastoral theology, is the best known.[14] The so-called *practical* seminary was founded by Pastor Wilhelm Löhe of Bavaria to meet the needs of German emigrants in America.[15] Here a two- to three-year course of instruction in a more practical training for the holy office is given to older, talented, Christian-minded youths. Here the subjects of instruction are chiefly exegesis—not in the original tongue, naturally—dogmatics, church history, homiletics, catechetics, and pastoral theology. Professor [F. A.] Crämer, previously a missionary among the Indians, is the head of the faculty there.[16] The students of this seminary attend several of the lectures held in the theoretical seminary. Here, too, great emphasis is placed on thorough acquaintance with the confessions of the church, and for this reason an attempt is made to have the students learn enough Latin to understand the confessional documents in Latin. Upon completion of the examination which all theological students must take at the conclusion of their study, different grades for different degrees of proficiency are not assigned. All who pass the examination receive the same testimonial of orthodoxy and fitness for office. He whose moral conduct or lack of orthodoxy is such that it would interfere with his appointment to office does not receive a testimonial but, no matter how erudite, is pronounced unfit or unworthy. At the moment, we have a score of Norwegian students in St. Louis, the majority of whom are in the practical seminary. Tuition here has been about $20 annually, but will in the future be higher for the Norwegian students, who have to rent a special house in which to live, because the seminary cannot house all the students, German as well as Norwegian.

Since Professor Larsen undertook the direction of our Norwegian Luther College, our synod has had no Norwegian instructor at St. Louis. It is our desire again to appoint such a teacher and our synod has granted $1,000 as an annual salary for one instructor at St. Louis.[17]

We now have seventeen pastors trained at St. Louis. If I were to compare them with those who come from the University in Norway, the latter certainly possess a formal training superior to that of our "practical" candidates, a training not to be disparaged in any way. But, as far as I can judge, there is a greater confessional clarity and certainty to be found among our men, just as their sermons are sounder, more potent, and simpler.

After having thus heard something about the state of our affairs relative to higher education in the church, it might interest some of you to hear a little about how large our college building is, how it is laid out, and finally what, together with its furnishings, higher education has cost our synod. This information will, in any case, witness to how vigorous a participation the congregations have undertaken in one of the church body's most important tasks.

Our college building is 126 feet in length. The main building is 52 feet wide and 44 feet in the wings. It has a basement 10 feet high; three main stories of 14, 13, and 12 feet; and while the third story in the wings is 16 feet without a loft, in the main building there is an "attic story" of 10 feet, and finally a roomy loft. In the basement there are, besides cellars, two kitchens for the household of the school, a dining room in which 100 can be fed, room for the servants and the family of the housekeeper, together with two washrooms for the students in which, without their having to leave the building, clean water is pumped from a cistern and disposed of by means of drains. On the first floor there are quarters for three instructors (two of them with families) along with a large study hall. On the second floor there are eight larger and smaller lecture and classrooms, along with a guest room for each of the two instructors' families. On the third floor there are four dormitories for thirty students, two infirmary rooms, and two study halls along with an assembly hall across the whole wing, also used for church services. Finally, in the so-called "attic story" there are four large sleeping rooms for fifty-five students in all. In addition to this there are rooms set aside in the main tower on the second and third stories; one can be used as a library and the other as a dormitory. By complete use of the available space, the building could certainly accommodate 100 students in addition to the teachers who now live there, and up to 120 if only the director were to live on the premises. The rooms are light and airy and warm at the same time. To be sure, it is rather difficult to keep the northwest wind out of the big windows

*The Luther College building in 1874 photographed by a pastor of the
Norwegian Synod, Andreas Larsen Dahl. (Courtesy of the Archives of
Luther College, Decorah, Iowa.)*

during the winter, but that can be accomplished with blinds and
other suitable furnishings. Outside the building we have an aque-
duct along with a well dug in 1863 which always holds water,
though not in great amounts, as well as four cisterns in daily use.
In addition there are plans for a large cistern to be used only in case
of emergency, and pipes have been procured for all stories in order
to have water from the cisterns at hand. We have procured a pump
to propel water up through the pipes into the highest loft.

The following accounts show the expenses we have incurred in
building for higher education.

Land for the college	$ 1,660
The old college and annex	4,140
The new college	75,000
Miscellaneous expenses	5,000
Professor's house	1,200
	$87,000

Linka Preus's sketch of the cornerstone-laying at Luther College on June 30, 1864. While the identification of the figures is uncertain, it is likely that C. F. W. Walther and F. A. Crämer are seated at left. The two figures at the far right may be Herman Amberg Preus (stooping) and Laur. Larsen (standing). (Courtesy of the Archives of Luther College, Decorah, Iowa.)

Of this only about $60,000 has been paid, with $27,000 remaining as debt. But since 1860 about $13,000 has been paid in professors' salaries, making a total of $73,000.

In the last synodical year our congregations contributed:

Gifts to the University Fund		$12,000
Professors' salary		2,000
School's household account		1,000
(besides donations *in natura*)		
St. Louis household account		300
Contributions to poor students		3,000
Synodical treasury		120
Mission to heathen	1,520	
Home mission	460	
		1,980
		$20,400

Voluntary contributions to the general work of the church body, chiefly to the school, thus amount to about $20,000–$25,000 per year. Beside these expenses each congregation naturally has to provide what is necessary for its own church, pastor, and school. If you take into account the total number of members of our church body, the sum of these voluntary contributions for the purposes of the church does not seem so very large. Yet for those who contribute they are not really paltry. In this instance one must bear in mind that the bulk of the members of our congregations are from the common people, who for the most part had neither the occasion nor the means when they were in Norway to make voluntary sacrifices for the church's purposes. When now, through the blessing of God, they come into possession of earthly goods, they need first to be taught to use them for the furtherance of God's kingdom. This task falls mainly to the pastor. He tries to do this not only by bringing these matters up in public at congregational meetings, and enlisting pledges there, but also by visiting homes, and by using the opportunities offered by meetings and chance occurrences to awaken interest in the kingdom of God and the will to contribute to its furtherance. To speak of authority or compulsion on these occasions is, naturally, out of the question.[19] On the other hand one cannot, of course, draw firm conclusions about the disposition of the heart from the gift. But recalling how many of our congregations are as good as without pastors and are visited by one of our pastors only a few times a year, and how much there is to do on these occasions, one can understand that these congregations cannot be counted on for much help and that in reality the yearly contributions on the part of many individuals are not so insignificant. The yearly contribution to the work of the church body the individual members of the congregations can be expected to offer thus varies from between $5 and $50, while contributions to the college building from a number of those concerned have been $100 or more. Sometimes, in pressing circumstances, a whole congregation will issue a call to the other congregations to take up a common concern zealously and willingly and offer their gifts. Because it so well illuminates our situation, both the way these things are done and the spirit in which they are attacked, I shall permit myself to read one of these calls, issued last autumn by the Koshkonong congregation.[20]

"To the dear congregations of our church body! Greetings of

grace and peace in Christ Jesus, Amen! It is well known to you all, dear brethren in faith, that a heavy debt rests on our school in Decorah. And it is about this matter that we make this brotherly recommendation to you. It must be a source of concern to us all that we have not hitherto been more zealous in this regard, when we consider the good gifts the Lord has given us in this school. It is our hope that pastors and schoolteachers can be sent out from here to further his Word and preserve the pure doctrine for us according to his ordinances. Since we must confess that his Word is our most glorious treasure, should we not then gladly make offering of the temporal goods God has granted us in order to maintain this school, which is meant precisely to serve the end of preserving this Word plainly and purely among us? We can see how many of our countrymen and brethren in faith there are among us who still do without the preaching of the Word. If we love and acknowledge its blessing among ourselves, should we not gladly help others toward the same blessing by furthering the progress of such a school? Think of how many souls are seduced away and perish because they are not watched over and led by faithful shepherds! Nor do we know how long God will allow us to keep the teachers we now have. Should we not gladly seek others to take their places when God calls them away? What use is it to have all the other earthly goods if we do without his proper preaching? And finally, when we think of the dear children, and how gladly we would work for them and sacrifice everything to make a good future for them, should we not first and foremost think of how, insofar as it is in our power, we can secure for them while they are young, so that they may later take our places in church and state, both competent schoolteachers and devout preachers?

"Think of how it would be if after we have passed on they had reason to complain about us that we provided better for them in everything else than the one thing most needful. Think of how it would be if on Judgment Day they were eternally lost through our neglect and they met us and accused us before God of sitting with our hands in our laps without procuring for them, while there was yet time, the one thing needful, but working only to bequeath earthly means to them. Yes, not only they will accuse us but many others of our countrymen, both of this generation and those to come. Our calling now is to build a church body. Shall we regard it as a burden or a yoke? Shall we begrudge this to those who follow us, who will share in the fruit without having first had to work for it? No, far be it from us! We would rather regard this as a gift of grace, an honor shown us by God that he let it fall to our lot to begin this nursery in the Lord's vineyard and above all to begin it on the proper foundation of the Word. And if we are afraid of being judged unfaithful on the Judgment Day and accountable for the loss, be it our own or strangers', should we not aspire to the honor and glory of being able on that day to hear testimony from many, known and unknown to us, that, because God was pleased through our work to allow his Word to reach them and they came in faith and were kept in it unto a blessed end, they must acknowledge us as the instruments used by God for their eternal salvation? Certainly the gracious recompense of the Lord will be returned a thousand-fold for whatever sacrifices we may now make. God has given us wordly blessings so richly, in any case sufficiently, that we can do what is needed here without loss. Would we not disgrace the name of God and his doctrine if we held back in this out of niggardliness or indifference, and this school were hampered or stymied by lack of support on our parts?

"Should we not all be afraid of committing such a sin and saddening the dear God who has been so good to us in this our new homeland and who up until now has so graciously blessed the efforts we, in all our weakness, have made? He has already gathered a church body large in numbers and sent out many orthodox teachers who have received their instruction here. How then can we expect God to bless our temporal work or our secular estate if he sees indeed that the more of peace and good days he gives us the more of his gifts we hold back and do not use to serve him where he clearly shows us that they are needed? Then we might well fear that he would take his hand from us and withdraw his blessing in temporal things. Again, what good would it do us, even in the richest circumstances, if we had to do without that? It is the Lord's blessing alone that makes us rich. Without that we are poor in the midst of the greatest wealth. With it we are rich in the worst worldly adversity. But even more, how can we expect the Lord to bless his Word upon our hearts if he can see that we do not cherish it enough to be willing to use his gifts to sustain this school whose purpose is to promote his Word, spread it, and preserve it for us from generation to generation? Should we not fear that he will at last take his Word from us and abandon us to terrible errors and to belief in lies? Therefore, dear brethren, let us all acknowledge that God shows us clearly here that he desires our poor service, that he thinks us worthy to use the gifts he has entrusted to us, to the furtherance of his kingdom, to our growth and the growth of many souls in piety!

"Let us not then grow weary or fainthearted when we think that the going is heavy or that it is so difficult for us to get this underway! We cannot expect that God will give us a school like this without exertion on our part. Until now no one has had to sacrifice beyond his means. No one has felt the pinch of what he has given, even the richest gift. No one is the wealthier for having held back even if he gave nothing. We must all confess that we could just as easily give again what we first gave without feeling the loss. Indeed, most of us must admit that through God's blessing we are in better circumstances now than we were when we started this task and that it would be easier, if necessary, to give a larger gift now than it was to give a smaller one then. Should we hang back now when less is required? Let us not watch others holding back and think that we should do the same. If we are not to repent of what we have done, let us not expect to be free of this obligation so that others can stand in the breach. Oh no, it is no burden of which we wish to be free; it is rather an honor to have had a part in this from the start, all the more because we have acknowledged the blessing of giving to the Lord. Therefore, if we love his Word, let us pray and work all the more zealously even as we see it neglected! Let us not grow fainthearted over this even if many oppose us in our work. God is still with us. He is present in his Word. And—praised be his grace!—that we have, plain and pure! And he is stronger than all his foes. It is this Word that we will advance. And there must be many among us who love it and who both can and will help us out of the present difficulty. Since we love his Word, we should be all the more ardent and, instead of waiting for others who have held back until now to come forth, we ought to press on so that our zeal might inspire them. By this means God may perhaps awaken them to reflection and allow them to understand that they stand in the way of their own joy by their aloofness from what they see has brought us a joy they did not before even suspect possible. Perhaps God will by this means put them in a frame of mind to begin to long for the Word of life which they see has the power to make us fervent in giving and happier and richer in such a simple message than they themselves were while they held aloof.

"Therefore, dear brethren, as many as love his truth and acknowledge the grace of God as he has entrusted it to us, let us pray to God to preserve us from the mockery of his name and doctrine that it would be should it turn out that even the church which rightfully praises his name because he gave it the pure Word and pure sacraments, and which always bears witness to the power of these means of grace to turn hearts and make possible all good works, did not have enough children willing to preserve the proper administration of these sacraments though God had entrusted them with worldly goods enough to do it! Then would we be put to shame by the many sects and nominal Lutherans around us who often show greater zeal and sacrificial spirit for their false doctrine than we do to preserve God's truth as a costly treasure, as a holy inheritance for ourselves and those who come after us.

"We have tried with these words in all simplicity to encourage ourselves and we pray God to help us take heart. We would with these words gladly seek to encourage you, dear brethren far and near, and pray that you do not disdain them but receive them with the same love in which they were sent. We know both of ourselves and of you that God alone can prepare a good place for us and convert all of our hearts and unite us in a powerful collaboration in common prayer and common work. He alone can give success and a good outcome. But should it be his good and merciful will, it is to be hoped that, if we all in his name earnestly take hold of the cause, this debt could be paid in a relatively short time, for example during this winter. There are enough of us, not merely enough reckoned by numbers, but enough of us who will gladly, by the grace of God, give to serve him and sacrifice for the furtherance of his kingdom. Let us first and foremost pray constantly in this matter, and the God who hears prayers and does more than we can pray for and understand, who has up until now so plainly done this for us in this cause and allowed everything to succeed beyond expectation, will now hear our prayers and incite us to energetic work and bless it to the glorification of his name. To him be glory and praise in all eternity! May he let it all prosper in Jesus' name! Amen!"

Missions

Another matter of general concern to the church in which the Synod has encouraged individual congregations to interest themselves is missions, both foreign and domestic.

The mission to the heathen receiving primary support from our church body in America is the one conducted by the German Lutheran Missouri Synod among the North American Indians. The reason we have adopted this mission especially is that over the course of the years we, as a part of the American people, have driven the Indians, the natives of the land, away from their homes and farther and farther west. We would like to make up a little for this and other injustices done to them. But, while we seek therefore to bring the saving message of the gospel to the awareness of these primitives, at the same time we also desire to come to the aid, in this its important work, of a church body to which we owe so much.

The Missouri Synod has had two stations among the Indians, one in northern Michigan and the other in northern Minnesota. The latter station, on the upper Mississippi where the German missionary [E. O.] Clöter labored, was disturbed during the war when the Indians revolted against their white oppressors.[21] It was only because at the last minute an Indian chief informed Clöter of the imminent danger that he and his family were able to save their lives by hasty flight. The missionary still hopes to be able to reclaim the abandoned station. The Missourians' missionary station in Michigan was previously at Bethany, where twenty years ago Professor Crämer began the work as the first missionary and where it was continued for a time by Missionary [E. R.] Baierlein, who is now in India.[22] Missionary [E. G. H.] Miessler later worked there for about ten years, but because the Indians among whom he worked moved to the reservation assigned to them in Isabella county he followed them there. These Indians belong to the Ojibway tribe.[23] The visible results of this mission have not hitherto been great, but it is no wonder, considering that this is a people systematically ruined by whites and laboring under burdens enough to overcome them, as most certainly few other heathen peoples have had to do. Therefore, neither hope nor the task may be abandoned. A son of Professor Crämer, who spent his childhood among the Indians and who has since often been among them to refresh his acquaintance with their language, is now receiving training in St. Louis in order to go out among them later as a missionary. Baierlein makes the following comparison between the American Indians and the Hindus of India.

"The people of America are magnificent and taciturn, few in numbers and spread out, full of character, free and independent as the game of the forest, and yet also just as inconstant, indigent, and dispersed. The people here in India are many in numbers, prattlers beyond all limits; they have been in bondage for thousands of years to native and foreign masters and are therefore practiced in the paths of serpentine deceit and masters of hypocrisy—a characterless mass.

"As with the people, so with the language. The Indian, silent as his forest, speaks hardly as many words in a month as the Hindu does in a day. In order not to use many words, he therefore packs as many thoughts as possible into every word, even if they are long ones. The Hindu piles word upon word for the same thought and, because when he has once gotten his tongue wagging he does not care to stop, will run the end of one word into the beginning of the next. Thus there are no pauses and no one can interrupt. Indeed even in written form, word is linked to word as if he feared separation or interruption.

"Religion *there* [among the American Indians] is simple, a childlike worship of the forces of nature, the 'spirits' who rule thunder and lightning, storm and wind, rainfall and earthquake, who live now in the skies above, now in the waters below, and now in human form as men with higher powers and authority who may change form when it pleases them. They can be well or ill disposed toward people, but never morally impure. Religion *here* [in India] is the most diverse and deliberate idolatry the world has ever seen, and the gods impose all kinds of burdens on the people.

"As with religion so with manners. *There* one finds great simplicity and little deceit, *here* no simplicity and great deceit on all sides. There, with respect to the Sixth Commandment, there is little to remember, here it is a sink of all kinds of obscenity.[24]

"But enough of these contrasts! There are similarities, too. There as here the wells are empty of the water of life. There as well as here are sorrowing hearts and absence of joy all around, and the way of peace is unknown. The many helpers, here as there, have gained us nothing and have nothing to offer and the *One* who has

91

earned for us and who can and will give us life and full salvation
—he is unknown, unsought, undesired."[25]

Our so-called inner mission is most specifically aimed at bringing the gospel to our countrymen in America who have settled
down in larger or smaller groups at considerable distance from the
general stream of Norwegian immigration and have for a long time
been without congregational organization and the ministry of the
Word. Small Norwegian congregations without the necessary
means to maintain themselves as churches can also receive assistance from the inner mission treasury. Among the chief places
where this missionary work has been conducted I shall mention
New York City and Texas. At the expense of the missionary treasury
we have sent to both places men capable of preaching God's Word
and arranging church affairs.

It would be well to point out that our missionary work, domestic as well as foreign, has preserved its ecclesiastical character. It is
not our goal in our home missionary efforts to organize lay preaching or, if I may put it this way, to establish or maintain an uncalled
and therefore improper office of lay preacher alongside the public
teaching office.[26] No, when "uncalled" preachers—be they lay people or pastors—are sent out it is because we believe that there is an
emergency authorizing them to administer ecclesiastical office publicly as "emergency pastors," without call. At the same time their
efforts are to be directed to meeting the momentary need and to
clearing the way toward making themselves superfluous by seeing to
it that a fit pastor is called to the proper service of the office as soon
as possible.

Next, our missions are a matter for the congregations. Neither
home nor foreign missions are carried out among us, as they are in
Norway, by an association formed for this purpose.[27] No, they are
conceived and conducted as they truly are, as a task for the whole
congregation and the whole church. We believe that it weakens congregational consciousness, that it is at root a declaration of the
bankruptcy of the Christian congregation to form associations for
all kinds of Christian purposes. It is entirely natural that this should
nourish partisanship and division as well as the self-importance and
arrogance that looks with misgivings, if not contempt, on those
who do not think it proper to take part in such unchurchly associa-
tional activity. One ought not to appeal to results; that they have by
God's blessings in many ways done good demonstrates nothing in

this case. The question is not whether the blessed effect would be greater and the dangerous consequences negligible, but whether the matter is handled in a way consonant with God's Word.

In the same way we have, without forming any association within the church body, worked toward publication and distribution of good Lutheran literature. A printing of 4,000 copies of Luther's house postils has sold out.[28] 3,000–4,000 copies of two volumes of *Luthers Folkebibliotek* have appeared and are also sold out, except for a few copies to be found at Dybwad's and other booksellers in Norway.[29] Similarly *Frelsens Olje* by Luther, the *Concordia*, and *Frikirken* by Professor Walther have been published in several thousand copies.[30] Our synod publishes Lutheran periodicals, *Kirkelige Maanedstidende* in Norwegian and *Lutheran Watchman* in English; they may be had at the cost of $1 annually, including postage.[31]

Efforts Toward Union with Other Norwegian Church Bodies

One matter always a source of worry and pain to our synod has been the ecclesiastical division of our countrymen. Our synod's efforts have constantly been directed toward smoothing this out and uniting the factions. We have shown ourselves forthcoming in this not only where we detected an inclination to effect a union but also where over many years our efforts to end the strife and seek unanimity have been met with ill will and coldness. With respect to the Augustana Synod, for example, we have not grown weary, but despite repeated rebuffs have continued our efforts to the present day, because we understand the sin that is perpetrated and the dangers to which souls are exposed by departing from the truth and following errors. On the other hand, we also see well how strife, sin, and harm come to both sides when such division among countrymen is continued over the course of years. In heartfelt earnest we seek to prevent this party division, sinful and displeasing to God, from continuing, and our synod's history will testify that we earnestly wish not to bear responsibility for it. But a union without unity of faith, a union in the Prussian mold in which God's Word and human propositions are tolerated side by side and have equal validity, this kind of union we will not promote.[32] This is an abomination to God and more dangerous to souls than open disunity and faction. We

*Peter Andreas Rasmussen (1829–1898), originally of Eielsen's Synod,
later a pastor of the Norwegian Synod and of the United
Norwegian Lutheran Church.*

have not wished to work for such a union to take place. Where we
have seen error among our opponents we have not tried to cover its
shame with the veil of false charity, but have openly and honorably
drawn their attention to it, running the danger of seeming un-
charitable. And if our opponents were to show us errors in our doctrine or practice, we would thank them for it and consider it a
demonstration of Christian love on their part rather than of hatred
or lack of love. We do not deny that sharp expressions can be used
in controversy; we believe that they have often been necessary and
the examples of Christ and the apostles show that they are permissible when needed. We regret that bitterness can creep in during the
heat of controversy, even when the scornful and hateful attacks of
our opponents have occasioned it. The candid person cannot allow
himself to abstain from rendering honor to the truth even though
he sees that some of the weapons used to defend it are of the flesh.

When hearts are given over to the truth and unity in faith is finally reached, there all bitterness is quickly pardoned, forgiven, and forgotten. Thus it was between us and Pastor [P. A.] Rasmussen and his friends.[33]

A little later I will go into more detail concerning the different factions in the church. Here I want only to point out the visible results brought about by our church body's efforts to establish peace and unity.

Pastor Rasmussen originally belonged to Elling Eielsen's church body, but along with many congregations he separated from it after complaining of false doctrine and an ungodly life on Eielsen's part.[34] He formed a church body by itself to which pastors [Nils] Amlund and John Fjeld were called.[35] Both before and after Pastor Rasmussen's defection from Elling, we carried on a violent battle with him. After we conferred with him and his followers in 1862, during which we achieved unity in faith, they were received into our synod the following year. Some Norwegian pastors and a few small Norwegian congregations here and there also belong to the Augustana Synod.[36] With them—of whom some, as we shall later see, have really been Reformed from the very beginning—we have waged open battle since the founding of our synod. Without being immodest we may dare to say that our attack and witness over against them has by God's grace been instrumental in drawing them back more toward the Lutheran Church and its pure confession. But that is not the only result of our struggle. Last fall pastors [Ole O.] Estrem and [Abraham] Jacobson left the Augustana Synod and joined our church body.[37] They could not, however, be received by us as pastors before taking further study at the theological seminary, even though the first of them had been named by the Augustana Synod as professor at its school. In the last few years, several more Norwegian congregations have severed their connection with the Augustana Synod and sought the service of pastors of our synod. They have been compelled to this step by the conviction that there is much in the doctrine and practice of the Augustana Synod militating against God's Word and the confession of the church, and that efforts made to put things right have been without result.[38]

LECTURE IV

The Spiritual State of the Congregations

H aving now considered the work of our church body at its common tasks, we will glance briefly at the spiritual state of the individual congregations. It will have been obvious from the foregoing sketch that this varies greatly with the different congregations. While some congregations are able to enjoy a rich service of the ministry of the Word, a great many others are as good as bereft of it, having to content themselves with a visit from a pastor a few times a year. There are congregations among us seeking diligently to allow God's Word to dwell among them, where household devotions are more common, where the Word is diligently applied in divine services and congregational meetings, where church discipline is exercised not just in exceptional cases but where an attempt is made to eliminate every public offense; congregations which occupy themselves in growing rich in good works, in meeting spiritual and physical needs out of their temporal goods, and in promoting the Kingdom of God in and beyond their own circles. At the same time there are unfortunately many congregations in our church body about which such things cannot generally be said. Where the public ministry of the Word cannot fully develop because of the lack of teachers, neither will the Word in other ways dwell richly there for the edification of the congregation, and there the fruits of the Spirit will be scarce. Contrariwise, open sins of the flesh will quite often cause public indignation, and for want of the exercise of Christian church discipline sinners will not be properly punished and their souls saved.

Here again we confront the need, the crying spiritual need, reigning in many parts of our church body primarily because of the lack of diligent proclaimers of the Word. But where this need has somehow been met or can be met, there we can have reason to hope for a happy future for our church body, in the sense that we may hope to see a healthy Christian life develop more and more. I believe it ought to be obvious on the basis of what has already been presented that the essential conditions for this are present to a far higher degree in our Lutheran free church than in the state churches. Where lay people are not only allowed but consistently required, and even pressed, to share in the work of the church by the instinct of self-preservation, to participate directly in the work of the individual congregations as well as in the tasks and governance of the church body as a whole, a greater interest in the church may and does come to prevail, a living consciousness of the congregation makes itself felt, and a fuller and stronger congregational life develops. Where a uniform and steady collaboration and exchange between the servants of the congregation and its members occurs, a more confident and intimate relation between them will develop that will not only ease and sweeten the burdens of office, but will also produce a much greater assurance that the work of the ministry shall not be without blessing.

And—God be praised!—this has already happened in many places. Had it not been so, I really do not know how many of those who have borne the burden with all its privations and pressures would have dropped under it. Yet—"My grace is sufficient for you," says the Lord.[1]

Before I leave this point behind, I would like to expand on a few details. It is chiefly in two respects that the clearer and stronger congregational consciousness mentioned above, as well as interest in the church, appears in our congregations.

Regarding the first, the obligation of every member of the congregation, insofar as possible, to "try the spirits whether they are of God," is rather generally acknowledged in our older, better served congregations.[2] As a result, many of the members of our congregations apply themselves to observing this admonition and grow more and more diligent in its observance. By no means do they just sit and take whatever it may occur to the pastor to preach to them. It is not their conviction that he bears the full responsibility, as if he could take the place of God's Word or alongside it preach his own opinions, human propositions, and errors, or speak confusedly and confusingly about the order of salvation while they sit mute. Nor will they take it equably if half in despair they find that their pastor and the shepherd of their souls has by frivolous and ungodly behavior publicly mocked the name of the Lord and of the ministry, scandalizing the congregation at the same time. Nor will they be idle spectators should he, through sloth or even incompetence, "render the Lord's work void" while the congregation of the Lord stands in danger of being divided or overcome. In the worst case, they will not peacefully allow the pastor alone to be responsible for their neglecting to go to church to hear his false or unspiritual preaching while they attach themselves to one or another lay preacher, seek edification from him, and let everything else go awry. No, there are many who would feel that they themselves bore the responsibility for not trying the spirits, for not admonishing and punishing a false teacher, an ungodly pastor, a careless shepherd, for not—where admonition and punishment were fruitless—exercising their authority, fulfilling their duty, and dismissing the unfaithful servant, thus all the more serving the glory of God and the salvation of the congregation rather than human personality and authority. They would indeed understand that by neglecting such doctrinal discipline instituted by God they would make themselves collaborators and accomplices in false doctrine, expose the members of the congregation to seduction, and finally suffer the fate of a church body united in error instead of Lutheran orthodoxy.

Far from any general tendency in the congregations to abuse this authority, there has occasionally been, as I must bear witness on their behalf, a tendency to show a forbearance and tolerance of megalomania and disrespect on the part of the clergy, on account of which tighter regulations might have been in order. On the other hand, the pastor, when he fears that the congregation is overreaching itself and that he is becoming falsely dependent on it, need only remember that he is not only the congregation's servant, but also God's servant, and that God's Word itself shows him when and where he can without sin "shake the dust off his feet."[3] In connection with this point, there is also the attention and energy awakened by controversy over doctrinal questions all across the church body. These battles are not restricted to clerical circles or individual congregations and considered pertinent only to them, but are rather of concern to the whole church body.

Regarding the second, interest in the affairs of the church manifests itself in the willingness with which the congregations as a whole, without external compulsion or authority, procure the necessary means for the maintenance of church, pastor, school, and even the common tasks of the church body. There remains in connection with these tasks much still to be desired from many individual congregations. Yet, when all the circumstances are considered, we must thank God that even in this respect things have gone as well among us as they have. In any case, we pastors do not suffer want. As a rule we more often have reason to accuse ourselves than our congregation.

The New York congregation occupies a special place in our church body.[4] Many of the oldest Scandinavian settlers are there; their number is extremely large and is annually augmented by city folk emigrating from the Nordic countries. And in addition to these Norwegian-American citizens, a number of Scandinavian sailors regularly stay in the city and sail from there for some years before returning home. As early as several years ago we tried, although vainly, to draw the attention of the fatherland to the spiritual need in which sailors, both those who live there and those who yearly visit New York harbor on Norwegian ships, find themselves in this enormous cosmopolitan city. In the meantime, in more recent years there have been earnest attempts here in Norway to be of spiritual help through this ministry to our less fortunate countrymen. There would be no place in which work on behalf of the spiritual welfare of Norwegian sailors would be so appropriate as in New York. In order to do my bit to interest you in these countrymen of ours I want here to give a sketch of religious conditions among the Scandinavians in New York.

Just as church affairs began to be put in order in the West, some families in New York began steadily to cry out to us: "Come over and help us! Send us a righteous servant of the Word who can break the bread of life for us."[5] The cry went to our hearts, but the need of our own congregations was so great that there could be no talk of sending them any of the teachers then to be found among us. Yet the church council often took the matter into consideration, consulted with the then Consul General [G. C.] Sibbern about it, and finally sent a petition to the Norwegian government for support for a Norwegian Lutheran pastor in New York.[6] Even at that time a large number of Norwegian sailors were regularly staying in New York, but the petition was not accepted.

During the years 1855 and 1856, the Danish pastor [P. C.] Sinding worked among the Scandinavians.[7] Had he been an orthodox, conscientious teacher, he would with God's help have succeeded in forming a congregation that could have sustained the preaching ministry in its midst. But the man either had no conception of congregational polity or he was concerned merely to get numbers of names on his rolls in order to get an abundance of daily bread from their contributions. It is sufficient to say that he accomplished nothing toward the end of establishing a Lutheran congregation. What is more, he occasioned indignation in a variety of ways, thus putting obstacles in the way of those whom the Lord would later send to work in this field.

In the year 1860, as emissary of our synod, Professor Larsen undertook his journey to Norway.[8] Both on the way and coming back he stopped for a few days in New York for the purpose of gathering and ordering a Lutheran congregation among the Scandinavians there. By God's grace he was successful beyond all expectations. In addition to divine services he held two meetings attended by quite a few people who showed no little zeal for the formation of a congregation. About seventy families, mainly Norwegian and Danish but also a few Swedish, united under the name: "The Scandinavian-Lutheran Congregation in New York," (Den skandinavisk-lutherske Menighed i New York). It adopted an orthodox Lutheran congregational order. The congregation delegated Professor Larsen to call a pastor from Norway and designated a yearly contribution of at least $400 for the support of the pastor. In addition several Scandinavians who did not wish to join the congregation promised to support it. Unfortunately, Professor Larsen did not succeed in getting a pastor in Norway to accept the call from the New York congregation. Many of the members consequently were again disappointed and their zeal cooled because the prospect of having their own pastor seemed far off, as far off as the time when it would be possible to send them a pastor from our church body in the West. Professor Larsen left after a stay of a few days in New York and the congregation was then without any pastoral service or leadership. A committee was selected to act on behalf of the congregation and gather it together when necessary, but it had no further significance for the congregation. To hold a part of it together as far as possible, the more zealous began to gather on Sunday mornings for lay reading services. But a certain Petersen, who took some sort of training at a Presbyterian seminary and in any event later associated himself with the Augustana Synod and was authorized by its president, Mr. [Tufve N.] Hasselquist, to work among the Scandinavians there, quickly disturbed all this by insinuating himself into the congregation and usurping its preaching ministry.[9] This had unhappy results, since little by little most of the congregation left and from that time on sought edification in their own homes or in the churches of other church bodies. In 1863 Pastor Ottesen conducted business for the congregation on his way to Norway.[10] In 1864, at the expense of the mission fund, Professor Schmidt traveled to New York.[11] He worked there for a little over a month. When the pastors' conference asked me to travel to New York in 1865, I decided with the consent of my congregations to go and with God's help to do all that I could in the short time of five or six weeks for the upbuilding of God's kingdom among our countrymen there.

The Scandinavian Lutheran congregation there still existed on paper, but that is about all one could say about it. There was no public activity, no common worship. One could hardly even speak of a cohesion among its members. They really were, as some of them put it, sheep without a shepherd, wandering hither and yon. Merely to gather them together again and to see that they were informed about the holding of divine services was a task fraught with no little difficulty and, in spite of every effort, it was only partially successful. Right up to the last day of my stay in the city, people came to my services explaining that they had not until then heard a word about my presence. That this can happen so easily will not surprise you when you hear that the city together with its suburbs extends a length of sixteen miles and along the whole of this length houses stand shoulder to shoulder, for all but brief intervals, and that the Scandinavians are dispersed throughout the whole city and its suburbs. This circumstance will always make the work of a Norwegian pastor in the city difficult and troublesome.

I did not find it immediately advisable to call a meeting of the older members of the congregation and others who might be interested in ordering the congregations afresh. I was working here with people who for a period of ten, sometimes even thirty, years had been without proper service of the ministry and of whom the majority had either not sought out any church affiliation or had attached themselves to church bodies erring to a greater or lesser degree. I did not know any of them nor they me, and even those interested in establishing a congregation were as good as unknown to one another. I thought it therefore appropriate to limit my work at the beginning to public preaching and visiting in homes. I thus decided to hold three worship services a week. The German Lutheran Church of the Missouri Synod generously allowed me the use of the "Marine Church" on Sunday afternoon. This church is used for sailors from every country and of every tongue without respect to confession. I believe, in fact, that as a rule the preachers there are Baptists and that the church is under their supervision as a missionary church. Since Monday evenings were set aside by established custom for the holding of Scandinavian services in the church, these evenings were given over to me during my whole stay in New York through the courtesy of the Swedish Baptist pastor, Mr. Anderson.[12] I was very happy about this since the church was right in the middle of the city, was well known to everyone, and had always been visited by Scandinavian seafarers. I also applied to old Pastor [Olof G.] Hedström of the ship Bethel for permission to preach there.[13] He gave many excuses for refusing me, since his congregation required that he himself should preach to them. Naturally I found his reasons good enough from his standpoint and the excuses superfluous. I answered only that it had been my wish that my countrymen whom I saw visiting his congregation might once again be allowed to hear *God's pure Word*. I also met here the Norwegian Methodist pastor, [Ole] Helland.[14] The ship Bethel with its old Swedish pastor Hedström is the Scandinavian Methodist church and is also well known to the Norwegian emigrants who come over to New York. Old Hedström rarely omits paying our newcomers a visit aboard ship or at Castle Garden, where all emigrants must now land. It has been very harmful not to have a Scandinavian Lutheran pastor living in New York, because not a few of our countrymen on landing have been seduced onto the ship Bethel and have either sought their spiritual nourishment there if they have settled in New York or have carried the Methodist contagion with them across the country.

So it was that I preached in the places mentioned above and tried insofar as possible to get acquainted with my listeners, partly through conversation after worship and partly by visiting them in their homes. I continued thus until September 21, for which date I had summoned a general meeting. At this meeting I first laid out the congregational constitution created several years earlier by Professor Larsen and accepted by the congregation. I then tried to present to them the idea of a Christian congregation and the importance of joining an orthodox congregation for the salvation of the soul, but at the same time I tried to draw their attention to how necessary it is for whoever wishes to join a congregation to have a penitent, believing disposition in order that his conduct should not amount to a hypocrisy harmful both to him and to the congregation. I thereupon invited all who had been members of the congregation to declare whether they wished henceforth to belong to it and work for it. These declarations made, some who had not before been connected with the congregation were taken in as members, while others for one reason or another did not wish to join the congregation but promised it their support. The congregation, thus organized, accepted the old congregational constitution, adding provision for the manner in which reception of new members of the congregation should take place in the future when the congregation might have its own permanent pastor, and decided to elect a congregational council. On Sunday the 8th of October, I held a final worship service with about sixty members of the congregation as communicants. By the time I left, ninety-five adults had joined the congregation. The greatest part of them were Norwegians, with about twenty Danes and a few Swedes.

When I arrived I was met everywhere with forthcoming friendliness, and by many with heartfelt joy, which cheered me greatly and will be a precious memory. On the basis of so short an acquaintance I will naturally not try to give a detailed sketch of the congregation's spiritual state. This much I can say: everyone expressed the wish for a permanent pastor as soon as possible, though whether it was out of an inner longing for God's unadulterated Word and sacraments I do not know. Many expressed their willingness to contribute what is necessary to the pastor's support and the maintenance of the congregation. Whether they will all be true to their word when it comes to it, time will tell. But I nourish no doubt that when a faithful shepherd of souls can regularly preach the Word of life among them, the dear God who has blessed them so abundantly in matters temporal will also bless his Word among them so that with hearts awakened to joy and thankfulness they will contribute their earthly goods to the maintenance of preaching ministry among themselves in order that the congregation may soon care for itself, even if it does need a hand at first. Many showed zeal for the preservation of the pure doctrine and said that they would not countenance anything other than an orthodox Lutheran teacher. Even if I cannot speak here of a living knowledge of the purity, preciousness, and nobility of the Lutheran doctrine, I can testify that I met members of the congregation of whom I have reason to believe that they were not only earnestly concerned for the salvation of their souls and heartily longed for the Savior and His Word, but also out of deep earnestness and rich spiritual experience combined a rare clarity of perception with a firm adherence to and deep love for the Lutheran Church. They were completely convinced in their minds that it — and only it — possessed God's pure and unadulterated Word, especially the Word of the forgiveness of sinners by faith for Christ's sake that renders souls confident, happy, and saved. In addition, some individuals were well acquainted with our Lutheran church body in the West. They were at home in the controversial questions that have exercised us. Indeed they have, so to speak, experienced our internal and external struggles and suffered with us as well as rejoiced with us when they saw the truth victorious. They were thus devoted from the heart to our synod and would not countenance a churchly affiliation other than with our synod. They came to this clear knowledge and confessional certainty in part through diligent reading of Luther's writings along with Holy Writ, and partly through their temporary affiliation with the Missouri Synod's German-Lutheran congregation in New York. Regular reading of *Maanedstidende* was also helpful.[15]

Now, so that on the basis of these remarks of mine no one gets an exaggerated idea of how far the congregation has progressed in its general spiritual condition or extravagant expectations for its future, I shall make a few further comments. After due consideration, there is reason to be sober in our expectations for this congregation's future. Just as we have before had to work in hope against hope and struggle steadily in prayer to God, the laborers here must be prepared for the same kind of adversity in the near future. We must thank God and rejoice when through our work a single individual is preserved in the true faith or when one or another of our precious countrymen is won back for God's kingdom, plucked like a brand out of a fire and saved for eternal life. We must be satisfied if we can gather the dispersed into a fine congregation, whether they come from those not so estimable in the eyes of the world or they happen to include many of the world's elevated, respected, powerful, and wealthy people. The main thing is not that the congregation grows large, but that it includes members who in their hearts hear God in faith and are saved.

The number of Scandinavians in New York is certainly very large. Reports vary between 10,000 and 30,000.[16] Of these perhaps the largest part belong to no Christian church body. The majority of them came from the homeland for the sake of worldly advantage. But unlike their countrymen in the West they were not met by a servant of the Word to preach the precious truth to them in their mother tongue, to remind them of the grace granted them in childhood and of the covenant concluded in their youth, to warn them of the many temptations and dangers to which their souls would be especially exposed in the great metropolis, to beckon them to the heavenly Fatherland, to show them its costly treasures, and to offer them their inheritance by faith. There no Lutheran congregation opened its bosom to them; there no brother met them with guidance, admonition, discipline, and comfort; there no congregation witnessed to them of the power of God's Word to make the dead live, to comfort the troubled, and to strengthen the weak. On the contrary what met them all there were the seductions of the metropolis, disruptive covetousness of this and that, incessant busyness, disorderly rushing from one thing to another, and a frenzy of speculation that even we American citizens cannot explain to ourselves.

Thus they existed for ten, twenty, even thirty years, their numbers increasing yearly while the religious situation remained the same—with no change for the better. Is it any wonder then that many allowed themselves to become so engrossed in their worldly occupations that they were carried away by a materialism murderous to all spiritual interests, with every earnest thought destroyed by the thirst for gold and the coveting of earthly happiness, so that at last they forgot the grace of childhood, the covenant of youth, their instruction in Christianity, and even their God and Savior? Is it any wonder that many of them were to be found among atheists and those who scorn God or even become completely indifferent to religion and the salvation of their own and others' souls? Is it any wonder that many, infatuated and enchanted with dulcet phrases and the appearance of philanthrophy, sought compensation for the lack of a church in sects and other human societies? It makes me absolutely sick at heart and brings tears to my eyes to describe all this misery, but it is no wonder to me, nor can it be to anyone who knows what a ruin the human heart is, who knows that it can be reawakened and reborn only by the power of the grace of almighty God through his divine Word and that life in God can only be preserved by discipline and admonition from the same Word, which is spirit and life from the Lord. No, more and more I only wonder that there are still some in this Babylon, I might well have said Sodom, who turn a longing gaze to a Jerusalem never forgotten and wish from the heart to see its beautiful worship of God, while there are still so many who hear the voice of the Lord and allow themselves to renounce it.

Still we dare not doubt that many of our countrymen who landed on American soil were earnestly disposed, many who perhaps through the absence of preaching and the customary divine services or through other circumstances came to fear for their souls. While some of these, in the manner I described above, little by little grew dull and worldly, and lost the gifts of grace that had been their portion, others—not a few—sought satisfaction for their needs in more or less erring religious bodies, since there was no place to be found to offer them the unadulterated milk of the Word. Many have thus gone over to the Methodists and some to the Baptists. The Methodist societies have done a great deal and still are doing a great deal to gather in the Scandinavians of New York. As I explained before, they have the ship Bethel very conveniently located for emigrants. The Swedish Methodist pastor Hedström has worked there for more than twenty years. In addition to him, the Methodist pastor Helland has also worked there.[17] Methodist services are regularly held in rented quarters over in Brooklyn. Unfortunately, many of our Lutheran countrymen have allowed themselves to be seduced by these false prophets, and we ought to be very worried by the thought that pious souls, for lack of understanding and guidance, have thus gone astray and are in danger of being spiritually overcome. To be sure, some have been so fanaticized by their blind guides that there is little hope of rescuing them, but some, we may be assured, will still let themselves find and follow the voice of the Lord when once they hear it. For others, the

Methodist Church has provided entrance into the land of the sects; they do not stay with it but go over to the Anabaptists, New Israelites, Spiritualists, Latter Day Saints, and whatnot.

In spite of this, many on arrival have been repelled by enthusiasm and indecency among the Methodists and Baptists, if not by their talk that often makes a mockery of God. Consequently, when these people have once learned the language of the land, they turn and seek spiritual nourishment in the "American Lutheran," Presbyterian, and Episcopal churches. Especially many have joined the latter and, I daresay, they have not fared worse than those who joined the pseudo-Lutheran congregations which, like the Reformed, deny clear Christian doctrines confessed by the true Lutheran Church. Of these, we can hope that many joined in ignorance, not knowing that there was any difference between those church bodies teaching false doctrine and the orthodox Lutheran. It is, of course, possible that sincere individuals may have preserved the orthodox faith in these church bodies, for the Lord says of his own that "if they drink any deadly thing, it shall not hurt them."[18]

As I said earlier, our congregation in New York was established as a Scandinavian Lutheran congregation, that is, it was founded for Norwegian, Swedish, and Danish Lutherans in New York. However, at about the time that I arrived, two Swedish pastors of the Augustana Synod, [Erland] Carlsson and [Andreas] Andrén, came to New York and a few Swedes formed the so-called Gustavus Adolphus congregation.[19] It is thus to be feared that not many Swedes will join our congregation. It might seem that this would be no great loss, and even entirely natural that there should be two congregations formed among such a large Scandinavian population; it must be acknowledged that there is some difference between the Swedish and Norwegian languages, but this difference is not actually significant enough to render difficult the union of Swedes, Danes, and Norwegians into one congregation. It would have been only proper for the Augustana Synod to have allowed there to be one Scandinavian congregation as it was first conceived and organized. If any discipline at all is to be exercised in reception of members, rather than merely trying to get as many powerful and wealthy people as possible into the congregation, there would be expense enough for a single congregation when it came time to get a church and a school and support a pastor and a schoolteacher. Then, when it had grown in vitality and size, two congregations, one Swedish and one Norwegian-Danish, could later have been formed to stand together in the inner bond of faith and in mutual respect. Now, on the contrary, it is to be feared that the Gustavus Adolphus congregation will in many ways be a hindrance to the up-building and extension of the true Lutheran Church among the Scandinavians of New York. This is because the Swedish Gustavus Adolphus congregation has been formed and hitherto served by pastors from the Augustana Synod, and is thus connected to this pseudo-Lutheran church body in which openly false doctrine is preached and tolerated. The position it has taken from the start is thus sinful, even if the members of the congregation, as I will gladly believe, have not understood the blunder they have committed but have thought themselves to be forming a true Lutheran congregation under an orthodox teacher.

It was fear of this that led a well-informed Swede, who was incidentally chosen as a member of a preparatory committee for the Swedish congregation, to try to arrange a conversation between the aforementioned two Swedish pastors and me immediately after my arrival. We briefly reviewed the various doctrines discussed in our Scandinavian conferences. When I drew their attention to the way these meetings had demonstrated that we held different beliefs and doctrines of "ministry, call, and lay preaching; of regeneration and its means; and of absolution," the pastors mentioned would not admit this with respect to the first doctrine, as if my well-founded complaints concerning the constitution of the Augustana Synod were only misunderstandings on my part. Unfortunately, I did not at the time have the documents at hand in order to convince the people concerned that I was right and spoke the truth. The dear Swede was later convinced that the Augustana Synod was established on the basis of error, as I had contended with the pastors. Even so, it was very hard on him to be separated from his countrymen, though for the sake of his conscience he dared not enter into connection with the Augustana Synod or call a pastor from it as long as the synod so named did not renounce its false doctrine as publicly confessed by its pastors and as long as it did not exchange the new, rationalistic Swedish manual and hymnal for the old, orthodox books.[20] He therefore declared to Pastor Andrén that he and his family would remain in our Lutheran congregation. I myself also declared to pastors Andrén and Carlsson that if they and their synod would confess the orthodox doctrine and preach the orthodox gospel I would gladly abandon the field to them and call upon all my countrymen to cleave to the Swedish pastors as orthodox, but that now I would all the more have to bear witness against them and their false doctrine.

In my reporting above I have spoken briefly of the Scandinavian sailors in New York. It is, of course, true that most of them cannot be considered among the Scandinavian inhabitants of New York whom we have in mind for our work. But even if they do live and dwell in Norway and can only be considered temporary guests in New York, they are still our countrymen and have confessed from childhood the same faith we have. Is then the Norwegian state church so crabbed at heart or choked by formalism that it will say not only to Norwegian emigrants but to its own children as well: "What have you to do with us? You ought to take care of yourselves or stay at home like good children! It is not our fault that you are spiritually overcome, even if because of your temporal calling you must spend the better part of your life beyond the borders of our country at sea or in foreign ports!" My dear friends! We should rejoice that the Lord stretches the ties that bind us enough to allow us to help them in their spiritual need at the same time as we labor in the field at hand shown to us by the Lord. How many Scandinavian sailors visit New York harbor annually and often stay there for a time I cannot say, but it must certainly amount to a couple of thousand. As a rule, they are usually out on long journeys, often of several years, and thus all the more need to hear a friendly word in earnest, a true word from God of warning, encouragement, and comfort. As simple and unrefined as these sailor boys often are, they often also have a deep and susceptible disposition in which God's Word can find good lodging. As a rule they are regular in attending church when they reach land. Thus it was that many of them were regular listeners to the Methodist pastor Hedström, and that I always met quite a few of them whenever I preached at the Marine Church. Some of them expressed great joy at hearing so far from home the word of truth they remembered learning in their catechisms. Indeed a few members of the congregation in New York, earnest in the truth as well as informed and grounded in God's Word, can recount the encouragement and strength they have drawn from association with the sincere Christians among these ingenuous, direct sons of the sea.

After I left the New York congregation, it was visited in 1866 by Pastor [U. V.] Koren, who worked there for five months.[21] At the same time Theological Candidate [Kristian] Magelssen worked there until Pastor O. Juul, who was trained in St. Louis and served a call in Wisconsin with great competence for two years, undertook the office of the ministry there as resident pastor in October of the following year.[22] At the general meeting of the Society for Mission to Sailors in Kristiansand in July of this year, $300 was granted as the society's contribution to the pastor of the New York congregation to the end that he should insofar as possible interest himself in the spiritual welfare of the Norwegian sailors in New York and make a yearly report to the society on this aspect of his work.[23] Thus we may dare hope that with God's help the existence of the Norwegian Lutheran congregation is secure for the immediate future and that the work of our pastor there will be a blessing both for the considerable Scandinavian population and for the Norwegian sailors passing through. Still, the congregation is certainly in need of support from countrymen in Norway in order to acquire its own church. For the sake of the sailors it is most important that it be conveniently located for them. The present location used for the church and costing $300 in annual rent is located in the vicinity of the Marine Church, a neighborhood very accessible to the sailors. In purchasing a church, the congregation will undoubtedly consider the support it has received on behalf of the sailors, but it will also have to try to find a place in which the church can be conveniently located for its resident members.

Having progressed thus far in consideration of our own church body, we will now take a look at the ecclesiastical field in which our church body has developed.

Catholics, Methodists, and Baptists

It is well known that the large majority of the American people are neither baptized nor acknowledge themselves to belong to any denomination. Indeed, we can hardly reckon the number of those who have joined one or another church body to be more than a fifth of the country's population.

The church bodies enjoying the greatest size in America are the Catholics, the Methodists, and the Baptists. The Catholics count something over three million communicants, and the Methodists and the Baptists one and one-half million each. While the Methodists seem to have been losing ground in recent years, the Catholic Church on the contrary has taken great strides forward. It carries on its work in America with all its characteristic cunning and energy. In recent seasons it has made significant advances and even exercises an influence in political life not lightly regarded by the government and certainly procuring for it more than one advantage. According to the Constitution, the civil government cannot make distinctions between the various religious bodies but stands impartially in relation to all of them. But if there is a religious body that can pride itself on being favored by the civil government it is certainly the Roman Catholic, the priests of which, for example, are exempted from military service. The French newspaper *Monde* also maintains that all the expenses of the Indian mission of the Jesuits are covered by the government. It explains that the Jesuit Father [Jean De] Smet "before his departure for Europe had a lengthy discussion with President Lincoln, who granted him considerable concessions in favor of the the the fathers of the Society of Jesus. The President and the government of the Union acknowledge that these missionaries (the Jesuits monks [*sic*]) alone are capable of keeping the inhabitants of the Rocky Mountains at peace and civilizing them."[24] It certainly cannot be denied that the non-Catholic segment of the population of the country in general is strenuously ill disposed to the Roman church and its pope, but this ill will is based mostly on hatred of the intolerance and tyranny the papist church embraces and has always shown openly rather than on a loathing of its profound and infamous apostasy from the Lord and His Word.[25] But where ill will, however legitimate, has no deeper foundation, it can quickly be converted into good will and devotion by force of circumstances and by spiritual influence. There is actually hardly any country where Catholicism has made such advances in recent decades as in America, and that not merely through immigration but through proselytizing.

The Catholics have not up to this point conducted any mission among the Norwegian population. The contrary is the case with the Methodist and Baptist as well as the Episcopal churches. While the latter church body in the last decade has had to yield most of the advantages it won in this field and now seeks to influence our youth only in a few places with its Sunday schools, the contrary is the case with the *Methodists*, who are prosecuting major work among the

Lutheran Scandinavians, whom they generally consider heathens, if not a good deal worse.[26] Other than in New York and perhaps Chicago, I do not believe that this church body can rejoice over any special progress among the Norwegians. The Norwegian Methodist congregations are as small as they are few. They would be smaller and fewer still did not the Methodist church body itself pay its missionary pastors out of its rich treasury.* As far as I know, all the Norwegians among these men are to a high degree ignorant of spiritual things. It is certainly a rare occurrence for any of them to have taken any training whatsoever for the office of the ministry. The Methodists themselves are beginning to acknowledge how deplorable this is and are seeking counsel on this point.

The *Baptists* have made considerable inroads among the Swedish population, but it is exceedingly rare to stumble on a Norwegian Baptist.

German and English Lutheran Synods

With respect to the number of its members, the Lutheran Church ranks fourth in America. It is supposed to number about two million souls. However, several of the so-called Lutheran church bodies are unfortunately Lutheran in name only. In reality they are something else and, if not out-and-out Reformed, they are very indifferent with respect to doctrine.

We might well immediately move on to a consideration of the so-called Lutheran church bodies among the Scandinavians beyond our synod, namely the Ellingians and the Augustana Synod, but because the latter has been so closely connected with and influenced by Lutheran church bodies of other languages, we will first take a look at them.

We may well call [H. M.] *Mühlenberg*, a pious and zealous Lutheran pastor, the father of the Lutheran Church in America.[27] The oldest Lutheran synod in America, over 120 years old, is the *Pennsylvania Synod*.[28] Its congregations are partly German and partly

---

*The Methodist have set aside $3,000 a year for their mission among the Scandinavians and $5,000 for their mission to Norway, Sweden, and Denmark. [Preus's note]

English. Until last autumns it belonged to the large so-called "Lutheran General Synod in America."[29]

This *General Synod* is comprised of more than half a score of synods, among which there are still to be found some who have never explicitly acknowledged the symbolical books of the Lutheran Church.[30] The General Synod itself only acknowledges the Lutheran confessions with reservations. In recent years, however, a more decidedly confessional Lutheran tendency has begun to make itself felt. This tendency finds its best champions in the bosom of the old Pennsylvania Synod and for the last four or five years has had its own organ, *Lutheran & Missionary*, edited by the gifted Professor [Charles Porterfield] Krauth in Philadelphia, as well as its own seminary in the same place.[31] "American Lutheranism," so-called in distinction to the supposedly superannuated old orthodoxy of Germany, is embraced by the dominant majority in the General Synod.[32] It has its headquarters at the seminary in Gettysburg and its champions in the recently deceased Benj. Kurtz and Prof. [S. S.] Schmucker.[33] Several years ago, the latter published his "Definite Platform," a confessional document in which the Lutheran doctrines of baptism as the washing of regeneration, of the Lord's Supper as the sacrament of Christ's body and blood, and of absolution were denied in Reformed fashion and scored as "papism."[34] Some years back, the Augustana Synod and last autumn the Pennsylvania and a couple of other synods separated themselves from this pseudo-Lutheran, loosely organized General Synod.[35]

The following large Lutheran synods have existed without any connection with the General Synod:

1) The German *Missouri Synod*, which is the largest of all the synods outside the General Synod. More about it later.[36]

2) The partly English, partly German *Ohio Synod*, which unreservedly acknowledges the confessions of the Lutheran church, but yet demonstrates great laxity in both doctrine and practice.[37] It has, among other things, experienced bitter controversy in its midst because several of its pastors belong to the Freemasons and other secret societies.[38]

3) The German *Iowa Synod*, the older pastors of which are without exception disciples of Pastor Wilhelm Löhe of Bavaria who persist in defending his Romanizing and chiliastic errors, which have occasioned several defections.[39]

4) The German *Buffalo Synod*, which until last year was under

the tyrannical rule of its leader, Pastor [J. A. A.] *Grabau*.[40] Its members emigrated from Germany primarily for the sake of their faith, it had existed for thirty years from its foundation, its clergy were learned and competent, it required a strict "Old Lutheranism," it was a decided opponent of the newfangled American Lutheranism, and it even severed church fellowship with the Iowa Synod on the basis of the latter's chiliastic doctrine, but in spite of all that it never made any progress.[41] Its doctrine of the ministry and church order as well as its practice were, in fact, so papistical that not only were its congregations under the tyrannical yoke of the clergy but so, too, most of the clergy were at the same time under the yoke of the leader, who ruled like a pope.

Since its founding, the *Missouri Synod* has battled incessantly, with great courage as well as skill and fidelity to the confession, against all these more or less un-Lutheran synods as well as against the German Reformed and Catholic church bodies. Against them all it has unfurled the Lutheran banner in all its free, shining glory. Even though every hand has been raised against it, even though it has had to put up with mockery, derision, and persecution from every quarter, it has stayed unwaveringly with "God's Word and Luther's doctrine." And the Lord has not allowed it to do battle without blessing. After a struggle of more than twenty years the Buffalo Synod last autumn conceded the rightness of the cause and called for a halt.[42] Last year it cast off the yoke under which it lay and expelled its leader, Pastor Grabau.[43] Additionally, last autumn's defections from the General Synod of which we have heard may well be considered as in essence an effect and fruit of the Missouri Synod's clear witness and self-denying struggle. I have already explained how we first came into contact with the Missouri Synod through the journey of pastors Ottesen and Brandt, how we found the fellowship of faith among these people of another tongue, how we sought it in vain among our separated countrymen and kinsmen in America.[44] I beg your permission to dwell a little on the significance of this synod for the whole Lutheran Church in America as well as on the love it has showed us and the spiritual and temporal help it has given us.

In 1839 a colony of Lutheran Saxons with five pastors settled in Missouri.[45] This was the parent stem of our Missouri Synod, first established in 1847, with fifteen pastors and ten congregations. Now, after the passage of twenty years, it consists of more than 250 pastors, with just as many congregations scattered all over the United States. It has extended its ties from the cities of the Atlantic to the coast of California on the Pacific Ocean, from New Orleans where the Mississippi empties into the Gulf to the northern regions where it has its source. It is divided into four district synods, each with a district president. The whole church body is governed and directed by the general meetings of the synod, which gathers every third year. Among its many extraordinary skilled theologians and pastors I shall mention here only the excellent dogmatician, President and Professor Walther; Professor Crämer; the self-denying former president [F. C. D.] Wyneken; and the honorable Dr. [Wilhelm] Sihler.[46] I described earlier its Latin school in Fort Wayne, its practical and theoretical seminaries in St. Louis, and their decided Lutheran character. Besides these, the synod has a normal school in Illinois and a Lutheran hospital in St. Louis.[47] It publishes a scholarly theological journal, *Lehre und Wehre*; a popular church paper, *Der Lutheraner*, which has already gone through twenty volumes; and a remarkable school newspaper.[48] I have previously described the peerless sacrificial spirit within the synod, posited even by its opponents as an example for congregations to follow. Among the theologians of Germany with whom the synod enjoys unity of faith I shall mention only President [G. C. Adolf von] Harless, Professor [Friedrich Adolf] Philippi, Licentiate [Karl] Ströbel, and Pastor [Friedrich August] Brunn in Steeden.[49] The latter, who has also enjoyed the benefit of support from this country for oppressed Lutheran congregations, has a proseminary underway from which he yearly sends ten or twelve students to the seminaries of the Missouri Synod for further training.

I ought to conclude with a testimony to these Missourians from opponents within the General Synod at a conference in Pittsburgh on the occasion of their defection from the General Synod.[50] It goes thus:

"It is saying but little, when we remark that these discussions were in the highest degree, able and instructive. The principal speaker, and indeed the soul of the whole conference, was the Reverand Professor Walther of Concordia College, St. Louis, a man of singular power as a logician, a controversialist, and a profound theologian. With the marks of great mental conflict and severe labor and study upon his countenance, he has yet the vigor and sprightliness of a young man, and enters upon the exposition and defense of his opinions with a profound reverence for the Word of God, and an earnestness which engages every sympathy of his soul. It was interesting to witness his thorough acquaintance with the Holy Scriptures, the older theological writings of the church, the minute history of the various errors and heresies which have appeared at different periods in her history, . . . And yet no one could listen long to his exegetical remarks, or the eloquent and truthful warnings which he gave to guard against Rationalistic tendencies on the one side and Romanistic ones on the other, without discovering that he had insensibly adopted the massive language, and with it to no small degree the spirit, of those iron men who waged the theological battles of former centuries, and were terrible to the enemies of the truth, while most gentle to its friends. For such combatants, thus armed and mailed, one must feel respect. . . . " The rectitude and impartiality of the conference made an especially favorable impression on us. We did not hear a single response which was not taken into consideration and weighed with tranquil deliberation. We are fully convinced of their deep earnestness and rectitude in holy things. There was no superficiality or triviality in their discussion or in their social behavior. No one could associate with these people without feeling how earnest they were for their own salvation and the welfare of their church. There was no put-on (affected) air of sanctity or refinedly sweet talk, but rather a healthy, manly way of expression which comes from an undaunted assurance of grace alone in the person and work of Christ. They are for the most part living Christians who preach Christ and him crucified powerfully and successfully. And the numerous churches gathered through their efforts and under most highly organized church discipline witness that their preaching is by God's power for the salvation of all who believe.[51]

117

LECTURE V

The Ellingians

We shall now turn to a consideration of the two Norwegian ecclesiastical factions in America claiming to be considered Lutheran but standing apart from our church body, namely the Ellingians and the Augustanans. As explained above, this will involve us here and there in a more detailed treatment of the doctrinal controversies occurring within our synod and especially between us and these two church bodies. I hope the presentation will make it plain that in these battles our synod has always stood its ground on God's Word, waving the banner of the Lutheran confessions.

The Norwegian ecclesiastical party with which we have had most contact and with which we were first in controversy is that of the Ellingians. They take their name from Elling Eielsen, a farmer from Voss who went to America twenty-eight years ago.[1] There he traveled around, preached among Norwegians, and gathered adherents here and there. His activity cannot be compared to that of a lay preacher in Norway, since he gathered around himself a faction separated from the rest of the Norwegian Lutheran church body, against which and its pastors—whom he tagged with the name "state church priests"—he railed and ranted as if against Babel itself. Within his own party he singly and solely conducted the ministry of the Word; as well as preaching, he conducted baptism and communion. Elling Eielsen has not received any training for the teaching office; he has not been examined by orthodox Lutheran teachers to determine his fitness for it. In those first days, of

Elling Eielsen (1804–1883) of Eielsen's Synod.

course, his work might in its place have been in order had he taught the pure, true Lutheran doctrine. That he never did this, but rather instead opposed and persecuted orthodox teachers and congregations, that was his greatest sin. Had he been concerned only about the salvation of souls it would have pleased him when competent and orthodox teachers entered the field where he had begun work as an emergency measure. Either he would then have entirely withdrawn of his own accord from the responsible work he had taken up, or he would have confined it to the places where there was immediate need, or, if he had been found fit to continue in the work of office, he would have accepted the call of individual congregations and advised his adherents everywhere to join the orthodox pastors and congregations already formed.

But he did none of this. He took it upon himself to form a faction. Through error, calumny, and patent lies he tried to keep his adherents away from our church body and to make the breach wider and wider. By insinuating himself into our congregations he constantly tried to win more adherents. For a long time he claimed for himself only an inner call, but later he found that it might serve his cause well to have something more on which to lean. Then he claimed that he had been ordained and directed those who desired proof of this first to one city and then to another where such proof was supposed to be found but never was.

The whole story of his ordination is sufficiently attested by eyewitnesses. The man who he maintains ordained him was a German, one F. Hoffmann, who was once a pastor and later an attorney, and is now a failed banker.[2] During his stay here in 1862, Elling explained in *Morgenbladet* that in 1844, after having been examined and called by emigrants, he was ordained by a pastor of the Missouri Synod, this Hoffmann, at the conclusion of a public service of worship in the presence of a large congregation in Chicago.[3] Eyewitnesses, however, declare that on that occasion there was a congregation of twenty or thirty emigrants in a little house in Chicago for whom Elling held a devotional service. Afterward a strange man entered; he read a little piece out of a book, which they believe to have been the Bible, spoke a few incomprehensible words, and left. To their great astonishment, Elling then explained that he was ordained. Since then he has never offered any proof that he was actually examined or called by any congregation. Had he never worried about being regarded as properly examined, called, and ordained, we would perhaps simply have thought of him as an enthusiast relying in good faith on his inner call; but now he has spread this story around and made a shameful mockery of holy things to deceive the simple folk; now he has shown himself to be a liar and a deceiver. All the same, we do not put so much weight on whether Elling is ordained or not. To us, the main thing is that he is a false teacher and the founder of an erring sect.*

Elling's friends first organized formally into a church body and adopted their own "church constitution" in 1846. There had already been a breach in his church body by that time, since pastors

---

*Since Mr. [S. M.] Krogness of the Augustana Synod has recently defended Elling Eielsen's ordination in *Aftenposten*, even though he warned against him during E.'s stay in Norway, I cannot see any other reason for this than that the Augustana Synod is now working for a union with the Ellingians, and that it is therefore necessary to whitewash Elling as much as possible. [Preus's note].[4]

Paul Andersen, Ole Andrewson Aasen and—I believe—Ole Hatlestad, who now all belong to the Augustana Synod, left him and joined the Franckean Synod.[5]

The Ellingians' constitution is, in the faction's own judgment, very important, since it is very nearly the only church document they have produced since they appeared on the scene, but there is also enough here—and nothing more is needed—to show how their position ought to be judged. When, in 1856 or 1857, Pastor Rasmussen along with a number of congregations left Elling's church body, he gave as his reasons for this step in part errors in the constitution which he had sought in vain to have altered and in part false doctrine and an ungodly life led by Elling Eielsen, of which he would not repent.[6]

It is especially the first two main paragraphs in the constitution that contain errors.

The first paragraph reads as follows: "This our church body shall forever continue to be, just as it now is, in conformity to the genuine Lutheran faith and doctrine, and built on God's Word in the Holy Scriptures in conjunction with the Apostolic and Augsburg Articles of Faith, which together with the Word are the rule for our church order."[7] The Apostolic and Augsburg Articles of Faith seem here to be placed on a level with the Holy Scriptures as containing the faith upon which a church body is built, and it expressly says afterward that these articles of faith together with the Word are the rule of faith. I do not believe the Ellingians have herewith confessed themselves to be in union with the Grundtvigians or that they have gone even further down the pathway marked out by them. No, I believe they just do not understand what they have written or what this paragraph contains.

In my opinion this is not the case with what follows in Paragraph 2. There it says: "Just as nothing common or unclean can enter the New Jerusalem, no one ought to be accepted as a member of our body except he has passed through a genuine conversion or is on the way to conversion."[8] Here the Ellingians identify their church body with the invisible church, and thus in donatist fashion make the visible church body into a body of the purely holy in which no hypocrites can be found.[9] This is what disposes them in conversation and preaching all the time to talk of themselves as "the little flock," in contradistinction to our church body which takes in the big flock, and also in their sermons, which are generally sharp and one-sidedly legalistic, to refer only rarely to their own members, but on the contrary to punish and scold those on the outside.[10] I hardly need to draw further attention not only to how objectionable this kind of preaching is, but also to how dangerous it is, how it can lull them to sleep in security because of the contention that those who enter or who belong to their church body are converted or on their way to conversion. Another error I have often noted in conversation with Ellingians resides in the paragraph adduced above and it is this, that they are in a position to judge with certainty who is converted or on the way to conversion. Since it actually says that none other than such a person can be received, there must naturally be found among them those who can separate the hypocrite from the true believer, in other words, who can discern heart and reins. It is presumption on our part to claim to possess this faculty, which indeed presumes omniscience. Finally, the Ellingians have not lacked those who have imagined and maintained that the way to conversion is through their church body, or that by entering it they were converted, and Elling's talk on many occasions has necessarily awakened and strengthened such faith.

Paragraph 6 of the constitution pronounces the judgment of excommunication on those who wear *clerical vestments* and annuls church bodies harboring such people.[11] That this paragraph conflicts with Article 7 of the Augsburg Confession requires no further demonstration, since that says: "For the true unity of the church it is enough to agree concerning the teaching of the Gospel and the administration of the sacraments. It is not necessary that human traditions or rites and ceremonies, instituted by men, should be alike everywhere."[12] This also applies as a matter of course to the judgment of the Ellingians on the *laying on of hands* in absolution. One might almost believe that they thought the laying on of hands and not the Word was the means by which the forgiveness of sins was imparted.[13]

Elling either does not use absolution or the loosing of sins at all, or he uses it only conditionally, while in his confessional addresses he has scored those of us who use it—and that always unconditionally—before the Lord's Supper and who also allow private confession to continue.[14]

I drew attention earlier to the fact that the Ellingians' ecclesiastical constitution is the only written confessional statement given to us by this church body. It is not therefore very easy to obtain evidence of the various errors not enunciated in their constitution but embraced within the church body, if not by all then at least by the majority and explicitly by the leaders. I do not believe that I would charge them with anything of which they are innocent if I were only to mention those errors attacked by us over a long period without having been refuted in any way or, on the other hand, recanted. In addition to the two errors just named, I will mention the following.

An essential distinction is sometimes made between "prayer in one's own words" and prayer according to a prescribed formula, between "public" prayer in an assembly and silent prayer. They claim that the public kind of prayer is much more powerful. Indeed, several have maintained that as long as one cannot offer a public prayer, one cannot be properly converted. From this stems the excessiveness in their prayer meetings, ordered in quite a Methodist fashion, during which up to a dozen people, among them women and even children, go up and offer so-called prayers, more often really sermons and most often about the person who is speaking. Contrary to I Corinthians 14:33–35 and I Timothy 2:11–12, the women speak and pray audibly in their public assemblies. In donatist fashion it is also generally taught that preaching avails nothing in our church body because the pastors are not spiritual. I have even heard this adduced as grounds for claiming that our baptism is false. "How"—it is said—"can anyone dead give birth to a living child?" These poor people do not bother their heads with Article 8 of the Augsburg Confession, even though they wish to be genuine Lutherans.[15]

Besides these points, controversy between the Ellingians and ourselves has chiefly involved the third article of the Apostles' Creed, the fourteenth article of the Augsburg Confession, and the Third Commandment or Sunday. We must therefore consider in detail their doctrine and ours on these points.

Concerning the third article of the Apostles' Creed, at first we used the various readings found in the different catechisms and explanations. It was our opinion that there was no essential difference among these readings. Which one or other of the various readings was used was not a matter of salvation. Our synod in 1855 did advise the use of the reading: "one, holy, universal, Christian church, the communion of saints, and life everlasting."[16] This reading is now used in parts of our church body, and in other parts the reading found in the old edition of the *Altar Book* is used.[17] The Ellingians maintained that the latter was the only correct reading, while the other was false. Indeed where it was used, it was often said, baptism was improper and invalid. It was especially the word "universal" which was an abomination in their sight. According to their faith it meant the same thing as "impure." When it was used in baptism, it was often said to parents that the children were incorporated into the universal impure flock, into the devil's synogogue, and even that they had been signed with the mark of the beast.

With respect to the fourteenth article of the Augsburg Confession, the Ellingians maintained that every Christian by virtue of his spiritual priesthood has the power and authority to preach publicly and does not therefore require any external call whatsoever.[18] "It is enough that he is called by God," as it is usually said. In contradistinction to this we teach that all Christians have the right privately to admonish, teach, and pray, and indeed also in public assembly to teach, rebuke, and admonish one another. On the other hand, we believe that wherever a layman steps up in meetings organized for public edification and prays aloud, teaches, and admonishes, then he is, in fact, exercising the public office of the ministry, but according to God's Word and the fourteenth article of the Augsburg Confession he has no right to this office. Only where an actual emergency prevails is it appropriate to breach this ordinance. Where, for example, there is no pastor, or he propounds false doctrine, or where he is so miserly in serving the congregation that Christians starve for lack of food and supervision, then there is an emergency and every Christian has the right and the duty to execute the pastor's task in the public assembly.[19] He does not do this by virtue of his spiritual priesthood, but as the congregation's temporary pastor who must breach God's ordinance in a time of need. The aim of this emergency administration of the ministry of the Word is to meet the situation so that souls do not starve, but where it becomes clear and apparent that the necessary gifts are quite lacking and that instead of meeting the emergency in such assemblies the situation is only made worse, so that many are led astray and seduced by perversions and vain abuse of God's Word or by scandalous arguing, then Christians must abstain completely from such gatherings, which do not fulfill their intention but only make the evil worse.

In order better to assist you in understanding our synod's doc-

trine on this important and timely point, a doctrine on behalf of
which we have been attacked not only by the Ellingians but also by
the Augustana Synod, I shall permit myself to read here a presentation of this matter which was the basis for our discussion at the
meeting of the Synod in 1862, where the question was decided almost unanimously.

"The holy apostle Paul says in Romans 3:2 about the church of
the Old Testament, or the faithful of that time: 'Unto them were
committed the oracles of God.' They were thus the possessors and
the administrators of God's Word or ministry. Because the Christians of Corinth were internally divided, because some were especially attached to Paul, others to Apollos, others to Cephas, and each
one boasted of the one he especially held to, the apostle reproved
them and wrote to them: 'Therefore let no man glory in men. For
all things are yours, whether Paul, or Apollos, or Cephas, or the
world, or life, or death, or things present, or things to come; all are
yours and ye are Christ's' (I Corinthians 3:21–23). Thus the apostle explains that everything possessed even by this high apostle and
servant of God himself belongs to the believing Christian. The
ministry of the Word is thus not a private possession belonging
only to the servants of the church but a common possession belonging to all members of the church, of which Peter says to them: 'But
ye are a chosen generation, a royal priesthood, an holy nation, a
peculiar people; that ye should shew forth the praises of him who
hath called you out of darkness into his marvellous light' (I Peter
2:9). Believing Christians should not therefore think that it is
enough for them to hear, receive, and believe God's Word; they
should not think that they have no responsibility for seeing that
God's Word is preached and the sacraments administered to
others, saying merely: 'That is what we have a pastor for.' No, he
to whom God has given faith he has also made into a spiritual leader and laid upon him care for the salvation of his neighbor.

"When the Lord himself said: 'Thus it is written, and thus it be-
hoved Christ to suffer and rise from the dead the third day: and that
repentance and remission of sins should be preached in his name
among all nations' (Luke 24:46–47), he spoke not only to apostles
and pastors, but to the whole church, that is, to all believing Christians unto the end of days. He, therefore, who does not wish to be
a preacher does not wish to be a Christian either, because a preacher and a Christian are one and the same thing.

Lecture V

"The whole New Testament is therefore full of admonitions to Christians to use God's Word not merely for themselves but also for their neighbors and for their brothers and sisters. Thus, for example, we read in Colossians 3:16: 'Let the Word of Christ dwell in you richly in all wisdom, teaching and admonishing one another in psalms and hymns and spiritual songs,' and Ephesians 6:14–15: 'Stand, therefore, having your loins girt about with truth . . . and your feet shod with the preparation of the gospel of peace,' and I Thessalonians 5:11, 14: 'Wherefore comfort yourselves together, and edify one another, even as also ye do . . . now we exhort you, brethren, warn them that are unruly, comfort the feebleminded, support the weak.' Further, II Thessalonians 3:14–15: 'If any man obey not our word by this epistle, note that man, and have no company with him, that he may be ashamed,' and Matthew 18:15: 'If thy brother shall trespass against thee, go and tell him his fault, between thee and him alone,' and I Corinthians 6:5: 'Is it so, that there is not a wise man among you? No, not one that shall be able to judge between his brethren?' Ephesians 5:11: 'Have no fellowship with the unfruitful works of darkness, but rather reprove them.' Philippians 1:27: 'Only let your conversation be as it becometh the gospel of Christ that . . . ye stand fast in one spirit, with one mind striving together for the faith of the gospel.' I Peter 3:15: 'Be ready always to give an answer to every man that asketh you a reason of the hope that is in you.' Matthew 10:32–33: 'Whosoever therefore shall confess me before men, him will I confess also before my Father which is in heaven; but whosoever shall deny me before men, him will I also deny before my Father which is in heaven.' Hebrews 10:24: 'Let us consider one another to provoke unto love and to good works,' and finally James 5:19–20: 'Brethren, if any of you do err from the truth and one convert him; let him know, that he which converteth the sinner from the error of his way shall save a soul from death, and shall hide a multitude of sins.'

"From all of this we can see that every Christian not merely holds office, but that in addition, if he is to conduct himself as a Christian, he shall and must administer it, that is, he too must confess the Word, teach, admonish, comfort, rebuke, and in every way exercise care for his neighbor's salvation, for his conversion as well as his preservation in the faith. In sum, wherever a Christian is, he shall show himself to be a spiritual priest to his spouse, his children, his own sisters and brothers, his household, his neighbors and friends, and to all people wherever and whenever God brings him together with them. For the sake of all, he shall administer the ministry of the Word in burning love and divine wisdom.

"But God knows that even his dear children are still made of flesh and blood and how weak and feeble most of them are. Therefore God at the same time established the holy ordinance of the ministry of preaching. Thus according to God's Word certain persons — who are prepared, gifted, equipped, and tested for this, who are always elected, called, and set apart by Christians to exercise the public ministry in their midst, that is, to administer publicly in their name God's Word and the holy sacraments — should lead their assemblies in common edification through God's Word and serve as the voice of Christians in these assemblies.

"Where the holy apostles established Christian congregations they did not, when they departed, simply leave the task of common edification through God's Word to the converted congregations so that everyone could publicly teach and preach the Word in the assembly. To this specific task they rather appointed certain persons whom they called elders or bishops or teachers or overseers. Thus Paul writes to his companion and collaborator Titus: 'For this cause left I thee in Crete, that thou shouldst set in order the things that are wanting, and ordain elders in every city as I had appointed thee: if any be blameless . . . For a bishop must be blameless as a steward of God . . . holding fast the faithful word' (Titus 1:5-9). Such elders or bishops do not, therefore, simply have the call like other Christians to use God's Word as spiritual priests on behalf of the neighbor. They rather have fixed congregations, in which the spiritual service of the public ministry is transferred to them alone. Thus Peter writes: 'The elders which are among you I exhort, who am also an elder . . . Feed the flock of God which is among you' (I Peter 5:1-2). This was not merely a good human arrangement, but an ordinance of the most high God himself. To be sure, the congregations themselves elected their elders or bishops or teachers, but these are described in the Scriptures as appointed by God just as the apostles and the prophets themselves were. Therefore the apostle Paul writes thus: 'And he (namely Christ, God's son) gave some . . . [to be] pastors and teachers' (Ephesians 4:11), and to those elected bishops by the congregation the same apostle writes: 'Take heed therefore unto yourselves, and to all the flock, over the which the Holy Ghost hath made you over-seers' (Acts 20:28).

"In addition to this, all Christians in their stations and callings can and should instruct *privately* or be teachers, but they are not to be teachers of the congregation as a whole or watch over it or work for it or judge it. This is to be done only by the specific persons called. Thus it stands written; 'Obey them that have the rule over you and submit yourselves: for they watch for your souls, as they that must give account' (Hebrews 13:17), and 'And we beseech you, brethren, to know them which labour among you, and are over you in the Lord, and admonish you' (I Thessalonians 5:12), and 'Let the elders that rule well be counted worthy of double honor, especially they who labor in the word and doctrine' (I Timothy 5:17). Such bishops are, therefore, called the angels of the congregations (compare Revelation 2:1, 8, 12, 18; 3:1, 7, 14).

"This is an incomparably gracious and sure institution from the merciful God, by whom above all everything shall be accomplished, to ensure that God's Word shall ever be preached rich, unadulterated, and pure in the Christian church, that false prophets shall be warded off, and that the holy sacraments shall properly and without adulteration be administered and proffered to Christians according to God's Word so that the divine economy of the Christian church and all Christian congregations can operate in a good, blessed order pleasing to God.

"Therefore, even though by virtue of faith all believing Christians hold the office the pastor administers, they ought not to administer it, thereby disturbing and usurping the ministry of public preaching instituted by God. So it is that though the Scriptures earnestly admonish all Christians faithfully and eagerly to exercise the office of the Word on behalf of their neighbor in whatever situation God has put them, still the Scriptures say: 'My brethren, be not many masters, knowing that we shall receive the greater condemnation' (James 3:1), and Paul says, 'God hath set some in the church . . . thirdly teachers,' and then puts a question to the Corinthians 'Are all teachers?' (I Corinthians 12:28–29). He means to say: Oh, no! Only those whom God in and through the congregation has appointed are to be public teachers or teachers of the congregation. Therefore the same apostle writes to the Romans: 'How shall they preach, except they be sent?' (Romans 10:15). To teach, admonish, comfort, rebuke, pray aloud, or publicly administer baptism or the Lord's Supper in public gatherings of Christians for edification — *all* this is not therefore something for ordinary Christians, but only for those whom Christians, according to God's Word and command, have properly elected, called, and installed for the administration of the public ministry.

"The dear Christians are not therefore bound to human beings for their salvation. If an emergency arises — if, for example, Christians do not have a regular public preacher or if the one they have is a false teacher, or if they are so little offered the means of grace by him that they nearly starve, if the business of the public ministry is not carried out among them — it would not be improper for lay folk in such an emergency to see to God's Word and prayer in public gatherings or even to administer baptism publicly. Thus, because as spiritual priests they already hold office by virtue of faith and do not exercise it in public gatherings of Christians only for the sake of order according to God's will, and because the order exists only for the sake of their salvation, it is right in case of an emergency for them to breach this order and confidently to exercise their original right in the sure hope that God will then look upon them and bless to them their public use of his saving means of grace. But they act not in consequence of their spiritual priesthood or of their general privileges as Christians, but as *emergency priests* or *emergency pastors*, much as once did the members of the household of Stephanas who devoted themselves to the service of the saints (I Corinthians 16:15–16). They indeed administer the pastor's office or the public ministry of preaching for the sake of souls in an emergency. Therefore the symbolical books of the Lutheran Church also say: 'In an emergency even a layman absolves and becomes the parish priest and pastor (*minister et pastor*), just as Augustine describes the two Christians together on a ship, one of whom baptized the other and was in turn absolved by him.' (Smalcald Articles, Tractate on "The Power and Jurisdiction of the Bishops," Müller's edition, p. 341, Latin paragraph 67)."[20]

The substance of this presentation was adopted by our synod in the form of the following theses:[21]

1) God has instituted the office of the public ministry for the public edification of Christians unto salvation through God's Word. (Unanimously adopted).

2) For the public edification of Christians God has not institut-

ed any other order to be placed alongside of this. (Unanimously adopted).

3) When one undertakes the leadership of the public edification of Christians through the Word, he undertakes and exercises the public ministry. (Unanimously adopted).

4) It is a sin when anyone *without call or in the absence of an emergency* undertakes this. (Unanimously adopted).

5) It is both a right and a duty in the case of an actual emergency for everyone who can to exercise in proper Christian order the office of the public ministry. (Unanimously adopted).

6) The only correct conception of an emergency involves the actual existence of a situation in which there is no pastor nor can there be one, or in which there is one who does not properly serve them or who propounds false doctrine or cannot serve them *sufficiently* but so inadequately that they cannot thereby be led to faith or preserved therein and protected against error *so that the Christians would perish spiritually from lack of supervision.* (Adopted with two voters dissenting, who voted thus because they feared the word "perish" could be misunderstood).

7) When an emergency is at hand, efforts should be made to relieve it by definite and fitting arrangements as the circumstances permit. (Unanimously adopted).

We come now to the third controversial point, concerning *Sunday* or the Third Commandment.[22] The controverted question is simply this: Is Sunday ordained and established by God himself? Is any one day established by God by divine commandment, which means that we are bound to keep it holy in the same manner the Jews were obligated to keep their sabbath? Or has the congregation, without divine commandment, decided of its own free choice to prescribe Sunday? Our synod maintains the latter. The Ellingians, along with the Augustana Synod as we shall later see, maintain the first position. Our *Augsburg Confession* emphasizes clearly enough, chiefly in Article 28, the importance of maintaining pure doctrine within Christendom on this point.[23] This has to do with nothing less than the preservation of our *Christian freedom*, purchased for us with the blood of the Lord, which we shall not allow ourselves to submit again to the yoke of a slavery to human propositions.

Here, too, I shall permit myself to read the theses discussed and almost unanimously adopted by the Synod's meeting in 1863.[24]

VIVACIOUS DAUGHTER

Thesis 1. When in the Third Commandment it says, "Remember the sabbath day to keep it holy," the term "sabbath day" does not for us Christians refer to a specific day as it did among the Jews. Compare Colossians 2:16, Romans 14:5–6, Galatians 4:9–10.

Thesis 2. On the contrary, for us Christians the "sabbath day" in the Third Commandment means that every day of our whole life shall be for us a spiritual day of rest in Christ.

Thesis 3. The spiritual sabbath, which consequently is the Christian's whole life, we should keep holy according to the Third Commandment, and this is done by diligent and proper use of God's Word. This is the moral element of the Third Commandment binding for all time.

Thesis 4. In order that our whole life can be kept holy as a spiritual sabbath day by diligent and proper use of God's Word, we must set apart certain times to consider God's Word, both each for himself in the daily life of the household (domestic devotions), and in public gatherings (congregational divine service). But when and how often this shall occur is left for Christians to decide freely, according to what is workable.

Thesis 5. For the times of such public consideration of God's Word, Christians from the most ancient days, in *freedom*, have chosen and set aside the Sunday of every week together with other annual holy days.

Thesis 6. a) In addition to setting aside Sunday and other days of remembrance for public worship, Christians have also made provision that on such days we should rest from all physical labor and use the day to further our sanctification. b) The Christian authorities in most countries have confirmed this Christian ordinance of abstaining from work on Sundays and holy days and made it into a secular law.

Thesis 7. A. That which should now oblige us Christians to observe Sunday is, therefore: a) the order and custom of the Christian church which we should observe for the sake of peace and love according to Philippians 4:8–9, Romans 14:3, and I Corinthians 14:33, and b) the command of our government in this matter which we should for God's sake obey, according to the Fourth Commandment and I Peter 2:13.

B. Consequently we sin by unnecessary work on Sunday: a) against the Fourth Commandment when we transgress the commands of government; b) against the Third Commandment insofar as we neglect or despise God's Word by working; and c) against love, when without valid reason we breach the order and custom of the church and thus give offense.[25]

Thesis 8. Proper obedience to this ordinance consists in using such sabbath days to further our sanctification so that both these days and every day of our whole life can be kept holy. This happens when: a) we regularly and devotedly attend public worship (Hebrews 10:25 and Ecclesiastes 5:1); b) we abstain from unnecessary physical labor as well as from everything prohibited by human ordinances on such days; c) we use our rest for devotion with the Word and prayer and divine meditation along with demonstrations of love for our neighbor; and d) we guard ourselves with God's help against all ungodliness and scandal, which is always sin, but would be doubly sin on such days as are consecrated to the promotion of our holiness.

Thesis 9. On the contrary, we are impeded in keeping the spiritual sabbath day of our whole lives and we profane the public sabbath day when we: a) without necessity stay home from church or during the rest of the day neglect consideration of God's Word or chatter while it is being heard or read or sleep or occupy our minds with alien thoughts; b) unnecessarily work or do other things prohibited by human ordinances (for example, buying and selling, public business); c) employ our day of rest in idleness or the satisfaction of sinful desires; or d) scandalize our neighbor either by neglecting demonstrations of love owed to him or by doing things in themselves permissible but which could cause a frail conscience to stumble.

Thesis 10. It is false doctrine, by which one sins against both God and one's neighbor, to maintain, as the sects of the whole Reformed church do, that for Christians Sunday morning or any other day is necessary or commanded as a divinely obligatory moral precept either in the Third Commandment or anywhere else in the Holy Scriptures.

Thesis 11. This false doctrine is so far from promoting the proper maintenance of the Third Commandment and Sunday that such doctrine will on the contrary only lead to superstition and disobedience to what is actually ordered by the Third Commandment and thereby to a false and improper observance of Sunday by a misguided conscience.

Thesis 12. On the contrary and conversely, only the true Lu-

theran, that is, biblical, doctrine of Sunday as a good human ordinance and thus as a gift from God through men will lead to its
proper observance by a happy and free conscience, thereby leading
toward a true obedience to the Third Commandment.

Thesis 13. It is always according to God's will and to his glory
and to the comfort of conscience to bring forth his truth and refute
false doctrine and doubly a duty to do this where we have seen from
experience that many are wrapped up in confusion and error which
burdens and misleads the conscience and leads it away from the
saving gospel to a false slavery to the law, while the pure doctrine
can comfort and rectify the sincere conscience and help to lead it
to the true evangelical freedom.

In connection with the Ellingians' false doctrine of Sunday or
the Third Commandment, it will not take us out of our way to consider their stance on the last seven articles of the Augsburg Confession. In one of the editions of Pontoppidan's *Double Explanation*
only the first twenty-one articles of the Augsburg Confession are
appended.[26] When we appealed to the twenty-eighth article during
the controversy over the doctrine of Sunday, we were often answered that the seven last articles are not authentic. At the meeting
in May of last year between the Ellingians and the Augustana Synod, the point also came under discussion as to how far the Ellingians acknowledged the last seven articles of the confession. One
of their younger pastors then said that he had always understood
that the whole confession, consequently all twenty-eight articles,
was considered as accepted by their church body. At this point Elling and some of the older members declared that they had never
seen more than twenty-one articles and never knew that there were
more. I think this declaration may be taken as characteristic of the
standpoint taken by Elling's church body in both doctrinal and intellectual respects. It is also just as characteristic, I believe, of the
standpoint of the Augustana Synod when one sees that these declarations on the part of the Ellingians with respect to the Augsburg
Confession were accepted as completely satisfactory by the par-
ticipants representing the Augustana Synod and were not the occasion of further discussion.

When the Ellingians intrude with their proselytizing, one reason they adduce as compelling for defecting from our congregations is the ungodly life and loose church discipline which they
maintain dominates our congregations. How valid a reason this

would be, even if things were as bad in our church body as the Ellingians maintain they are, informed Lutherans will know how to decide. As to what is actually done about the exercise of church discipline in our church body, I have informed you of this earlier in my presentation. In respect to this point, I shall add only the following. I have already drawn your attention to how the Ellingians in their sermons castigate "the big flock" without, but not "the little one," their own. In his confessional addresses Elling usually invites everyone, known and unknown, to come to the Lord's Table, and I know that he has received those who have just previously been denied access to the sacrament in our congregations on account of their ungodliness. Among the Ellingians there is no confession or counsel before the Lord's Supper as there is among us.

The Ellingians have always shown a certain fear, even disdain, of scholarly training and accomplishment. They usually talk of the higher schools as if they were necessarily nurseries of arrogance and false doctrine. The degree of jealousy Elling Eielsen and the real old Ellingians have shown toward those of their pastors, Rasmussen for example, who have come to possess some basic skills is remarkable.[27] It has been one of the contributing causes of division in their church body. Most of Elling's pastors, whom he naturally has examined and ordained himself, are as a rule just as ignorant and erring as he is.

Some time back there was for a couple of years among the Ellingians a high school, as it was called, "for schoolteachers to learn at least to read and write." The teacher at this school, who naturally called himself "Professor," is a Mr. [Andreas P.] Aaserod, who was for a time one of our students at the seminary in St. Louis but had to leave because he showed a lack of capability and intellectual power.[28]

Recently, controversy with the Ellingians, in any case in our older congregations, has died down. After they became known among our congregations, they let up on their proselytizing when they saw that continuing it would yield them nothing. Even though as a rule there are a few Ellingians who live within the boundaries of our congregations because they have defected from them, everyone goes his own way and tries to avoid unprofitable controversy by having as little as possible to do with each other.

With the defection of Pastor Rasmussen and his congregation, the Ellingians' church body received a jolt from which it will not

so easily recover.[29] Thereby they lost not only their most competent teacher and many of the most pious and active members of
their congregations, but since that time a certain distrust and dis-
content has prevailed in the church body, especially in relation to
Elling himself. Whether anything good will come of a union with
the Augustana Synod is highly doubtful, because even if both factions unite in the battle against us a very different spirit still prevails
in the two church bodies. Among many Ellingians, especially the
older ones, there is still a certain earnestness for the weal of souls,
a warmth and a zeal, even if it is mixed up with a great lack of clarity in doctrine, a very Methodist enthusiasm and emotionalism, on
the one hand, and a very falsely pietistic legalism and rigidly moral
conduct on the other. In the Augustana Synod, on the contrary,
there prevails a speculative spirit, meaningless activity, and a sys-
tematic expediency alongside of a hierarchical church politics and
a false humanism, none of which will be to the taste of the more
earnest, old-fashioned Ellingians, even if it might perhaps commend itself to the younger and more Yankeefied generation.

In conclusion I shall only mention, but not dwell further on, the
thoughtless credulity shown on the part of many in this church
body toward Elling Eielsen, its founder and leader. It is known that
his immoral life was one of the reasons that caused Pastor Rasmussen, with his friends, to separate himself from the Ellingians after
he had vainly complained of this and sought to lead Elling to repentance. In truth it can be said that a large share of the Ellingians are
pitiable seducees, blind prey having no wills of their own in the
hands of a cunning seducer.

LECTURE VI

The Augustana Synod

We shall now turn to the Augustana Synod, which we have so often had occasion to mention earlier in our presentation and with which our church body is at present carrying on its fiercest battle. In order to understand this battle and rightly to judge it as well as the stance of both synods toward God's Word and the confessional writings of the Lutheran Church, it will first be necessary to summarize the historical development of the synod in question.

As explained in the previous section on the Ellingians, pastors Paul Andersen, Ole Andrewson and presumably also Ole Hatlestad separated from Elling Eielsen's church body and joined the American Franckean Synod.[1] These pastors, insofar as they had any pastoral training, had received it at a Reformed college. The Franckean Synod has never explicitly accepted the Augsburg Confession as its own doctrinal basis, and this was the cause of the controversy stirred up in the General Synod when it applied for membership in that body. It did not even pretend to be regarded as Lutheran. These Norwegian pastors manifested the same attitude in the whole of their doctrine and practice, which was through and through Reformed, without even the appearance of being Lutheran. At that time they published the *Racine Kirketidende*, in which there were constant attacks on the Lutheran Church and its most characteristic doctrines, for example, that baptism is the washing of regeneration.[2] Here I shall address only the confessional formula required by the synod in question for the reception of

137

Paul Andersen (1821–1891), president of the Synod of Northern Illinois and a prominent figure in the Norwegian Augustana Synod.

members into its congregation. The confirmands shall, it says, "call heaven and earth to witness that you acknowledge the Lord Jehovah, Father, Son, and Holy Ghost, to be your God—your Redeemer and your Sanctifier—and the supreme object of your affections, and your portion forever."[3]

Later, Pastor [Lars P.] Esbjørn was the first Swedish pastor to join these Norwegian pastors.[4] Either shortly before or after this, they severed their connection with the Franckean Synod and entered into a new connection with the Synod of Northern Illinois.[5] This change meant that something, even if not very much, was accomplished in the direction of a rapprochement with the Lutheran Church. To wit, the Synod of Northern Illinois belonged to the fragmented General Synod. But when this synod, with its conditional acceptance of the Lutheran confessional documents and practices, granted constitutional rights to those who condemn the chief doctrines of the Lutheran Church and allowed them to lodge within its precincts, was it not a sin for the Synod of Northern Il-

(0. 3. Hatlestad.

Ole Jensen Hatlestad (1823–1892), a leader of the Norwegians of the Scandinavian Augustana Synod and the first president of the Norwegian Augustana Synod.

linois with its Scandinavian pastors to enter into a church body with these patent enemies of the Lutheran Church? And did it set things right that they were able to obtain tolerance for themselves and their more Lutheran views and confession? Should Paul Andersen have acclaimed such an erring synod, as he did at a general gathering in 1857: "Where, then, shall we go for pastors, except to you?" Could the same pastor in good conscience "beseech them over their fathers' graves not to withdraw their hands from the poor Norwegian Lutherans?" Was that bearing witness to the truth?[6]

Little by little, several pastors, both Norwegian and Swedish, joined their countrymen in the Synod of Northern Illinois. It was owing partly to this and partly to the earnest attacks they had to suffer from us on account of their errors that a retreat into a more orthodox Lutheran direction little by little showed itself among them. In individual congregations, the Lutheran formulae for baptism and the Lord's Supper were accepted and confirmation was similarly reintroduced. In the meantime, the Swedish Pastor Esbjørn was appointed professor at the synod's seminary in Springfield, where the Norwegian and Swedish students were to obtain a training of sorts for office. Experience has shown that this training cannot satisfy the requirements that ought to obtain in the matter of a Lutheran pastor's competence. How could it? Both Professor Esbjørn and his fellow teachers, professors [Sidney L.] Harkey and [William M.] Reynolds, lacked the necessary theological knowledge and skills for this, not to mention the orthodoxy.[7]

Before 1859, we had little contact with the Swedish pastors. Naturally, however, our attack on the Norwegians also touched their Swedish brethren in faith and communion, and our witness against their truth-denying connection with the General Synod was naturally also a witness against those who had committed the same sin. At that time, in spite of all their confusion and aberrations, we still had more faith in the Lutheran disposition of the Swedish pastors. Thus we nourished the hope that if, by God's grace, we could rescue them from their situation, there might occur a rapprochement between them and us. We repeatedly manifested a favorable attitude toward them, and this finally resulted in the first Scandinavian-Lutheran Conference, in Chicago in July, 1859.[8]

Attending were seven Swedish and five Norwegian pastors from the Synod of Northern Illinois and ten Norwegian pastors from our side. The discussion revolved chiefly around the following three points: 1) Whether our synod harbored Grundtvigian views. Explanations from our side demonstrated that such charges against us were unwarranted, and our opponents declared themselves satisfied. 2) On their sinful connection with the General Synod. We emphasized this in particular as something that would make union with us impossible. They explained, however, that it was their conviction that not only could this ecclesiastical connection of theirs be continued without sin, but that it was their duty to continue in it and that it would certainly be a blessing to their church body. Only Pastor [O. C. T.] Andrén, now returned to Sweden, found the connection not only "undesirable, but a cause for sorrow," even though he did not for that reason feel conscience-bound to sever connections.[9]

The third point under discussion was Article 14 of the Augsburg Confession.[10] Here we could not agree. I have presented our synod's doctrine in the foregoing section on the Ellingians. The Augustanans on this point declared themselves in disagreement with us. They also attacked on this point later, when the synod at its meeting last autumn mentioned this as one of the points of doctrine on which it still disagrees with us.[11] At the conference in Chicago, Professor Esbjørn declared that when at gatherings for edification a pastor calls on one man one evening and another a different evening, then they have been properly called. Later the same Professor Esbjørn delivered a report on this point that was adopted by their conference, although it deviates from the doctrine of the church in essential points. We shall see later that the constitution of their church contains paragraphs giving evidence of their errors on these points. In addition, their practice of allowing lay members of congregations to preach and pray aloud in public gatherings when there can be no question of any emergency shows that they controvert Article 14 of the confession. Augustana's publication *Hemlandet* calls our teaching "a new-fangled doctrine of church and ministry" and expresses itself in a highly derogatory way on precisely that point of doctrine where we maintain "that when Christians choose for themselves a teacher, they give him authority to administer the ministry of preaching in their place and on their behalf" and "that teachers *in the congregation's place* shall conduct and administer the ministry they all possess."[12] It is clear that our doctrine on this point does not tally with the high-church views reflected in their constitution. To be sure, Pastor Carlsson explained to me in New York that his synod agreed with ours on this point, but at that time he was interested in getting those concerned to believe there was no difference between our synods. In any case, at the meeting last year the Augustana Synod itself contradicted his assertion and did not retract its earlier error on this point.

But we must return to the historical development of the synod.

Early in the spring of 1860, Professor Esbjørn resigned his office as professor in the seminary of the Synod of Northern Illinois in Springfield, and in April of the same year it was decided at a pastoral conference in Chicago that the Norwegian and Swedish congregations should sever their connection with the Synod of Northern Illinois and thereby also with the General Synod. On our part we greeted this step with joy in the hope that it would make a rapprochement with us easier. In order not to offend them we refrained for an entire year from any detailed criticism of their conduct on that occasion. After we tried without success to arrange a meeting with them, through a committee, through the church council, and finally through our pastoral conference, and after our well-intentioned invitation was disdainfully declined, we tried to show them how sinful their method of departure had been. Both Professor Esbjørn and the other pastors, before they departed from their synod, ought to have borne witness against the errors and ungodliness they later declared to have been openly permitted there, but they neglected this. Next, they ought to have acknowledged the sin they committed by entering this divisive synod. Nor was there a single word about this. On the contrary, they tried in departing to make it appear as if they were martyrs for the truth and that they departed because the synod wished to deprive them of their costliest treasure, the pure Word of God.

When, some months earlier, at the joint conference in Chicago, we maintained that they had sinned by remaining in such a connection to an unlutheran synod, they denied both parts of the accusation and charged us with a lack of love. Indeed, barely a month before their departure we were abused by them in their publication for our warning.[13] When they departed, however, Professor Esbjørn explained that for two whole years he had not been able to partake of the Lord's Supper in the congregation to which his Norwegian and Swedish students belonged and of which his two fellow professors of theology, Harkey and Reynolds, were pastors. On this occasion all the pastors declared that there was "a definite difference of doctrine in the synod," and that they therefore had to break the synodical bond.[14] And, indeed, they all now attack their erstwhile American brethren with a bitterness and hatefulness with which they cannot charge us, even in our most pointed articles attacking their ungodly institution. Nor have they since shown the slightest sign that they have acknowledged their great sin against the truth as well as against the souls committed to their care. And we who have constantly had to tolerate harsh judgments from them for our witness against the General Synod still have to listen to abuse as thanks for it.

In June of 1860, the defecting pastors and congregations organized themselves into a new synod under the name Augustana Synod.[15]

This synod's statistics for 1861 show that it included 60 congregations, with 5,600 communicants and 32 pastors.[16] Of these, 11 were Norwegians, with 17 congregations and 1,400 communicants. The synod's statistics for 1865 show that the number of congregations had climbed to 72, with 8,400 communicants and 39 pastors. Among these were 20 Norwegian congregations, with 1,700 communicants and 15 pastors. On the basis of the above we draw attention to the following facts: 1) The Norwegian element in the synod is only 1/5, amounting to the negligible sum of 1/20 relative to our synod. We ought also to note that their largest Norwegian congregation, namely the Chicago congregation with 722 communicants, has now left the synod, which is thus down to 1,000 Norwegian communicants with 19 pastors.[17] 2) The ratio of pastors to communicants in the Augustana Synod is on the whole favorable, averaging one pastor for 200 communicants, but with reference to the Norwegian congregations the number of pastors is so high that it averages out to one pastor for 50 to 60 communicants. This is certainly the reason that one or several of the synod's Norwegian pastors are regularly without a position and seek to maintain themselves in other occupations. 3) The Norwegian congregations are as a rule very small, several having fewer than 50 communicants. 4) Consequently, there has not been nor can there be any talk of a need of pastors for the sake of the Norwegians in Augustana, since the number of Norwegian pastors is more than sufficient to meet the need.

As for the synod's territory, it is a different one than our synod's as far as the Swedish congregations are concerned, since several of the Swedish congregations are located in Indiana, Michigan, and Illinois, where we have no congregations. On the other hand, most of the synod's Norwegian congregations are located within the boundaries of our congregations, and several of them have arisen through the intrusion of Augustana's pastors into our congregations and the withdrawal of members from them on schismatic and sectarian grounds.

With respect to intellectual attainments and competence, the Norwegian pastors in the synod stand on a very low rung of the ladder. As of last autumn, none of them had received a true scholarly theological training. But even worse, there are several of them who, even overlooking their errors, may be said to be quite unfit for the ministry because of lack of essential skills. One can hardly expect it to be otherwise in a synod like the Augustana which has received first this person and then that person without any real preparation for the ministry. What kind of examinations are administered can be ascertained by reading the proceedings of the ministerium or clergy for 1860 when eight pastors were examined in one afternoon, basically in this fashion — as it says — "their special gifts and scholarly qualities were taken into earnest consideration" and "each one especially described his conversion, spiritual experience, and call from the Lord," and then it says that "the ministerium has *assured* itself of the candidates' conversions."[18] I know less about the Swedish pastors, but I do believe that properly competent individuals are to be found here and there among them, although none of them has actually shown at the general conferences or by authorship that he possesses the really basic theological knowledge. It is highly probable that the Swedish pastors who have taken their training at the extremely poor and erring seminary in Springfield stand just about on a plane with the Norwegians who have come out of this seminary.

The synod also has its own seminary in Paxton to which a sort of Latin school is attached.[19] That not so very much is to be expected from these schools, however, will be evident, considering that for both institutions there are only two teachers, the Swedish Pastor Hasselquist and an American by the name of [William] Kopp.[20] I had never heard of the latter before he became a professor at Paxton. The first certainly is, as Pastor Muus has recently portrayed him, "a kindly, hospitable man, a good Union man," but as a theological professor he is seriously lacking in the necessary skills and confessional clarity.[21] Recently a student [John] Olsen from over here served as a teacher at the school, but he hardly possesses the ability necessary to raise the level of the institution to that of a theological school.[22]

The means necessary to defray the expenses of this school are not, as they are among us, sought exclusively through voluntary contributions from the congregations. On the contrary, only the smallest part comes in this way. The synod has received its largest contributions from Sweden. The Swedish king has, in fact, permitted an offering for its support to be gathered in all the churches of the realm.[23] Likewise, the synod has received support for the school as well as for individual congregations from the Gustavus Adolphus Society.[24] And finally, the synod has had a not inconsiderable annual income through association with a railroad or land company in Illinois and from selling land for it.[25] The records of the synod for 1865 thus show the following receipts: gifts from Sweden for the library, $563; offerings in Sweden for a general fund, $2,229; interest and gifts from the Gustavus Adolphus Foundation, $599; commission for land sold, $1,851, altogether amounting to $5,242.[26] This year saw no contributions come in from the synod's own congregations. The previous year's interest and contributions from the congregations amounted to $438, while the offering from Sweden was $1,973 and commission on land sold $2,722, and about $5,000 more was subscribed for a future Norwegian professorship.[27] Many have asked in amazement how a church body as small as the Augustana Synod could take on such large undertakings and display so much activity involving such significant expense. The answer lies in the figures reported above. It is not difficult to develop extended work without fear of objection and conflict among the congregations when, though so over-extended, it has others to pay the bill and then lets its own congregations peacefully be. We are in principle opposed to this way of doing things. We consider it harmful to the congregations and unfair to the other contributors. When opportunity in America is so great that it is precisely that which invites emigration, it is not right to allow the poorer fatherland to pay the expenses while one sits back and takes it easy in well-situated congregations, at the same time weakening their interest in the tasks of the church and nourishing instead love for this world's goods.

The president of the synod is the above-mentioned Professor Hasselquist, but the real leader is Pastor Carlsson of Chicago, a man of ability, although unfortunately he uses it as a solicitor more often than as a servant of the Lord.[28]

The synod has a religious-political publication, *Det gamla och nya Hemlandet*, and a devotional one, *Rätta Hemlandet*.[29] The sometime seminarian now Pastor Krogness last fall began publishing, in Norwegian, *Den Norske Lutheraner*.[30]

Before we consider the activities of the synod and the condition of its congregations, it will be necessary for us to take a close look through the synod's constitution.[31] In essence it follows the constitution of the Synod of Northern Illinois, but with changes in its confession.

In Chapter 1, Article 2, the synod acknowledges the Holy Scripture as the highest rule for faith and life and adheres to the confessional writings of the Lutheran Church. Indeed it even asserts that it wishes to have the Augsburg Confession interpreted in harmony with the symbolical books of the Lutheran Church not acknowledged by the Norwegian part of the church. It may well be an oversight that the Small Catechism is not mentioned in the listing of the symbols of the Lutheran Church.

Consequently, we can see that on paper the synod's confession is proper. The following will enable us to judge how far this is sustained through the remainder of the constitution and in its public doctrine and practice.

In Chapter 1, Article 4, it says that the number of lay votes may never exceed the number of pastors' votes, and that a delegate from a congregation with a pastoral vacancy shall have the right to a seat and to speak, but not to cast a vote unless the synod decides otherwise.

This article demonstrates that the Augustana Synod has quite misconstrued the concept of the *Lutheran synod*. This is likely part and parcel of a false concept of *church and ministry*. According to this article, the Augustana Synod considers pastors the essential element needed to form a synod while the delegates are considered an accident, an appendage. If the pastor is not present, then the delegate has no right to take part in any decision. Consequently, it is the pastors who actually constitute the synod. Such a false conception of the synod can only originate in and be based on a false, catholicizing concept of the church, according to which pastors alone, as a special order appointed by God, not only must be present but must be present as the most essential element in the formation of the church. A true Lutheran instantly knows this as a false idea of the church. With the fathers in the Augsburg Confession, he says that the church is a "communion of saints," whether or not they hold the office of pastor.[32] He says that the ministry of "preaching the word and administering the sacraments" is entrusted to the church and that the administrators of the ministry, the pastors, are gifts granted to the congregation by its Lord, Christ.[33] Consistent with this genuinely Lutheran conception of the church, a synod, which is concerned with the responsibilities of the congregations, is an association of these congregations disposing of their responsibilities through plenipotentiaries at general meetings of the synod. At these meetings pastors are seated and vote as the called and authorized servants of the congregations and do so only as such, for which reason a pastor who does not serve in the ministry of a congregation belonging to the synod ought not to vote in its meetings. On the other and contrary hand, the congregations do have a right to send one or several plenipotentiaries from among their lay membership. Indeed they ought in this case to count it all the more important to authorize lay delegates when they cannot be represented by their pastors. — These delegates ought, because they represent congregations constituting the synod, not only to be seated but to vote, whether a pastor is present or not, whether the congregation even has a pastor or not.

That the synod must have a false conception of the church is made even clearer in [Chapter I,] Article 5 with its provision for a hierarchy. Article 5 runs as follows: "It shall be the duty of the synod to see that the polity and discipline here recommended in the Constitution for the Evangelical Lutheran Congregations in North America and accepted by the Chicago and Mississippi Conference on March 18–27, 1857, is maintained by all congregations and pastors united with the synod, to receive and act on all appeals from the congregational councils and the decisions of special conferences when the same are brought forward in orderly fashion, to examine and decide upon all charges against pastors (*errors in doctrine excepted*), to attend to all such business as has to do with the congregations united with it, when the same is brought forward in orderly fashion, and to consider and enact such fitting measures as may promote a true, living faith and the active fear of God."[34] This paragraph should be taken together with Chapter 7, Article 2, which runs as follows: "At each synodical assembly there shall always be a meeting of the ministerium, consisting exclusively of the ordained pastors united with the synod, with the intention to examine and ordain candidates for the office of the holy ministry of preaching as well as to make inquiry and *dismiss or suspend* pastors and catechists for errors in doctrine, to examine the testimonials of pastors from other church bodies who seek entrance into the synod, and to hold colloquies with them, as well as to give attention to other affairs concerning the teaching order alone."[35]

Pastors are granted greater power here in the governance of the church than is due them according to God's Word and the confessions of the church and more than it is wise to convey to them. One should also compare here Chapter 12, Article 2, where it says: "At all synod meetings one-third of the ordained pastors shall be necessary for a quorum."[36] — The congregations, the faithful, are thus deprived of one of the most important rights given them, that is, to examine and judge doctrine. — Further, the congregation is deprived of the right to suspend or dismiss a pastor, since this right is put partly in the hands of the synod and partly in the hands of the pastors. One can also compare here the sixth chapter, Article 2: "Charges against a pastor shall not be accepted without two or three witnesses (I Timothy 5:19). Should he unfortunately go astray, in doctrine or in life, then the church council in all humility and love shall warn and admonish him, but if this should not have the desired effect, then the matter should be referred to the consideration and *judgment* of the *synod* or *ministerium*."[37] In summary, a legislative authority over against the individual congregations, to which they are obligated to bow, is given to the synod.

We run up against the same sharp distinction between the clergy and the synod (its lay element) in the provision that not the synod but the ministerium, the pastors alone, shall adjudicate all complaints against pastors for false doctrine, while the synod is within its rights in adjudicating all other complaints which do not have to do with false doctrine, but that the ministerium alone has the right to judge and dismiss pastors for errors in doctrine as well as to see to what concerns the clergy alone. But this is not the saddest thing about this provision. No, the worst is that it violates the most sacred privilege and equally weighty obligation of the congregation, the right to try the spirits and judge doctrine.[38] That this provision of the synod is completely contrary to the Scriptures is clear from various passages of Holy Scripture, for example, Matthew 7:15–16, where the Lord bids us to be on guard against false prophets, which one cannot indeed do without testing and judging; Acts of the Apostles 17:11, where Luke praises the Bereans for ransacking the Scripture daily to bear themselves in all things as the apostles had taught; and further, I Corinthians 10:15, where Paul says to the Corinthians, "I speak as to wise men; judge ye what I say"; and finally I John 4:1, "Try the spirits!" And last, the Acts of the Apostles 15:15 and 12:22 are utterly decisive and incontrovertible with respect to the layman's right to test and judge doctrine.

Certainly it belongs to the ministry of the church to try and judge doctrine, but this right must and does pertain to the layman as well according to the passages of Scripture adduced above. I must also draw attention here to the vote of no confidence the Augustana Synod gives to the truth and to the lack of authority this provision attributes to the congregations. If one has unlimited confidence in the power of the truth, then one will not be afraid of the company of laymen going into questions of what the truth is. But if one is proud of one's own wisdom and cleverness, then it is natural to be fearful when too many people get involved, especially if one is of the foolish opinion that a majority vote can decide what the truth is. — There is still one more thing I must explain before I leave this point behind, namely, the provision that the ministerium shall suspend and dismiss pastors. This is an intrusion into the sacred privilege of the congregation. No human power has the right to step between a congregation and its called pastor to separate them. In their relation to one another they stand under no other authority than that of the Lord and His Word. The synod (not the ministerium) can expel a pastor from the synod, it can earnestly admonish the congregation to separate itself from him, and if necessary it can dismiss the congregation from the synod, but only the congregation, to which God has given the right to call its own pastor, has the right to dismiss him from office — naturally according to the Word.

We have heard that legislative authority and even a partial power of assessment over against the congregations is abandoned to the synod. This resides in Article 5 *implicite*, but is expressed even more clearly in Articles 13 and 14, in which the congregations are obligated to abide by the synod's constitution and decisions whether they are appropriate and workable or not; in cases to the contrary, they are to be punished for *refractoriness* (just as if they were under temporal authority), by being denied representation in the synod. Consequently, unconditional obedience is required not to God's Word but to the synod's decisions, while stipulation is never made for the congregation to answer for itself before the synod through a representative.

The constitutions obtaining in the congregations of the synod, which are drafted by the pastoral conferences of the synod and put before the congregations for approval, also reveal the same hierarchical tendency we see running through the synodical polity. Here, too, there appears encroachment on the part of the synod over against the congregations.

According to Article 3, Paragraph 4, of the congregational constitutions — which sounds just like Article 2, Chapter 6, of the synodical constitution cited above—the synod shall decide whether a congregation can retain its pastor or not, while the congregation itself shall have no voice in this discussion but finds itself abjectly subject to the synod's decision. This was also the synod's procedure in the case against Pastor [C. J. P.] Petersen in Chicago.[39]

We ought also to pay attention to another peculiarity in the polity of this synod, since it exercises a penetrating influence in churchly life both in the synod and in its congregations. I mean the so-called majority principle, so very dangerous to the self-government of the congregations and to their Christian freedom, by which the synod arrogates to itself not merely an advisory but also a legislative and an assessing authority. The majority shall rule, and the minority shall bow to it, not merely in somewhat more indifferent matters, but also in matters of doctrine and faith and in cases of conscience. This is clearly evident: 1) in Chapter 7, Article 3, of the synod's constitution, which says: "A two-thirds majority of the ministerium is required to ordain a candidate, to receive a pastor from another communion, or to *dismiss or suspend* a pastor from the ministry";[40] 2) in the congregational constitution, Article 7, Paragraph 5, which says: "A majority *decides* in all cases not otherwise provided for";[41] and 3) in the congregational constitution, Article 3, Paragraph 5, which says: "The pastor shall not against his will be discharged from the congregation unless two-thirds of the congregation votes thus, nor shall a decisive vote on such a discharge occur before sixty days has elapsed after a charge has been made at a public meeting of the congregation."[42]—It is especially noteworthy in this last paragraph that it allows a congregation to dismiss a pastor with a plurality of two-thirds, even though it cannot adduce any valid ground for dismissal according to God's Word. Thus the congregation is given a formal right to act contrary to God's Word if it can merely summon a two-thirds majority for a decision.

Before we leave the synodical constitution behind we must draw attention to the statement in Chapter 7, Article 4, "that the ministerium, through personal conversation or in another way, shall assure itself of the applicant's living faith and *sincere* fear of God."[43] This provision is like in kind to the one I described the Ellingians as adhering to, according to which no one can become a member of their church body without being converted or being on the way to conversion. Of course, it is in accord with this provision that the ministerium of the synod declared in 1860 that it had "assured itself of the conversion of the aforementioned candidates."[44] God alone can see into the heart. Along that line, we humans can only have certain expectations.

Finally, before we set aside the congregational constitution, we shall pause for a bit over its Article 5, Paragraph 5. Here the exercise of church discipline is transferred to the congregational church council, which it seems is to exercise it in the first, second, and third degrees, although the sinner retains the right of appeal to the congregation. To be sure, in subheading 1 under paragraph 5 it says that "The Savior's precept in Matthew 18:15–18 shall be observed *as far as possible*," but the provision for the church council to exercise discipline is of itself of such a nature that it and Christ's precept cannot be observed at the same time.[45] Subheading 3 allows for the requirement of a civil oath and the case of the ecclesiastical discipline of Pastor Petersen shows what sad consequences such improper provisions involve.[46] Rather than allowing the affair to be decided by witnesses, as God's Word invites that it be done, accuser and accused were allowed to swear oaths against each other, and thus the case has nearly collapsed for lack of witnesses. Having finished with the constitutions of both the synod and the congregations, were we in conclusion to summarize our judgment of them in a single sentence we might say that they build on *unevangelical principles,* since: 1) a voting majority rather than God's Word is made decisive, so that even an upright pastor can be legally dismissed; 2) the rights of the congregation over against the synod are violated as are the rights of the laity over against the clergy; and 3) the ordinances for church discipline are not in accord with God's Word.

Now that we have examined the synod's constitution in this way, let us consider how it is put into practice, and in so doing we will also cast a glance at the *conditions in the congregations.*

Turning our attention, then, to the *synod meetings* themselves, we note that *doctrinal questions never come under discussion.* The case is the same to a great extent in the congregation. The Augustana Synod and its congregations lack the emphasis we place on both synodical and congregational meetings and the blessings they bring us in promoting knowledge of God and unity in faith. Of course, the report to the Gustavus Adolphus Society does read: "Between pastor and congregation there is unity based on oneness in doctrine and spirit."[47] Our conferences with them, however, have shown us that they are not united in even basic doctrines, but that their apparent unity is based in part on pure ignorance and in part on indifference with allows them to keep silent while their brethren in the synod preach quite contradictory, false doctrine. In addition there has been violent controversy among them concerning the use of the altar book and its formulae.[48]

We shall take further note of the following characteristics of the synod's practice:

1) The synod, or rather its ministerium, has granted ordination to persons who either have no call or whose call is invalid (for example, to Pastor [Johan] Hveding).[49]

2) It not only tolerates the intrusion of its pastors into our orthodox congregations but even encourages it, thus raising altar against altar (for example, Pastor Hatlestad in Whitewater and Neenah).[50]

3) It has allowed some of its pastors to intrude into and provoke division in congregations served by its own pastors (for example, Pastor Hveding in Pastor Petersen's congregation in Lee county and Pastor Ole Andrewson in Pastor Am[und] Johnson's congregation in Leland).[51]

4) It has allowed its pastors to accept a call from a congregation which has tied its own hands by turning out its own rightful pastor, and that without the congregation first repenting of its sin (for example, pastors Hveding and Krogness in Chicago).[52]

5) It has allowed its pastors to use the Reformed formula for the Lord's Supper and the conditional form of absolution, to omit the renunciation of the Devil at baptism, and to baptize children without the presence of sponsors.[53]

6) It has allowed Methodist pastors to be teachers in its Sunday schools and a Congregationalist pastor to preach at the dedication of one of its churches.

7) It has allowed prayer meetings and "revivals" to be conducted Methodist-fashion in its congregations.

8) Through its pastors it has repeatedly issued calls to the American synods for financial help. To get such it has portrayed its congregations as very poor and presented the Scandinavian situation in a partially false light, as if there were no other Lutheran synod than their own among the Scandinavians, as if it alone had to meet the great religious need among the Scandinavians.

9) The synod and its pastoral conferences have not only refused forceful invitations on our part to meet jointly with us, but they have even declined to discuss disputed doctrinal points with those among their own pastors who are troubled in conscience and have therefore requested that they do so.

In my opinion all this sufficiently demonstrates the indifference reigning in this synod, how it is all for extending itself and winning respect, how it therefore seeks to avoid strife and controversy and prefers to allow errors and abuses and departures from both the doctrine of the church and good Lutheran ecclesiastical order. There has entered in here a genuinely American speculative spirit, a spirit that does not ask whether something is right, but whether it is clever or "expedient." Thus, in this synod, the Lutheran confession is in reality a display sign to decoy the naive, since both its doctrine and its practice manifestly controvert this confession and God's Word.

That this spirit of indifference also holds sway in *congregational life* speaks for itself. It naturally happens that there is a reciprocal effect between congregations and the synod. I am not personally acquainted with the Swedish congregations, but I know of the prevalence among the Norwegian ones of what is in part gross ignorance and in part indifference to pure Lutheran doctrine. This is revealed in their life by the characteristic traits of a Methodistic, false pietism as well as by emotionalism and the external appearance of meekness.

LECTURE VII

Doctrinal Controversies with the Augustana Synod

We shall now turn to the points of doctrine over which we have entered into controversy with the Augustana Synod. At its annual meeting last year that synod mentioned the following four such points: 1) the doctrine of the spiritual priesthood and lay activity, and those concerning 2) absolution, 3) the Sabbath, and 4) slavery. To these we might also add: 5) the doctrine of regeneration through the Word, and 6) the question of chiliasm.

As for the first point of doctrine mentioned, in the piece on the Ellingians I have already expressed myself sufficiently and presented our doctrine in its conformity with God's Word and Article 14 of the Augsburg Confession, which the Augustana Synod clearly controverts when it rejects our doctrine on this point.[1] I shall here only draw attention to how in the above-mentioned report on this controversial point our opponents clearly speak of "the spiritual priesthood and lay activity," while the controversy actually concerns the doctrines of church, ministry, and call. Concerning the spiritual priesthood and lay activity, certainly everyone who heard my earlier lecture will have been convinced that if there is any church body where the spiritual priesthood has come into its own, where an attempt is made at exercise of lay activity, and where it is practiced in conformity with God's Word, then it is our synod, where church polity as well as congregational practice elicits and

155

indeed requires the collaboration of the congregations and the laity in many different ways.

Next, concerning the doctrine of the Sabbath, in the piece on the Ellingians I have had occasion to present our doctrine on this point, too, and I believe I have demonstrated its complete conformity with Article 28 of the Augsburg Confession as well as God's Word.[2] The Augustana Synod must consequently controvert both when it rejects our doctrine on this point.

I come now to the doctrine of *regeneration through the Word*. After many invitations, we were finally able to hold a Scandinavian conference in Chicago in 1863. We first discussed the concept of regeneration and were agreed on it. But when we came to the question of the means of regeneration, our agreement was at an end. All the pastors of our synod together with several Norwegian pastors of the Augustana Synod adhered to the old Lutheran doctrine that the Word in itself is a means of regeneration, just as baptism is also.[4] The other group could not assent to this. To be sure, when it came to the final vote only one of the Swedish pastors was candid enough to say that not the Word in and of itself but only baptism was the means of regeneration. But all the other Swedish pastors and a few of the Norwegians were agreed in denying that the Word alone can regenerate, for example, a heathen who through the law has come to repentance and contrition and now longingly reaches out for comfort and salvation in the gospel.[5] They believed that such a person could come to the true justifying faith and be regenerated not through the Word but only by first being baptized. They conceded that, as an exception but not ordinarily, the Word could effect this if the man died before receiving the water. According to their doctrine, the Word does not have life-giving power except in connection with baptism; it is that alone which creates new life. But how, then, can Paul say that faith comes by hearing God's Word, and Peter that we are reborn from the imperishable seed that is God's Word, and James that God has begotten us chiefly by the Word of truth?[6] During several days of discussion we sought through God's Word to demonstrate the rightness of our doctrine, but it was all in vain. To this day, the pastors of the Augustana Synod have not recanted their error—that the Word alone can in no way regenerate—although individuals among them at their meeting with the Ellingians wanted to delude the latter into thinking that agreement had been reached between us at our conference.

The real truth of the matter is that on this issue the Ellingians were in agreement with us; the Augustanans, now desiring to unite with the Ellingians, could not have touched on a sorer spot than in denying that the Word alone can regenerate.

From the position of the Augustana pastors in regard to the doctrine of the Word, the life-giving power of which they basically denied, it was rather certain that they would also disagree with us on the doctrine of *absolution*. It was at the Scandinavian conference at Jefferson Prairie in 1864 that this point of doctrine came under discussion.[7] A report received with great interest and unanimously adopted by our synod in 1861 was taken as the basis for our discussion.[8] It goes as follows:

1) Absolution, or the forgiveness of sin, is, according to Luther's teaching, the gospel, whether it is proclaimed to many or to individuals.

2) Private absolution is consequently not a power outside or alongside the gospel to forgive sins, but rather is nothing other than the preaching of the gospel to the individual sinner.

3) The stewards and dispensers of absolution in the public ministry are the preachers of the gospel, but otherwise this privilege belongs to all Christians, since the whole church originally was the keeper of the keys. But He who forgives sin through their service is the Triune God.

4) Absolution does not consist in this, that the confessor sits as judge and returns a verdict over the inner state of the penitent, nor in an empty announcement or wish for the forgiveness of sins, but in a powerful communication of it.

5) The effect of absolution does not depend on human repentance, confession, and satisfaction, but absolution requires faith, it creates and strengthens faith. Without faith it benefits man nothing, although it is not therefore a faulty key.

6) By private absolution there is imparted no essentially different or better forgiveness than in the preaching of the gospel. Nor is it in any way necessary to receive such forgiveness as if without it no absolution had taken place. Still it has its own particular values and use, because by it the individual is made more certain that the forgiveness of sins belongs also to him.

After protracted discussion it seemed as if we were agreed on the first three of these theses, but when we reached the fourth, there was apparent disagreement. The pastors of our synod along with four Norwegian pastors of the Augustana Synod insisted that "absolution consists of a powerful impartation," that is, that the gospel is and always remains the same, whether people accept it or not, and consequently that God in the gospel always gives and grants the same thing, and that our faith just as little gives the gospel its content or adds something to it as our unbelief can take anything of its content from it.[9] This doctrine of the content and essence of the gospel was from the first definitely denied and rejected by the other pastors of the Augustana Synod. What they advocated was essentially the Reformed doctrine that the Word is only declarative (explanatory) rather than collative (imparting), that it does not of itself possess and give the forgiveness of sins. According to their contention, the gospel is but an empty offer which takes on forgiveness as its actual substance only when faith in our part enters in. Faith is then assumed by them to be not merely the means by which a person accepts the forgiveness of sins, but—and this is what was false—to be the conditional element by which the gospel can actually contain and bring the forgiveness of sins as a gift from God. Where the conditional element, faith, is not present, the gospel is then an empty offer, a "faulty key," which our church rejects as a Catholic error. Faith, which acts through the power of the gospel, is consequently posited as a conditional element by which the power, through which it should itself be active, can be present in the gospel.

Our opponents from the beginning have plainly shown a great deficiency of clarity and a lack of understanding and insight into this doctrinal issue. The president of the Augustana Synod himself declared that he was little prepared for this question, although everyone had had the theses to study for quite some time before our discussion of them. After listening to our counter-arguments, refutations, and demonstrations of how completely their positions harmonized with the doctrine of the Reformed Church, they let themselves be induced to give way somewhat and tried to formulate what they had to say according to Luther's usage. They finally declared "that the gospel proclaims and contains, offers and proffers the forgiveness of sins to all who hear it, but this forgiveness is given, granted, and imparted only to those who receive it in faith."[10] We said to them that we had absolutely nothing in and of itself to object to in the expression that "the gospel proclaims, contains, offers, and proffers the forgiveness of sins to all," but rather acknowledged them as good Lutheran expressions, and that we absolutely would not controvert them over words, if we could only be assured that they understood these words according to a genuinely Lutheran way of speaking. But, because at the same time they maintained that the forgiveness of sins was not granted by God in the gospel, and was consequently not present in the gospel as a gift on God's part where faith did not appear to receive it; because furthermore they used the expression that God is in no way reconciled with a Judas, a Caiaphas; because Pastor Carlsson, to defend his false doctrine, explained the word "them" in II Corinthians 5:19 as referring to *believers* but not to the world;*[11] because these and like expressions and explanations clearly showed that our opponents did not understand the expressions according to a genuinely Lutheran way of speaking; because we knew that they used and defended a conditional absolution—we considered ourselves forced, if we were not to be entrapped in ambiguous expressions, to put a very sharp point on the issue and use expressions upon which it was impossible to put a Reformed construction, expressions to which no one could assent without actually agreeing that the Lutheran doctrine is not merely declarative, but also collative, that the gospel always has the forgiveness of sins as its full content, and that God in the gospel, wherever it is heard, always proffers the forgiveness of sins as a gift on his part to all who hear the gospel whether they believe it or not at the time.

Then the following formula, which we believed we could accept, was proposed by one of the Augustana pastors who agreed with us: "The gospel (absolution) gives, grants, and imparts the forgiveness of sins to all who hear it, whether they believe or not; it cannot be accepted by all but only by believers; these alone are saved."[12] We added the final phrase in order to defend ourselves against those who could misunderstand the words, "give, grant, and impart," as if these expressions simultaneously contained the

---

*The passage reads: "To wit, that God was in Christ, reconciling the world unto himself, not imputing their trespasses unto them." It was only after repeated calls to do so that Pastor Carlsson would read what was actually *written* so that the people who were listening could know what was actually written, that it was "them," "the world," for whom God "did not impute trespasses," and not merely the believers, as Pastor Carlsson would have it. [Preus's note]

concept "receive." But, although by such an addition we were simply trying to avert misunderstanding, and although the doctrine that all, unbelievers as well as believers, are saved, is indeed so insane, so patently false, that hardly anyone would believe us to hold it even if we said that thus it was we taught, our opponents have still tried to make the matter turn on the contention that the people would believe we maintained that the unbelievers who heard the gospel also accepted the forgiveness of sins and were saved, and consequently that the issue around which the controversy revolved was whether faith was necessary to accept the forgiveness of sins, as if all, even unbelievers, were saved. But there has been no controversy over this. About this we have agreed with them from the start: that faith is absolutely necessary to accept forgiveness and be saved. No, that around which our controversy with them revolves is not the effect of the gospel, not how it comes to work unto salvation, but the *essence and true, actual content of the gospel.*[13]

The Augustana Synod itself has mentioned *chiliasm* as another point on which it disagrees with us.[14] We have, of course, known for a long time that a rather crass chiliasm has been publicly propounded within the synod, but it was not until last autumn that we found expressions of this sort in their church publication. Not only is the (presumably mass) conversion of the Jews to Christ proclaimed in *Hemlandet*, the organ of their synod, but also their return to the land of their fathers. The same article stated that this doctrine is "a matter of faith just like all other doctrines in the Holy Scriptures," and that on this point of doctrine most of the Reformers and their successors have erred or they "have had eyes but do not see."[15] Our synod, of course, has never discussed this question. In this matter as in all others we hold to the clear witness of God's Word and therefore, with the Augsburg Confession, Article 17, reject all Jewish opinions about a thousand-year reign of glory on earth.[16] It is hardly to be doubted that this doctrine of the Augustanans on the return of the Jews to Canaan is of a piece with everything else that goes with chiliastic enthusiasm. Here, however, I shall restrict myself only to what has explicitly been said by them. With respect to this we naturally do not believe that the Jews are rejected in such a way that none of them can ever be saved. On the contrary, in harmony with the Scriptures we believe that those among them who do not remain in unbelief shall be engrafted, because God is mighty enough to engraft them again. We believe that these people who are by nature branches of the olive tree shall be engrafted into their own olive tree and that this engrafting of Israel shall continue every day until the end of days.

We do not find taught in Scripture, on the other hand, the so-called "mass conversion" of the people of Israel. Insofar as anyone talks of this matter as an idea, a private opinion he has formulated for himself that he will naturally not preach as God's Word nor adhere to as a doctrine of the faith that is firmly grounded in the Scriptures, then it will not indeed be anything of concern to the general public or the congregation. But this is not the position of the Augustana Synod in this matter. As we have heard, they have not only expounded this doctrine but also that of the return of the people of Israel to Canaan as a matter of faith which everyone consequently must believe as much as any other doctrines of the Scriptures under peril of the loss of salvation. We must protest against this on our own behalf as well as that of the Reformers. This is as little the doctrine of the Lutheran Church as it is of the gospel itself. I would just as little dare deny that God could possibly arrange for a mass conversion of the Jews and that the same thing might happen to other people, but the Lord has not clearly revealed this in his Word and so it shall not be made into a matter of faith as the Augustanans wish it to be. Besides, we cannot see anything other than that this doctrine must lead to denial of the doctrine we find expressed in many places in the Holy Scriptures, namely, that we can expect any day the advent of Christ and the revelation of judgment. If anyone intends to adhere to this doctrine along with the idea of a mass conversion of the Jews, this is certainly not so difficult as the other alternative, but we find it to be without basis in the Scriptures. Naturally all of this pertains to an even greater degree to the doctrine of the return of the Jews to Judea, a doctrine entirely controverting God's Word and Spirit and nothing other than a gross, Jewish-chiliastic enthusiasm.

I come finally to the last doctrinal point upon which the Augustana Synod declares itself in disagreement with us, namely *slavery*.[17] There has, to be sure, never been any controversy carried on between us and the Augustana Synod nor have I seen any detailed presentation of its doctrine on this point. In the records of its ministerium last year, it is only stated that "it was said about slavery that it is sinful and irreconcilable with the Spirit of Christianity and that this position was in agreement with the opinion of the theological faculty in Christiania published in the Norwegian newspapers."[18] However, because of the controversy caused in our own synod, this point is of such significance for us that I will take the present occasion to express myself somewhat more fully on this question. I know what harsh judgments have been passed on us by many here in our fatherland both for our position on the slavery question and for our relation to Pastor C. L. Clausen on account of his position on the matter.[19] But I also know that many here judge us as a blind man might judge colors. I shall, therefore, try to put the whole matter in its proper light. If I were to put you, my listeners, in a position to grasp clearly the course of the violent strife carried on among us over this question for six years now and at the same time to judge the controversy this has occasioned between us and the theological faculty here, it would be necessary for me to read all the various pertinent documents. This would require that I take a special evening for it, and because I do not know if my listeners would sacrifice so much time to this question, I shall attempt to pull it together as briefly as possible.

It was at our synod meeting in 1861 that this question was brought up for discussion. The frightful Civil War was then in full course, and everyone knows how it was related to the institution of slavery as it existed in the southern states. Most of us definitely wished that the handling of such a burning question could be postponed to a time when more tranquil dispositions could consider it. This was doubly desirable to us, since we knew both that there were those who wanted the matter handled as a *political* question and that it would be exceedingly difficult for us to keep the political element completely out of the discussion in order to consider the question as a purely ecclesiastical one. However, the issue was bound to surface, and the Synod decided to discuss the question of what the *Scriptures* teach concerning slavery. Several people, indeed, tried to get the discussion to revolve around American slavery, but they did not succeed, since protests were lodged against the Synod as an ecclesiastical assembly occupying itself with a purely historical-political question.

As might be expected, opinion showed itself to be divided. Some opined that it was in itself sinful to hold slaves. Others were convinced that so far from condemning and abolishing slavery, the Scriptures quite to the contrary sanction it as a civil institution modified and sanctified by the spirit of Christianity. Finally the pastors of the Synod jointly made the following unanimous declaration: "Although, according to the Word of God, it is not in and of itself a sin to keep slaves, nevertheless it is in itself an evil and a punishment from God. We condemn all abuses and sins connected therewith, and furthermore, when our official duties require it and when Christian love and wisdom demand it, we will work for its abolition."[20] As to the question of whether the Synod was satisfied with this declaration from the pastors, twenty-eight lay representatives answered "Yes," ten "No," and twenty-eight abstained.[21] Nine of the representatives then offered the following counterproposal: "Slavery, viewed as an institution, can only exist under definite laws, and since the laws upon which it is based stand in manifest conflict with the Word of God and Christian love, it is a sin; and since slavery in the United States has been one of the country's greatest evils for both church and state, we look upon it as our absolute duty as Christians and good citizens to do everything in our power, by legal means, to alleviate, lessen, and if possible abolish slavery when our country's welfare and Christian love demand this of us."[22] It will be seen that what the controversy revolved around was precisely this, whether it is in itself, that is, under all circumstances and in every case, sinful and reprehensible for one person to keep another as a slave, consequently whether it is as sinful as murder, adultery, or theft.

When the Synod's discussion and the pastors' declaration became known among the congregations, they created not only a sensation but also widespread opposition and exasperation. As a rule the issue was misunderstood, as if the pastors and their friends approved and would support the extension of slavery. Additionally, there were in many places mistaken notions of Christian freedom confused with civil and physical freedom, which were naturally not without their blind admirers and defenders among us. It was not long before many of the better and more thoughtful members of our congregations understood what the heart of the matter was and were enlightened by God's Word on the truth of our doctrine or, if they could not get that far, felt themselves so stricken by the testimony of God's Word that they no longer dared gainsay us. But then there was an event that made our opponents bolder and set the controversy in full swing. The Danish pastor C. L. Clausen had hardly come home from the Synod to his congregation, where for several reasons the commotion was perhaps greater than in any

Claus Lauritz Clausen (1820–1892), pastor of the Norwegian Synod and its critic in the debate over slavery.

other place, when he acknowledged to the congregation that the declaration he had put forth together with the other pastors was false; when somewhat later he also publicly recanted and attacked our doctrine, it was naturally necessary for us publicly to defend the truth we confessed. In the course of a year, however, public controversy began to abate, especially when the discussion of the matter at nearly every subsequent synod meeting was by a preponderant majority deferred because the Civil War and the circumstances of the times made discussion of this issue inadvisable.

However, the controversy broke out again with renewed violence last summer. In 1861 the Synod's then-President, Pastor A. C. Preus, transmitted the declaration of the pastors to the theological faculty in Christiania and asked their opinion in the matter; their reply came to me, since in the meantime, in October of 1863, I had become president.[23] After first consulting with my ministerial brethren and then with our church council, I desisted for a time, until last year, from making this opinion public at a synod meeting.

The first page of the opinion on slavery of the theological faculty in Norway. (Courtesy of the Archives of Luther College, Decorah, Iowa.)

Our reason for this was that it was clear to us that the opinion consisted of two parts, so internally contradictory that it articulated two opposed interpretations and answered "Yes" and "No" at the same time. This did not seem to us to be good theology. We therefore considered it our obligation both to our church body and to the faculty, whose opinion we had requested, to try and see if we could not reach agreement through discussion. Consequently, in the spring of 1864, I transmitted a rejoinder prepared by professors Larsen and Schmidt for the consideration of the faculty.[24] Since it did not find any occasion to make changes in its opinion, our church council, at the request of our pastoral conference, directed a new communication to the faculty.[25] There was still no response to this, and since our synod was to meet last year,* I therefore considered it my duty to lay before the Synod the faculty's opinion along with the rest of the correspondence. It was decided that all the documents should be printed in the proceedings of the Synod. Hardly had this taken place than the controversy broke out freshly with increased violence. Pastor Clausen immediately came forward with an attack on the doctrine we confess and appealed to one portion of the faculty's opinion, and he was quickly imitated by a whole crowd of authors who all appropriated this part of the faculty's opinion, while they most often passed over the other part in silence.[26]

Many of the productions which thus appeared were obviously of the sort that every Christian, of whatever conviction he might be in this business, would blush and be saddened over. We were sharply criticized, grossly abused, lied about, and sneered at, the main thing for some. There were among our opponents not only worthy and pious, if in this instance misled, members of the congregations, but also men who stood outside the church and did not seem to bother themselves about God and his Word, men who embraced a false humanism and were intoxicated with the modern rage for "natural and inalienable human rights," who considered outward, temporal freedom *absolutely* necessary to human beings. But the more the deep significance of the question came out of the controversy and the more we saw that we had actually to do battle with an aspect of the antichristian spirit of the times, naturally the less we dared to keep silent and thus betray the truth. We tried again to defend from God's Word the doctrine we confessed and to this end got excellent assistance from the second part of the faculty's opinion.

---

*I now know that the faculty wished to make a new statement, but was hindered in doing so by heavy loads of work among its members. [Preus's note]

Historisk Fremstilling

af den Strid, som

i Aarene 1861 til 1868

indenfor den norske Synode i Amerika

har været ført

i Anledning af Skriftens Lære om Slaveri.

———— ◆ ————

Udgiven af
navnte Synodes Kirkeraad.

———— ◆ ————

Madison, Wis.
Trykt i B. W. Suckows Bogtrykkeri.
—
1868.

Title page of the Norwegian Synod's historical account of the slavery controversy published shortly after the "Seven Lectures."

I shall now attempt to render a presentation of our doctrine as briefly as possible.

1) According to our declaration, slavery is not a divine institution, nor is it something glorious and good, but rather in many situations something much more sorrowful and evil, even though it can be turned to good for those who fear God.

2) It does not occur according to God's original will as creator, but as a punishment for sin; it does not originate in Paradise, but is a consequence of the fall into sin.

3) It is not merely an evil for the slave, but also perilous to the master, whose responsibility is greater, whose obligations are most difficult, and for whom temptations to the abuse of power are great.

4) Such abuses are condemned as, for example, fornication with slaves, obstruction or disturbance of proper marriage among them, withholding of God's Word, burdening them with work beyond their powers, maltreatment, and withdrawal of sustenance.

5) Masters are obligated to obey Matthew 7:12 ("Therefore all things whatsoever ye would that men . . . "); they should therefore see that slaves are able to lead industrious and godly lives, get instruction and edification from God's Word, enter into lawful marriage, have moderate work and the sustenance needful, including food and clothing.

6) Slaves are entitled to fitting work, shelter, and recompense, that is, food and clothing (I Timothy 6:8).

7) The law of love does not always compel the freeing of slaves, because it does not abrogate distinctions of station among people. On the other hand, it does require a manifestation to the neighbor, including slaves, of everything good according to his wants and needs in the station and occupation in which he is placed.

8) Slaves are the possessions of their masters according to Genesis 26:14 and Leviticus 25:45 ff., although only for service and use harmonious with the commands of God.

9) Masters do not have power over the consciences and souls of slaves; that belongs only to God and His Word (I Corinthians 7:23, Galatians 5:1).

10) The slave is thus a servant who is obligated for his lifetime to serve, obey, and work, although he has a right to board, clothing, sustenance, and time to further his salvation and fulfill the will of his heavenly Lord in the calling in which he is placed.

11) When the master shows this to the slave, he shows what is just and fair, according to Galatians 4:1.

12) If it is objected that this is an ideal slavery, but that in actuality it is sinful, it is certainly conceded that a sinless perfection is not to be expected in this situation more than in others, yet master as well as slave can fulfill their duties in the sincerity of an evangelical spirit, grow in it, and be preserved from the sin of malice.

13) As in other permissible social relations, for example between married people, masters and free servants, the authorities and those subject to them, only a very few strive to fulfill the commandment of love, without it therefore meaning that the station itself is sinful, so that one can hardly expect anything other than that masters will for the most part abuse their powers, without the station therefore being sinful in itself.

14) Galatians 4:1 shows what disposition the master is to have toward the slave, but the temptation to tyrannize is so much greater because the slave is bound to lifetime servitude.

15) Therefore every Christian humanitarian will thus wish and work for the continuing abolition of this severe servitude.

16) No Christian can therefore be a "pro-slavery man" in the fullest sense of the term, nor have we ever been that. History also demonstrates of Christianity that where its spirit penetrates it has by degrees ameliorated and then fully abolished slavery.

17) However, we cannot declare it to be sinful in itself, that is, to keep slaves in all circumstances, because God in the Old Testament allows his people to have such possessions and even calls this a blessing (Genesis 24:3, 5; 26:12), and even though Christ and the apostles meet slavery widely extended everywhere (sixty million slaves in the Roman Empire, according to Gibbon), the New Testament still does not contain prohibitions of it, but rather admonitions both for slaves to hold their masters worthy of honor and serve them faithfully and for masters to show their slaves how right and fitting it is to remember that they themselves have a master in heaven (I Timothy 6:1).[27]

18) That the Greek Word δουλος is translated as "bondservant" [*træl*] and "servant" in Ephesians 6:5–9; Colossians 3:22–24, 4:1; I Timothy 6:1f.; Titus 2:9f.; that I Peter 2:18 actually means "slave" can be seen by the contradistinction to "free" in Ephesians 6:8, I Corinthians 7:21, and Galatians 4:1f. The accuracy of this explanation is also evident from the testimony of history

in which all servants were once as good as slaves; this is attested by the Weimar Bible, Bishop Gislesen's *Catechism*, the opinion of the theological faculty, Webster's *Dictionary*, and Pastor C. L. Clausen.[28]

19) When our opponents say that the apostles well knew that it was sinful but did not wish or dare to say so, that they therefore did not require the freeing of slaves and did not castigate masters, but forebore, and rather admonished slaveholders as believers and beloved brethren to deal with their slaves properly, this is essentially to deny that the Holy Scriptures are inspired by God and that the apostles were guided by the Holy Spirit, that is, to deny the Holy Scriptures as the only perfect rule for faith and life. It is to mock the dear apostles who regarded it as an honor to be despised for Christ's sake (II Corinthians 11:23–28).

20) Over against these clear passages in the Holy Scripture we cannot thus say that it is in itself, that is, always and everywhere by anyone who may do so, a sin to hold slaves, or that one always commits a sin by the act itself of holding slaves, however lovingly and well one may treat them.

21) This does not depend on everyone understanding the agreement of the passages mentioned with the commandment of love or other words of Scripture, because we know that the Scripture cannot contradict itself, even if it may seem to us to do so.

22) Nor does it depend on understanding how slavery could ever have properly arisen, because God's Word must be believed, even if we cannot understand it as a whole.

23) Still, we do not declare and never have declared unchristian all those who do not perceive the truth of our doctrine and its harmony with God's Word, especially if they have doubts and scruples on the basis of passages of Scripture and do not show open recalcitrance toward the Word of God.

24) We do not regard and never have regarded this doctrine as a chief or fundamental doctrine of Christianity, but we cannot therefore regard it as unimportant or consider it an indifferent matter for each to believe after his own fashion, first because errors on this point stand in close conjunction with other errors concerning the Fourth Commandment, and second because we are obligated to believe in every word of God, even the most insignificant.

25) We have not sought controversy in this matter, but we have

tried to confess, as we have been able and where we could not stay silent without sin, what we know to be the truth of God's Word.

Since appeal to the opinion of the faculty has often been used against us, I shall point out that in its second part, in which it restricts itself to our declaration on the question at hand and responds only according to God's Word, it expresses exactly the same opinion we have taught and expounded: "The New Testament contains no express prohibition of slavery, no outright judgment rejecting or condemning it, no law commanding its abolition. It no more calls it a sin to be a slave or a duty for the slave to break his bonds than it makes it unconditionally a sin to hold slaves or a duty for masters to free their slaves. On the contrary, it puts the relation of slavery—alongside the social relations established by God between man and wife, parents and children—under the Fourth Commandment (Ephesians 6:5–9, also 5:21–26 and 6:4; Colossians 3:22, 4:1, and also 3:18–21). Based on the presupposition that within Christian congregations there were both Christian slaves and Christian slaveholders, the former are admonished to consider their earthly masters, be they believers or unbelievers, good and fair or perverse, as representatives of their heavenly master and to serve them as such respectfully, submissively, and faithfully (Ephesians 6:5–8; Colossians 3:22–25; I Timothy 6:1–2; Titus 2:9–10; I Peter 2:18). On the other hand, masters are to bear in mind that they, too, have a master in heaven, who is no respecter of persons, and to treat their slaves with paternal love, justice, and fairness and, insofar as they are Christians, as brothers in the Lord (Ephesians 6:9; Colossians 4:1; Philemon [1]:12–16).

"The general Christian rule: 'Let every man abide in the same calling wherein he was called. . . . let every man, wherein he is called, therein abide with God!' (I Corinthians 7:20, 24) is expressly applied by the apostle Paul to the state of slavery as well (vv. 21–23). He admonishes the Christian slave not to worry or to be dissatisfied with the state of slavery, as if it could mean any diminution of the power or glory of his station as a Christian, but rather to esteem his spiritual freedom in Christ as higher than the yoke of his outward bondage. He is so far from representing outward freedom as an especially important object of the Christian slave's endeavor that, on the contrary,—according to an interpretation of v. 21 which does not in any event lack able spokesmen—even if he should be able in a proper manner to achieve such a change in his

outward station, he advises him — presumably in consideration of
the church's status at that time (v. 26) — to 'use it rather,' that he
is 'called being a servant,' and consequently to abide with God in
the station in which the call of his grace reached him. In conformity
with this, the apostle thus sends the runaway slave, Onesimus,
back to his master, Philemon, without requiring of this his brother
in the Lord the liberation of the slave who has now become a Christian, but only prays that he will receive him with love and treat him
as a brother in the Lord (Philemon 10–18). Thus we see that the
New Testament at the same time as it emphatically maintains the
basic principle that for Christ and in relation to him there is no distinction between master and slave, yet far from deriving from this
any justification for the slave arbitrarily to break his own yoke or
any absolute obligation for the master to set him free, on the contrary it makes such a change in the outward relation an entirely
subordinate factor in relation to the inward equality of both, even
though, by positing such a basic assumption, it has at the same time
passed a judgment on the essence of slavery so that without any
course of coercive external action it must cease, or in any event lose
its sting everywhere this basic assumption is acknowledged."

When Pastor Clausen, though holding with us that slavery
designates a relation of ownership, at the same time maintains
against us that slavery in itself is sinful and that the slavery spoken
of among Christians in the New Testament is not a relation of
ownership but only a relation constituted by compulsory service or
by obedience and is therefore not slavery at all but has only the
name and form of slavery, he certainly has no grounds for maintaining an appeal to the faculty's opinion. It nowhere denies that
"slavery" in the New Testament designates a relation of ownership
and even if some individual expressions could seem to wish to
avoid acknowledging slavery in the New Testament as an actual
slavery, it was certainly not the intention of the faculty to assert
this, but only to say that an originally heathen slavery was altered
considerably by Christianity. In any case Professor [Gisle] Johnson, a member of the faculty, explained these expressions this way
during the discussion Pastor Clausen and I had with him in the
month of February this year.[29] When Pastor Clausen claimed the
support of the faculty's opinion for the assertion mentioned above,
Professor Johnson had to declare that he must admit that in the
opinion under discussion the expression "slavery in name only"

was not an adequate expression for what the New Testament calls "slavery," and therefore should not be urged as such. He added that Clausen ought not to claim the opinion of the faculty for himself when he would not acknowledge in agreement with it that the relation of ownership continues in the New Testament and that it is consequently an actual slavery.

Finally, with regard to the accusation against us in this matter that we have proceeded against Pastor C. L. Clausen with loveless rigor, I confidently reject such an accusation as a falsehood. Pastor Clausen himself at one time testified to the contrary. As for our proceedings against him, I believe that we have been justified and obligated by both the love and the truth owed to him. As for anything else, I shall not enter further into this point. It grieves me that I had to take this up at all. Those who desire further information on the relation between Pastor Clausen and us during this controversy can read about it in *Luth[ersk] Kirketid[ende]*, VIII, No. 20, where it has been necessary for me to explain the situation.[30]

I have now presented the doctrinal points on which the Augustana Synod disagrees with our synod and departs more or less from the truth. Our battle with this synod has—God be praised!—not been without fruit. Last autumn, three of its Norwegian pastors together with several of the congregations forsook it for the sake of their faith and united with us.[31] And even within the synod itself a more earnest consideration of the importance of the pure doctrine and here and there a somewhat clearer perception of the truth may well have been the fruit of our witness. In any event, we hope so. Additionally, in recent years we have repeatedly sought conferences with the Augustanans, but so far in vain. We may still hope that the new Norwegian pastors the synod has received in recent years in the persons of the theological student Olsen and the seminarians Krogness and [Johannes] Møller Eggen will not allow themselves to be led blindly by the Swedish pastors.[32] Even though they may have a considerable lack of competence, there is reason to hope that they possess a more Christian earnestness, a healthier life of faith, and simpler Lutheran awareness than some, in any case, of their Swedish brethren. May God's grace help them to open their eyes and see that with their congregations they should annul their present sinful association and join our orthodox synod if they hope to preserve Lutheran faith and doctrine. God help them to this for Jesus' sake.

*Linka Preus's sketch of a discussion of slavery in the home of her sister,
Hanne, Marie Bang, and her husband, Hans Fredrik Bang, in Drammen,
Norway. The conversation, involving Linka Preus's brother, Johan
Carl Keyser, Bang, and Herman Amberg Preus, illustrates disagreement
on the slavery issue in the Preus family. (Courtesy of the Archives of
Luther College, Decorah, Iowa.)*

Conclusion

I am, then, finished with my portrayal of our religious situation
in America. I have had a dual purpose in mind. I have wanted to give
our mother church an opportunity to learn about our situation in
order to be in a position to judge it properly, because it is not a matter of indifference to us how we are regarded and judged by our
brethren in faith and especially by brethren in faith among our
countrymen. But I also wished to awaken sympathy for the spiritual
needs of their countrymen and brethren in faith among the younger
theologians and, if possible, to get some of them to hear and heed
the cry to "Come over and help us!" Perhaps in conclusion it will
therefore be permitted me to address some words especially to Norway's young theologians.

I shall first remind them of the great, great spiritual need among
us, of the many vast congregations without pastors, of the multi-

tude who cry out for the bread of life so that they do not perish for want of it; remind them of the countless dangers and seductions to which their countrymen in such congregations are exposed, of the multitude of their countrymen and brethren in faith from here who come over to us every year and increase our state of need. Again this year a thousand score of our countrymen have departed. How many candidates have felt their hearts powerfully stirred by the thought of their spiritual need, how many have felt themselves so strongly moved in the spirit by the sight of this mass of dearly purchased souls of whom many shall now go astray like sheep without a shepherd, that they have left behind the temporal bonds that bind them, set every inessential consideration aside, and declared themselves willing to follow after them and break the bread of life for the hungry? I blame no one for taking an interest in Jews, Turks, and heathens, for working to spread the gospel of Christ among the most distant of peoples unto the ends of the earth. But could not your countrymen, brethren in faith, lay claim to your compassion and love? Are they to be regarded as lepers or victims of the plague from whom one recoils and flees? Even if that is what they are — Christ did not treat them so, he came unto them and helped them, he sought out the lost, and it is his love that we should seek to appropriate and emulate.

We are, of course, ourselves working to meet the need. To this end we hope in the course of a few years to be able to send out a score of teachers among our countrymen. But, as I explained earlier, most of these have only practical training, and we are sorely in need, and in the immediate future will be in even greater need, of competent, scholarly, trained, pious theologians. Therefore we will gladly receive competent theological students and help them complete their theological training among us. First and foremost, however, we need candidates who can help us immediately in our work and help us cast out the nets in which souls are to be caught for the kingdom of God.

But I hear so many objections, so many excuses!

1) "We feel no call!"—Brethren, here is a cry, here is a call from God's congregations! You know that our need is the more crying, the need for you to extend a hand greater, than it is here at home. You know beforehand that your work there will be received and grow great with blessing. You who have consecrated yourself to the

work of the gospel and have been found worthy, look! You have the call, the call from God.

2) "But I do not feel the inner call, the desire to leave!"—Then you must strike the old Adam a good blow to the head and rebuke yourself that you do not feel the desire, the desire of a new spirit to do that to which God calls you and love should impel you—then stand up, and even without the desire, indeed even against your own desire, cast off old Adam's chains and in God's name get about the preaching of God's gospel and pray that the Lord will give you a desire for the work and you shall have it.

3) "But it is a matter of freedom and I can do as I like"—Yes, that is what they say who cry: "Let us cast off His bonds! We do not want Him to rule over us!" But the Lord's disciples follow the Lord's voice in everything, indeed they attend to His slightest beckoning. Their whole lives are a sacrifice made in love and in obedience to faith; they have forsaken all willfullness and self-interest along with the Devil.

4) "But there is need here at home; the fatherland has need of us!"—This is partly true, and to those who remain at home to meet the needs of this church I do not direct these words. But when calls stand vacant in Finnmark or elsewhere, or when it is difficult to get them filled, the cause is not a lack of candidates but rather that the candidates have not taken the needs of *their own* church to heart. It is no wonder, then, that any true feeling for the needs of *our* church is also lacking.

5) "But the schools require our abilities!"—This is also true for some.[33] The theological candidate is not specifically trained or set apart for work in the schools, except insofar as religion is the chief subject. There is something to be said for candidates preparing themselves for the ministry by working for a few years as a teacher in the common schools, but not so that he works himself weary there and loses both understanding and appreciation for theology and the work of the ministry. Naturally, there is no rule without exception, and for some it can appear late in life that work in the schools rather than in the preaching ministry is their proper place.

6) "Circumstances with our parents and ties of family make it necessary for us to stay here."—Yes, there are such circumstances. But certainly there are only special instances in which these circumstances are of such a nature that they force us for God's sake to stay. We should perhaps seek counsel from parents and Christian friends,

but we should not be bound by flesh and blood. And also, let us not forget the Savior's words: "Whosoever forsakes father and mother for my name's sake, he shall gain a hundred-fold over." We have experienced the truth of this promise. In a foreign country we have found father and mother and sister and brother to take the place of those we had to forsake here.

7) "We are not fit for such difficult situations."—When they are not too old, most theological candidates surely are theologically competent. And as a rule it is also best to let others judge that. It is certainly true more than it is here that the pastor's task in America requires especially a practical competence, a gift for leading a congregation and maintaining both inward and outward order during discussions in meetings. But it would certainly be exceptional if a competent, orthodox, pious theological candidate did not possess or could not gain through practice this gift from God for the conduct of the ministry.

8) "But the demands over there are so great, and so much trouble and exertion are required."—True enough, but not as a rule to the same degree as earlier. Besides, has not the Lord purchased us for this by His blood? Has He chosen us to be His instruments for the preparation of congregations in order to seek comfortable posts and good days, or in order daily like the apostle Paul to sacrifice ourselves in His service? We should regard it as the highest honor to be worthy to bear His saving message to dearly purchased brethren. We should rejoice when we are counted worthy to suffer privation, tribulation, and mockery for His name's sake.

9) "But incomes, temporal existence are so insecure. There are no guarantees."—The Lord is our hope and comfort and great confidence! He is our guarantee, and we consider Him the best one. When have you seen a child of righteousness forsaken by Him? Cast your burdens on Him and He will care for you! Besides, preach in the power of the Lord in season and out of season, the law for the discipline and mortification of the flesh, the saving gospel for refreshment, for comfort and life; gain for souls the taste of grace, the sweetness of the gospel, and then you will see that hearts are opened to your bodily needs and will be willing to share all the temporal goods necessary!

10) "Yes, but the spiritual pressure over there is too strong."—We endure no spiritual pressure other than from God's Word. This Word, we believe, is clear enough for everyone who properly oc-

cupies himself with it. We are all, pastors and lay people, obligated to bow to it. If we err in anything, we are willing to allow ourselves to be disciplined and guided by the Word and will thank the person who will come over and do this for us. Hardly anyone will argue that we are so far off the track that a really orthodox Lutheran could not or would not stand in the communion of faith with us.

11) "But we could never turn back."—That is not the case. Not least because of the present need, certainly no one for considerations of the flesh should forsake his congregation without valid reason, but where the matter is decided according to God's Word and in heartfelt certainty, so that the step is not taken in doubt but in faith, we would certainly insofar as it was up to us not put any obstacle in the way of a return. I could give examples of this.

I have herewith mentioned and answered the most essential objections made to coming over to us. But I shall now also permit myself to adduce some reasons for theological candidates to heed the cry.

1) I have earlier mentioned our desperate need. Congregations disintegrate, souls languish, pastors overexert themselves and still cannot do what is essential for the upbuilding of our far-flung congregations.

2) For the god-fearing theological student, pastoral work in our free church will be an excellent school both for his inner life and for the completion of his training for the ministry. From his own experience there he will learn to understand and appreciate the Lutheran free church, in which every activity can be directed according to God's Word. There he will easily learn to judge the situation of the state church, its great flaws and deficiencies as well as the ways in which they can be remedied. There he will be tempted less to look to so many temporal considerations, to require and build upon all kinds of human guarantees, and to make flesh his arm. He will be driven more to put his confidence in God's Word, assured that by it God will uphold both him and the church.

3) Those who, by reason of circumstances in the state church here in Norway, have reservations about entering into ministerial service can satisfy among us their longing to work for the salvation of souls as servants of the Word without being hemmed in by the prejudices, constraints, and burdens of the state church. There he does not, as here, need to shudder to think of having perhaps to work in the same congregation, or in any case the same church

body, together with false teachers, whom according to God's Word he is obligated to shun, after having rebuked them in vain. There he need not, as in the situation of the state church, fear that when he must leave his congregation it could just as easily fall into the hands of an erring teacher as be entrusted to an orthodox servant of the Word. In short: he need not be anxious about having to be in a church body which, despite its orthodox confession on paper, may ultimately be found to be heterodox. There he can bind himself to exercise a church discipline harmonious with God's Word, without fearing that it shall be made as good as impossible even by conditions within the congregation as well as by external prejudices and pressures. There he can collaborate with the congregation in a situation allowing all spiritual power to be put to work in harmony with God's Word for blessing to both the congregation and the church. To sum up, there, by the grace of God, he can conduct his ministry according to God's Word in a congregation and a church body ordered and guided according to God's Word and secure in its future so long as it holds fast to the Word, and he can thus avoid the struggle endured by a conscientious pastor in the state church, because so much in it is not arranged or disposed according to the direction of God's Word. In it there is as good as no church discipline to be found, because the congregation is excluded from public activity and participation in the governance of its own affairs, by which not only are its edification and development restricted, but its lay people are altogether too often tempted to activity not warranted by the Word of God, which, when exercised without such warrant, can never be without injury to God's congregation.

And now, brethren, forgive me if I have spoken harshly. My heart is on fire with the need of my countrymen. I thank God who has granted it to me to see again fatherland, kindred, and friends after such a long time away. But in the happiness of the moment, I still cannot forget her who is the bride of my heart over there. Even here I still cling to that congregation with all the love of my soul, follow its struggle, and pray for God to stand by it and bless its work to His glory and the salvation of souls. And if you, brother, can take an effective part in this struggle, then I say: "Come and you will be cordially welcome among us!" And, I know it for certain, the Lord also says to you: "Go!" And the same Lord will bless your work in America.

179

APPENDIX I

The Constitution of the Norwegian Synod

As Preus remarks in the "Seven Lectures," the leaders of the Norwegian Synod quickly realized that the synodical constitution adopted in 1853 was not entirely suited to the North American context or consistent with the Synod's theology.[1] In 1861 the Synod's church council undertook a first attempt to revise the constitution, but a lack of time prevented thorough consideration and presentation to the congregations.[2] The church council later appointed U.V. Koren, F.A. Schmidt, and Laur. Larsen to a committee charged with preparing a new draft.[3] This committee presented a draft for discussion when the Synod met in 1865.[4] Substantial disagreement emerged during the course of this debate over the title, duties, and term of office for the Synod's elected head.[5]

At the Synod meeting of 1867, this document was again thoroughly reviewed, somewhat revised, and approved except for Chapter 3, sections 2 and 3, which contained the much debated provisions for officers of the Synod.[6] It was not until 1868 that the Synod approved the constitution as a whole, deciding finally to use the term "president" (*formand*) rather than "bishop" (*biskop*) or "chairman" (*præses*) and to establish a term of six years for this office rather than the virtually permanent tenure proposed in the preliminary draft.[7]

The official text of the constitution of the Norwegian Synod was printed in complete form in the synodical report for 1868.[8] The present translation is a very slightly revised version of the English text which appeared in the *The Lutheran Watchman* the same year.[9] Minor revisions have been made on the basis of the Norwegian text of 1868.

VIVACIOUS DAUGHTER

CONSTITUTION OF THE SYNOD FOR THE NORWEGIAN EVANGELICAL LUTHERAN CHURCH IN AMERICA

I.N.I.

CHAPTER FIRST.

Of the Name, Confession, and Church-Usages of Synod.

SECTION 1. — The church body [*Kirkesamfund*] hitherto called "the Norwegian Evangelical Lutheran Church in America" herewith adopts the name of "the Synod for the Norwegian Evangelical Lutheran Church in America."

§ 2. — The only source and rule for the faith and doctrine of Synod, is God's Holy Word, revealed in the canonical Books of the Old and New Testaments.

§ 3. — Synod adopts as its confession of faith the symbolical books or confessional writings of the Norwegian Lutheran Church, because these present a pure and incorrupt exhibition of the doctrine contained in the Divine Word. These Confessional writings are:

a. — The three ancient symbols: the Apostolical, the Nicene, and the Athanasian; b. — the unaltered Augsburg Confession; c. — the smaller catechism of Luther.

NOTE. — The only reason why the other symbols of the Lutheran Church are not yet mentioned among the symbolical books of our Synod, is the fact that they have hitherto been little known to our congregations.

§ 4. — To preserve uniformity in the ceremonies connected with public worship, Synod recommends to its congregations, so far as this is possible, to continue employing the Norwegian church-ritual of 1685 and the Liturgy of 1688.

CHAPTER SECOND.

Of the Composition of Synod and its Representation in Synodical Sessions.

SECTION 1. — Synod is composed of the congregations who have combined themselves into a whole by adopting this Synodical constitution.

2. — Standing members of the Synodical Union, such as in reference to their official position always are subject to the supervision of Synod and whose duty it is to attend the meetings of Synod, are: a. — ministers having charge of congregations belonging to Synod, whenever they are admitted into Synod, and b. — the members of the church-council.

§ 3. — Besides, the following may be received as standing members: a. — teachers in the institutions of Synod; b. — pastors having charge of congregations not in connection with the synod; c. — permanently appointed school-teachers of Lutheran congregations within or outside of Synod.

§ 4. — Whenever a congregation desires to become connected with Synod, it shall forward an application to that effect to the President of Synod. This petition is to be accompanied with: a. — a copy of the congregation's constitution and bylaws, together with evidences showing that the doctrine, confession and church-order of the congregation are genuinely Lutheran; b. — a legitimately certified declaration to the effect that this Synodical constitution has been adopted in a public meeting of the congregation. These documents are to be laid before the Synod, which thereupon decides whether the petition shall be granted.

182

§ 5.—Whenever a person desires admission into Synod in the character of a standing member, he must forward to the President a suitable application accompanied with the declaration that he absolutely concurs in the doctrine and confession of Synod, and submits to its constitution. If the person applying for admission is a pastor, he must at the same time, before his admission can take place, produce satisfactory evidence that he is properly examined, regularly called, and in a churchly way consecrated to the ecclesiastical office. The matter, together with the accompanying papers, is laid before Synod, subject to its decision.

§ 6.—In conformity with the Apostolical prototype, as given in Acts Chap. 15, the common concerns and interests of Synod are regulated and conducted through: Synodical meetings. These consist of: a.—the standing members of Synod; b.—representatives elected by congregations in connection with Synod.

§ 7.—These meetings are held at intervals of not more than two years, at the time and place which has been selected by the previous meeting.

§ 8.—Every congregation connected with Synod ought to be represented at the sessions of Synod, either by a representative chosen from its own midst, or by a representative chosen in conjunction with one or more congregations ministered to by the same pastor. The representatives must be men of good report and they shall bring with them evidences of their election by the congregation.

§ 9.—Members of the Synodical meetings are:—

A.—**Entitled to vote.**—1. pastors belonging to Synod and having charge of congregations in connection with Synod; 2. representatives elected by congregations that have joined Synod.

B.—**Advisory.**—1. standing members who are not entitled to vote in pursuance of A. 1. & 2.; 2. delegates whom congregations within Synod might send besides their representatives, and of whom each congregation may send one; 3. theological candidates in connection with our church body; 4. guests who may, by a resolution of Synod, be admitted as advisory members.

§ 10.—The Synod shall:

a. watch over the purity and unity of doctrine, (Eph. 4, 3–16, 1 Cor. 1, 10.) as well as the development of the Christian life, and therefore in its meetings particularly canvass such doctrinal questions for the discussion of which a peculiar need might reveal itself within the Synod, make mention of and warn against invading sects, errors and sins, together with unchristian tendencies of the age;

b. carry on supervision in respect of the official conduct of all standing members, as well as the churchly condition of the congregations, to which end the pastors are required to forward yearly reports to the President of Synod;

c. seek to adjust ecclesiastical contentions, whenever the parties concerned desire it, and further, to communicate advice and judgments in religious questions;

d. whenever the circumstances might require this, in the meantime divest a congregation or standing member of its privileges in Synod, and if they, in spite of repeated admonition should stubbornly continue in false doctrine or ungodly life, finally and utterly dissolve the Synodical connection with such persons;

e. establish and manage institutions

of learning for the training up of orthodox pastors and school teachers, and
promote missions at home and abroad;

f. promote the use and dissemina-
tion of the Holy Scriptures and of orthodox text-books, hymn-books, and
devotional writings;

g. manage a school treasury for
defraying the expenses connected with
the Synod's public institutions of learning, the salary of the teachers, and the
erection, furniture and repair of their
buildings, etc., and also a Synodical
treasury for defraying the expenses
connected with the discharge of the
functions of Synod, the Church Council, and the President.

h. elect its officers and more explicitly define their range of business, and
also revise their report of proceedings
and their accounts;

i. examine the credentials of
representatives, amidst congregations
and members, and exercise the requisite Christian discipline during the sessions of Synod.

§ 11. — With the exception of
changes in the constitution (see Chapt.
IV.) and questions of doctrine or conscience, all matters are decided in Synodical meetings by a simple majority,
and if the votes are equally divided that
of the President effects a decision.

§ 12. — Questions of doctrine or
conscience cannot be decided by a
vote, but only in accordance with the
Word of God and the Symbolical
Books of our Church.

§ 13. — Over against the congregations in their separate capacity, the session of Synod is no more than an advisory assembly. Hence, if a congregation believes that any resolution is in
conflict with the Word of God, or that
it is not conducive to its welfare in its
peculiar circumstances, the congregation ought to report this to the Church

Council and state its reasons in the
case. If no such report is forwarded
during the six months following upon
the publishing of the resolution of Synod, said resolution is regarded as having been accepted by the congregation.

CHAPTER THIRD.

**Of the Officers of Synod, Their Elec-
tion and Activity.**

Section 1. — The officers of Synod
are: — 1. The President of Synod; 2.
The members of the Church Council,
to wit: the President of Synod who also
acts as President of the church-council,
together with two pastors and three
lay-members; 3. A secretary; 4. A
treasurer.

§ 2. — The President shall be elected
at the session of Synod for 6 years.
Thereafter new elections for the other
officers shall occur at every other regular session of Synod.

§ 3. — At each regular session of Synod two revisors are appointed whose
duty it is to examine the accounts of the
treasurer and report to Synod.

§ 4. — The church-council is called
to meet by its President whenever he
deems it necessary, or whenever at
least two of the remaining members of
the same call upon him to do so.

§ 5. — It is the duty of the church-
council in the name of the Synod to execute its resolutions, and upon the
whole to exert its influence in the interval between the Synodical sessions to-
wards promoting the object of the
Synod.

§ 6. — The church-council shall
thus: —

a. attend to the management of and
exercise supervision over the institutions of learning established by Synod,

according to the method prescribed by Synod;

b. in conjunction with the pastors of Synod and the permanently appointed teachers in the institutions of learning belonging to Synod, elect new teachers in these;

c. make provisions for the examination of candidates for the ministry and, whenever this is deemed necessary, also of pastors who, having previously been members of other communities, may desire to connect themselves with our Synod;

d. mediate in case of contentions whenever its service is called for by the parties concerned;

e. have the right to inflict a provisional suspension from membership between the sessions of Synod, upon such a standing member as continues in manifest false doctrine or ungodly life notwithstanding repeated admonitions from the Word of God;

f. exercise supervision in regard to the treasuries of Synod;

g. whenever peculiar circumstances require this, call an extra session of Synod.

§ 7.—The proceedings of the church-council are duly recorded and an abstract of them is published.

§ 8.—The President of Synod shall:—

a. either personally or through other pastors of Synod, among whom preference is due to the members of the church-council, hold a visitation in the charges of Synod provided with pastors, and also at its institutions of learning, if possible at least once in the course of every three years;

b. ordain and install pastors, or, if he is prevented from doing so himself, appoint other pastors to do so;

c. as far as possible attend at least the more numerous pastoral conferences held by the pastors of our Synod;

d. in like manner as the church-council mediate in the case of dissensions, whenever his service is especially petitioned for by the parties concerned, or the service of the entire church-council cannot be had;

e. call meetings of Synod and the church-council in accordance with the rules contained in chap. II. § 7, and Chap. III. § 4.

f. preside over transactions at the sessions of Synod;

g. appoint committees or essayists as well before as during the sessions of Synod for a preparatory treatment of more important matters, unless the Synod itself resolves to appoint such;

h. at each regular session of Synod present a report respecting the activity of himself and the church-council, as well as the condition of the church-community upon the whole.

§ 9.—In the exercise of his official duties the President shall, as far as circumstances permit him to do so, seek the advice and aid of the entire church-council or of its members individually;

§ 10.—The Secretary of Synod shall register a protocol of the proceedings of Synodical sessions, make provision for the publishing of an abstract which has been approved by the President, compose the documents issued in the name of the Synod whenever it or its President instructs him to do so, and also publish the time and place of Synodical sessions, and the subjects for consideration that may have been duly appointed.

§ 11.—The Treasurer of Synod shall administer the means of the school and Synodical treasuries. He pays out moneys only under the direction of the church-council, or of its President in its name, and shall give an account of his functions at each meeting of Synod.

CHAPTER FOURTH.
———

Of Changes in the Synodical Constitution.

With the exception of chapt. I. § 2 and 3., and chap. II. § 5., the contents of which must never be changed, an alteration in this Synodical constitution may be effected in the following manner: A proposal for alteration is laid before Synod, and if the latter approves of the same with a two-thirds majority, the proposition is to be published in order that the congregations connected with Synod may forward their declarations respecting it to the church-council. Those congregations which forward no declaration until the next Synodical meeting are regarded as having given their consent to the amendment. At this next meeting of Synod the matter is again taken up for consideration, and if the proposal then gains the approval of two-thirds of the votes, it is finally received.

APPENDIX II

A Sequel to the "Seven Lectures"

The following article originally appeared in *Luthersk Kirketidende* in 1868 as a sequel to the "Seven Lectures." More than the "Lectures," this report illuminates the interests of Herman Amberg Preus and the other leaders of the Norwegian Synod in the larger American Lutheran scene. Their early engagement with the question of Lutheran unity and the rigorous position they took in this matter illustrate the way in which these pioneer pastors quickly looked beyond ethnic lines as they worked out their sense of Lutheran identity in the United States. Like the "Seven Lectures" this essay underscores the role of doctrine in the adaptation of this religious tradition to a new cultural context.

This brief article reveals as well the early development among Norwegian-American Lutherans of an antipathy toward the traditions of American Lutheranism first planted along the eastern seaboard during the colonial era. The sharply critical attitude toward the General Council of the Evangelical Lutheran Church in North America is a portent of decades of strain between the Lutheran bodies that would eventually become the American Lutheran Church in 1960–1963, on the one hand, and the churches that would merge to form the Lutheran Church in American in 1962, on the other hand. Charging the Lutherans of the General Council with hierarchical tendencies in polity and laxity in doctrine, Preus here sounds themes that would appear over and over again in the literature of the coming decades.

The Lutheran Church in North America
by
Herman Amberg Preus

In my "Seven Lectures" I also briefly described the most important of the German- and English-speaking Lutheran synods over here and reported the principal matters on which they have disagreed, as a result of which they have hitherto remained separated from one another.[1] Since the last few years have been abundant in important events for the Lutheran Church in America, I have thought it might be of interest to the readers of *Kirketidende* to have a simple explanation of what, by the grace of God, has happened here and what may well, with the help of God, be of extraordinarily great significance for the future of our Lutheran Church in this land.

Among these synods, I dwelt especially in my lectures upon the Missouri Synod because of the great faithfulness with which it has held fast to God's Word and the confession of the Lutheran Church and with which, in spite of all opposition and derision, it has sought to put the Lutheran faith into practice.[2] Its zeal for purity of doctrine and confession, its courageous and definite witness and struggle against all sorts of error and unchristian practice has, from its very first appearance on the scene, won for it the bitterest enemies in two camps, those of the Romanizing Lutherans and the unionists. In the meantime, the Lord has apparently blessed its witness and permitted its results to be made manifest in a way that, indeed, hardly anyone could have dared hope only ten years ago.

The Buffalo Synod is about 30 years old, a few years older than the Missouri Synod.[3] It consists primarily of "Old Lutherans" from Schleswig, who emigrated under Pastor [J.A.A.] Grabau essentially to escape the Prussian Union.[4] This synod wishes to be regarded as authentically Old Lutheran, but a strong Romanizing tendency has been revealed to even the weakest eyes. Its *Senior*, Pastor Grabau, ruled with the power of a pope, and lately it has become altogether too evident that he relied on papistical errors to establish and preserve his lordship over the pastors and people of the synod.[5] Right from the outset it was with this synod that the Missouri Synod had its bitterest battle.[6] As early as 1846, the Missourians proposed a colloquy and they have since repeated this request, but in vain because the Buffaloans required first the retraction of the doctrinal theses which were to be discussed! In 1866, in the meantime, Grabau was exposed as a false teacher and a cunning tyrant, and was deposed as president of the synod. He and a few people of like mind had hardly left it before it decided to act on the old proposal from the Missouri Synod. After preliminary discussions in Fort Wayne, the conference opened in Buffalo on November 26, 1866, and lasted fourteen days.[7] Among the delegates chosen by the synods and present as colloquists were Professor Walther, President Wyneken, and pastor [H.C.] Schwan of the Missouri Synod and pastors [H.K.G.] von Rohr and [Christian] Hochstetter of the Buffalo Synod.[8] There was discussion of the points of doctrine around which controversy had turned for some years, and by the grace of God everyone agreed, except von Rohr. After one of Buffalo's colloquists had expressed agreement with a declaration made by one of the Missourians and his complete agreement with them in doctrine, the Missourians responded: "To the declaration of the Buffalo colloquists we, the delegates of the Missouri Synod, with thanks and praise to God also declare that as a result of this conversation we acknowledge complete unity of doctrine and that we therefore publicly offer them the hand of fellowship."[9] Pastor von Rohr did his best to disrupt this unity; he won to his side the president of the Buffalo Synod, [Friedrich G.] Maschhopp, who on his own summoned an extraordinary meeting of the synod to which only like-minded pastors and congregations were invited.[10] Pastor Hochstetter and six other ministers protested against this; they summoned all the members of the synod to gather for an extraordinary synod meeting which was held in Buffalo on February 25, 1867.[11] A new president was elected, and the synod declared that both von Rohr and Maschhopp had excluded themselves since they had publicly declared the existing differences in doctrine to be church-dividing. Following this the synod discussed the points of doctrine which were covered in the discussions with the Missourians, voted to approve the declaration of the colloquists, and retracted point by point all errors formerly embraced, of which the following were the most essential:[12]

"1. Concerning the church. a) The visible Lutheran church is not a particular church, but the one flock, of which Christ speaks in John 10:16, outside of which God gathers none of his sheep. b) No one can be saved outside of the visible Lutheran church. c) False churches do not have the invisible church within them and cannot, therefore, *per synechdochen*—because of the hidden believers among them—be called churches. d) The church possesses the highest and final authority to judge or "the keys," not directly, but only insofar as it has the clerical office to hold confession, i.e., this authority is given only to those who hold the holy preaching office.[13]

"2. Concerning the ministry. a) The proper, divine call or the ministry gives the Words of Institution, in the Lord's Supper, for example, their power and effect. b) A congregation without the regular ministry does not have Jesus in its midst and cannot comfort itself with his promises; Christ is not present among us on account of faith but is only present on account of the vows of the minister. c) It is false doctrine to maintain that the congregation has the right to transfer the office of the ministry to a preacher.

"3. Concerning the Ban and the right of layfolk to judge doctrine. The right to judge and declare a sinner to be a heathen and a publican does not belong to the congregation but to the ministerium (the pastors). Lay folk have no right to render public judgment of doctrine.

"4. Concerning church order. The congregation may, for the sake of peace and love, permit its pastor to hold to ordinances which are not contrary to the Word of God, because even in indifferent things they owe their pastor obedience on the basis of the Fourth Commandment."

Following this, the synod unanimously declared:[14] "1) We confess that our synod has unfortunately allowed itself not only to be seduced into tolerating and teaching these false doctrines and rejecting the witness now and then made against them by individual pastors and delegates, but also into judging as sectarian (factionalist) all of those who were, because of these doctrines, excluded and banned, as well as all of those who have been in fellowship with such. We retract, therefore, all sentences of banning which have been pronounced over those who for the sake of these points of doctrine have been separated from our synod and seek their forgiveness. 2) We declare that the Missouri Synod has rightly battled against the false doctrine mentioned above and has taught the pure doctrine on the basis of God's Word in accordance with the witness of the confessional writings and the fathers. Since we approve the final declaration of our colloquists, we likewise confess that there has now been achieved unity in doctrine with the Missouri Synod. 3)

We confess that we, because we were ensnared in error, falsely declared the Missourians heathen and publicans and a sect; we acknowledge that in the synodical decision of 1859 touching on this we have sinned grossly and hereby publicly beg the forgiveness of the Missouri Synod.[15] With this we hereby also publicly retract all the contemptuous talk with which we have persecuted the Missouri Synod in synodical letters and publications.[16] 4) For all of these reasons we will no longer consider the old synodical letters, the 1st through the 7th, and other synodical publications, which were written primarily to justify the false doctrine mentioned above, as in any way authoritative in doctrine."

It is, indeed, truly precious to see so open and humble a confession from an entire synod. What more noble witness to the victory of truth could there be than that those who contend for the truth shall never be put to shame and that in the end the upright shall prosper, even if he was for a time entrapped in error?

As a result of these decisions by the synod, there have in many places now occurred cordial reconciliations between the congregations of the synods so that they united and formed one congregation where there had previously been two. The pastors of the Buffalo Synod have ceased the publication of its synodical newspaper, dissolved the synodical bond, and united with the Missouri Synod.

The Devil, of course, would not allow the children of God the joy of seeing all of the Buffalo Synod's members united with their former opponents in the one truth. Pastor Grabau and three other pastors have formed their own synod.[17] Pastor von Rohr, Maschhopp, and two or three other pastors have done the same thing.[18] Finally, one Pastor Habel left the Buffalo Synod some years ago and in connection with three or four pastors has formed his own "Brotherhood."[19]

Things have come to a pitiful pass for a good part of the once so proud Buffalo Synod which looked down with such contempt on the insignificant little Missouri Synod. But the Lord has allowed the Missouri Synod to prosper; it now numbers more than 300 pastors with 300 congregations and 40,000 communicants. It holds itself faithful and fast to God's Word and Luther's doctrine, and therefore the Lord has given it the victory.

The so-called "Lutheran General Synod" in America is not merely unionistic, but actually a union church, whether one considers its constitution or its public confession, or the teaching of doctrine within its confines, or finally its ecclesiastical practice.[20] In the meantime, to be sure—essentially as a result of the witness of the Missouri Synod—a more confessional Lutheran tendency has certainly made itself felt within it in recent years. Indeed, for a time it seemed as if it might win the upper hand in the General Synod and that it might succeed in effecting a thoroughgoing reformation within it. But the more acute the Lutheran-minded appeared in their witness, the more effectively they made it felt that God's pure Word and the Lutheran church's confession should actually obtain in life and doctrine within the synod, the more the unionist tendency, the so-called "American Lutheran party" sought to gather its forces to break the power of its opposition and eradicate all so-called "confessionalism and orthodoxism" from the General Synod, in the event that they could not succeed in weakening and misleading their opponents through compromise.[21]

The fight broke out in earnest at the meeting of the General Synod in Fort Wayne [Indiana] in 1866. The result was an open breach; the great old "Pennsylvania Synod" and four other synods withdrew from the General Synod.[22]

After this schism had occurred, the withdrawing synods, through a committee, issued a call to the various Lutheran synods in America with an invitation to form a *common Lutheran General Synod* on a strictly confessional basis.[23] When several synods approved this proposal, a convention of delegates from the Lutheran synods was summoned for Reading, Pennsylvania, on December 11th, 1866. Our synod's church council also chose delegates for this convention, Pastor Koren and Professor Schmidt, of whom only the latter attended.[24]

The convention accepted the following "Fundamental Principles of Faith":[25]

"1. There must be and abide through all time one holy Christian Church, which is the assembly of all believers, among whom the Gospel is preached, and the Holy Sacraments are administered as the Gospel demands. To the true unity of the Church it is sufficient that there be agreement touching the doctrine of the Gospel, that it be preached in one accord, in its pure sense, and that the Sacraments be administered conformably to God's Word.

"2. The true Unity of a particular Church, in virtue of which people are truly members of one and the same Church, and by which any Church abides in real identity, and is entitled to a continuation of her name, is unity in doctrine and faith and in the Sacraments, to wit: That she continues to teach and to set forth, and that the true members embrace from the heart and use the articles of faith and the Sacraments as they were held and came into distinctive being and received a distinctive name.

"3. The Unity of the Church is witnessed to and made manifest in the solemn, public, and official Confessions which are set forth, to wit: The generic Unity of the Christian Church in the general Creeds, and the specific Unity of pure parts of the Christian Church in their specific Creeds, one chief object of both classes of which Creeds is, that Christians who have a Unity of faith may know each other as such, and may have a visible bond of fellowship.

"4. That Confessions may be such a testimony of Unity and the bond of Union they must be accepted in every statement of doctrine in their own true, native, original, and only sense. Those who set them forth and describe them must not only agree to use the same words, but must use and understand those words in one and the same sense.

"5. The Unity of the Evangelical Lutheran Church, as a portion of the holy Christian Church, depends upon her abiding in one and the same faith, in confessing which she obtained her distinctive being and name, her political recognition and history.

"6. The Unaltered Augsburg Confession is by pre-eminence the confession of that faith. The acceptance of its doctrines and the avowal of them without equivocation or mental reservation make, mark, and identify that Church which alone in a true, original, historical, and honest sense of the term is the Evangelical Lutheran Church.

"7. The only churches, therefore, of any land which are properly in the Unity of the Communion, and by consequence entitled to its name, Evangelical Lutheran, are those which sincerely hold and truthfully confess the doctrines of the Unaltered Augsburg Confession.

"8. We accept and acknowledge the doctrines of the Unaltered Augsburg Confession in its original sense as throughout in conformity with the pure truth of which God's Word is the only rule. We accept its statements of truth as in perfect accordance with the Canonical Scriptures: we reject the errors it condemns, and believe that all which it commits to the liberty of the Church of right belongs to that liberty.

"9. In thus formally accepting and acknowledging the Un-altered Augsburg Confession, we declare our conviction that the other Confessions of the Evangelical Lutheran Church, inasmuch as they set forth none other than its system of doctrine and articles of faith, are of necessity pure and scriptural. Preeminent among such pure and scriptural statements of doctrine, by their intrinsic excellence, by the great and necessary ends for which they were pre-pared, by their historical position, and by the general judgment of the Church are these: The Apology of the Augsburg Confession, the Smalcald Articles, the Catechisms of Luther, and the Formula of Concord, all of which are, with the Unaltered Augsburg Confes-sion, in the perfect harmony of one and the same scriptural faith."

It will be apparent from these "Fundamental Principles of Faith," as it was from the discussions, that a large part of the delega-tion was animated by a sincere and earnest desire and intention to promote the cause of divine truth and to rest our dear Lutheran Church on its own true foundation. When the Fundamental Princi-ples of Faith were unanimously accepted, it was the opinion of the majority that nothing now essentially stood in the way of proceed-ing immediately toward the formation of an external organization to bind together the various synods. The desirability of such an or-ganization was commonly acknowledged; many especially hoped for great blessings on the church from a higher seat of judgment and similarly many looked for great benefit from the introduction of similar hymnbooks, church usages, etc. Virtually unanimously, therefore, it was decided to form the "General Church Council for the Lutheran Church in America." A committee was named to write a constitution to be sent to the presidents of the synods represented in the convention. When ten synods ratified the constitution, a sec-ond convention would be gathered to accept and organize the syn-od. Representatives from the Missouri Synod and our synod, how-ever, declared themselves against these resolutions. While they also desired such a bond of unity among the orthodox Lutherans in America, it was their opinion that it could only be established among those who actually stood on the ground of one faith and who were from the heart united in the doctrine of the Lutheran church. They were convinced that this was not the case with several of the synods represented in the convention in spite of their assent to the Fundamental Principles of Faith. The publications and prac-tice of the synods concerned gave sufficient evidence of this, and indeed several of these synods are actually in controversy with one another over important points of doctrine. Thus it was that on account of the discussions on church order our delegates feared in the convention a common tendency to transfer many of the privileges and much of the authority of the individual congregations to the Church Council and thus to strengthen their bonds by permitting the individual congregations and synods to be bound by the enactments of their representatives and consequently to draw the strength of the association more from the compulsion of law than from love and humility springing from a common faith. Our delegates therefore maintained that for the time being they ought to stand by and, as often as possible, hold conferences for the discussion of the various doctrines, especially those about which there has been controversy between the various synods. When in this way, by the grace of God, unity in faith is achieved and a complete confidence among the synods is secured based on a consciousness of a common faith and doctrine, then, in their opinion, the time will have arrived for the formation of a common Lutheran general synod. But for now it is too soon; a true unity in faith is lacking and without it the new synod like the old one will from the day of its birth bear within itself the germs of disunity and strife and will again end in division and dissolution. That our delegates were right has, unfortunately, already been demonstrated.

As a result of decisions taken at the meeting, a constitution has been prepared, sent to the participating synods, and accepted by a number of them. Thereafter a new meeting was held in November in Fort Wayne in Indiana. The constitution was again reviewed, amended, and accepted and the new association was organized under the name of "The General Council for the Evangelical Lutheran Church in America."[26] The following synods immediately entered this Council:[27]

	Pastors	Congregations	Communicants
Pennsylvania Synod with	125	300	50,000
New York Synod	48	52	12,000
The English Ohio Synod	11	11	2,500
Pittsburgh Synod	64	124	9,000
The German Wisconsin Synod	50	100	12,750
Iowa Synod	60	80	7,000
The English District-Synod of Ohio	38	90	10,000

	Pastors	Congregations	Communicants
Michigan Synod	15	24	3,035
Augustana Synod	45	85	11,800
Minnesota Synod	22	53	3,000
Canada Synod	26	55	7,211
Illinois Synod	34	37	5,000
	538	1,030	133,296

However, even before the conclusion of the meeting the Iowa Synod withdrew from the General Council. The cause of this will be apparent from the following.

The Joint Synod of Ohio, one of the largest of the Lutheran synods, wished to join the General Council but wanted first to assure itself that the Fundamental Principles of Faith adopted at Reading would be reflected in practice. It therefore required the Council's answer to the following four questions:[28]

"1) To what degree would the General Council consider it right to admit to participation in the Sacrament of the Altar those who belong to unlutheran societies and who do not consequently believe the Lutheran doctrine of the Sacrament of the Altar?

"2) To what degree would the General Council consider it right to allow pastors who are not Lutherans to preach in its churches?

"3) Would the General Council accept such pastors who are members of secret societies (e.g., Freemasons, Odd Fellows, etc.)?

"4) What standpoint will the General Council take over against false doctrine on the so-called thousand-year reign, in which Christ will appear on earth at the day of judgment, and all that is related to it?"

These four questions dropped on the assembly like four bombs.[29] It was quickly apparent how afraid people were to permit themselves to answer them because they knew that there was thoroughgoing disagreement on them and that a decision would elicit controversy and perhaps division.

It was the opinion of the majority of the synods that it would be possible to respond only if the questions were put forward by a synod belonging to the Council. The questions were then referred to a committee consisting of a member from each synod. To it was given a statement from the Missouri Synod as well as a document from the Iowa Synod which handled several of the points the Ohio Synod had put on the table.[30] The committee proposed the following attempt at a response: "1) The General Council rejoices that the Ohio wishes to join it. 2) The Council is aware of nothing in its basic principles or constitution which can cause doubt about the answers that would be given to the questions of the Ohio Synod that would not be in agreement with the Word of God and Confessional writings. 3) Whenever official evidence is presented that unlutheran doctrine or practice is propounded or tolerated in any of its synods, it will take measures against such. 4) Because the Iowa Synod has set forth similar questions, the Ohio Synod is requested to consider as an answer the resolutions taken in response to the intervention of the Iowa Synod."[31] On the same occasion a statement of response was made to the Missouri Synod in which it was greeted as a synod "which has won for itself a place in the devotion and respect of every Lutheran by its faithfulness in word, deed, and suffering for the pure truth of the Holy Scripture as our church owns it."[32]

The Ohio Synod, therefore, would have its answer in the answer to the Iowa Synod. One of this synod's representatives was in the meantime a member of the committee, and when during the course of discussion it became apparent that practice permitting the admission of non-Lutherans to the Sacrament of the Altar would not be denied, he explained that it had now become clear to him that his synod could not remain in full membership in the General Council, but would permit itself only participation in debate. For this reason, no further answer was given to the synod's remaining questions. Later, however, the *Lutheran and Missionary*, a publication by the most influential members of the Pennsylvania Synod and the General Council, answered thus: "It was evident that neither the Committee nor the General Council were prepared to endorse the conclusions arrived at by the Synods of Missouri, Ohio, and Iowa. The General Council is not prepared to close its pulpits to *all* non-Lutheran ministers, its Synods have never discussed and decided the matter of secret societies, and they are not prepared to issue a declaration against them; and Chiliasm, as was well said during the debate, is a term so wide and vague, that it is utterly unprepared and unwilling to commit itself by giving a vague answer to a vague question."[33]

Given the expectations we nourished when the old General Synod ruptured we have been sadly disappointed by the General Council's position in this matter. What good are any constitutions and orthodox confessions on paper when at the same time one's life displays such weakness, when truth is suppressed, and when a blind eye is turned to error? What confidence can anyone have in the orthodoxy of such a society which will, by a conspiracy of silence, permit non-Lutherans to enjoy the body and blood of Christ in spite of the fact that they do not believe them to be present in the sacrament and which will tolerate the abandonment of the pulpit to those who will propound false doctrine and ensnare souls? What a pity that a Lutheran body does not dare "decide anything" over against societies which, according to the Word of God, are as patently unchristian as the Freemasons and other secret societies in which by oath one pledges oneself to something one knows nothing about and enters into brotherhood with Turks and Jews and other Christ-deniers and blasphemers. And finally, what weakness to be silent and not to repudiate openly chiliastic enthusiasm and fantasies already condemned by our articles of faith in the Small Catechism! Unfortunately it is clear to us that the new General Council has not been able to free itself from the *unionistic* spiritual tendency that was the old General Synod's distinctive characteristic and its ruination. The future will show that this spiritual tendency which is in its essence indifferent and truth-denying will dominate the General Council. God grant that this may not be the case.

NOTES

INTRODUCTION

1. A critical biography of Herman Amberg Preus (1825–1894) is a *desideratum*. Existing biographical sketches are all in the form of appreciations written by friends, colleagues, admirers, or members of Preus's family. The best of these is "Herman Amberg Preus," in *Livsbilleder fra den lutherske Kirke i Amerika* (Decorah, Iowa, n.d.), 55–94. The genealogy of Herman Preus and recollections by a son, a grandson, and a younger ministerial colleague are included in a privately printed work by Johan Carl Keyser Preus, *Herman Amberg Preus: A Family History* (1966).

2. An excellent brief introduction to this period of Norwegian church history is Einar Molland, *Church Life in Norway, 1800–1950*, trans. by Harris Kaasa (Minneapolis, 1957). A more extensive study is Molland, *Norges kirkehistorie i det 19. århundre*, 2 vols. (Oslo, 1979). See also Andreas Aarflot, *Norsk kirkehistorie*, Vol. 2 (Oslo, 1967), and Carl Fr. Wisløff, *Norsk kirkehistorie*, Vol. 3 (Oslo, 1971).

3. An account of the journey is included in the published diary of Caroline Dorothea Margrethe Preus, *Linka's Diary On Land and Sea, 1845–1864*, trans. and ed. by Johan Carl Keyser Preus and Diderikke Margrethe Preus (Minneapolis, 1952).

4. For a revealing look at Preus's work as a parish pastor, see selections from his ministerial diary and commentary by J.C.K. Preus, "From Norwegian State Church to American Free Church," in *Norwegian-American Studies*, 25 (1972), 186–224.

5. A thorough and sympathetic study of the early history of the Norwegian Synod is Gerhard Lee Belgum, "The Old Norwegian Synod in America, 1853–1890" (Ph.D. dissertation, Yale University, 1957). The bibliography appended to this dissertation is an excellent guide to primary and secondary sources for the history of the Norwegian Synod.

A balanced account of the entire history of the Norwegian Synod, set in the context of the history of Norwegian-American Lutheranism as a whole, is included in E. Clifford Nelson and Eugene L. Fevold, *The Lutheran Church Among Norwegian-Americans: A History of the Evangelical Lutheran Church*, 2 vols. (Minneapolis, 1960). For criticism of this work by a grandson of Herman Amberg Preus, see J.C.K. Preus, *A Critical Look at the Lutheran Church Among Norwegian-Americans by Professors E. Clifford Nelson and Eugene L. Fevold of Luther Theological Seminary, St. Paul, Minnesota* (Minneapolis, 1978).

6. J.A. Bergh, *Den norsk lutherske kirkes historie i Amerika* (Minneapolis, 1914), 80.

7. See, for example, comments on this matter by a ministerial colleague in Adolph Bredesen, "Pastor Herman Amberg Preus as I Knew Him," in J.C.K. Preus, *Herman Amberg Preus*, 105.

8. See "Rev. Herman A. Preus" in J.C. Jensson, *American Lutheran Biographies; Or, Historical Notices of Over Three Hundred and Fifty Leading Men of the American Lutheran Church From Its Establishment to the Year 1890* (Milwaukee, 1890). J.C. Jensson (also known as Jens Christian Roseland) belonged first to the Norwegian Augustana Synod, later to the United Norwegian Lutheran Church in America, and finally to the Norwegian Lutheran Church in America.

9. Decorah, Iowa, 1876. Preus wrote this book in response to August Weenaas, *Wisconsinismen belyst ved historiske kjendsgjerninger* (Chicago, 1875).

10. "Herman Amberg Preus," in *Livsbilleder*, 85.

11. "Til vore Brødre i den evangelisk-lutherske Kirke i Norge fornemmelig til dens Præster og theologiske Candidater," in *Kirkelig Maanedstidende*, 5 (1860), 233–234.

12. For the events surrounding Larsen's journey to Norway, see Karen Larsen, *Laur. Larsen, Pioneer College President* (Northfield, Minnesota, 1936), 115–125. Laur. Larsen's lecture, originally published in *Morgenbladet*, November 6 and 7, 1860, was later reprinted as "Foredrag over de kirkelige Forhold blandt de Norske i Amerika," in *Kirkelig Maanedstidende*, 6 (1861), 40–51. For Larsen's report of his journey, see "Beretning om min Reise til Norge," in *Kirkelig Maanedstidende*, 6 (1861), 67–78, and "Tillæg til min Beretning om min Reise til Norge," in *Kirkelig Maanedstidende*, 6 (1861), 133.

13. See, for example, Bernt Julius Muus, "Fra Nordamerika," in *Luthersk Kirketidende*, 7 (1866), 369–377. This article also appeared as "Correspon. fra Nordamerika til et norsk Blad," in *Kirkelig Maanedstidende*, 12 (1867), 37–44. Portions of it also appeared as "An Extract from a Correspondence from North America to a Journal in Norway," in *The Lutheran Watchman*, 2 (1867), 26–29.

14. The narrative of the family's travels can be reconstructed in outline from "Uddrag af Reiseberetning til Kirkeraadet fra H.A. Preus," in *Kirkelig Maanedstidende*, 11 (1866), 129; "Pastor H. A. Preus's Reise til Norge," in *Kirkelig Maanedstidende*, 11 (1866), 380; "Efterretning fra Pastor H.A. Preus," in *Kirkelig Maanedstidende*, 12 (1867), 143–144. See also "Herman Amberg Preus," in *Livsbilleder*, 64, 67–70. Linka Preus recorded moments from the journey and the family's stay in Norway in her sketchbook, now in the archives of Luther College in Decorah, Iowa. For discussion of these sketches, see Gracia Grindal, "Linka's Sketchbook: A Personal View of the Norwegian Synod," in J.R. Christianson,

ed., *Scandinavians in America: Literary Life* (Decorah, Iowa, 1985), 258–266, and Grindal, "Linka Preus' Sketches of Iowa," in *The Palimpsest*, 67 (1986), 118–129.

15. J.F. Halvorsen in *Norsk forfatter-lexikon, 1814–1880* (Christiania, 1896), s.v. "Preus, Herman Amberg," indicates that Preus lectured in a variety of places in Norway during 1866–1867.

16. The thematic reference is to Acts 16:9–10.

17. See "Bestræbelser for at faa Prester fra Norge," in H. Halvorsen, ed., *Festskrift til den norske Synodes jubilæum, 1853–1903* (Decorah, Iowa, 1903), 119.

18. "Bestræbelser for at faa Prester," 121.

19. For reports of the lectures, see *Aftenbladet*, May 25, May 29, June 1, June 5, June 8, June 15, and June 20, 1867.

20. Letter of Niels Kr. Høimyr to Todd W. Nichol, June 22, 1984. Relations between the Norwegian Synod and Det Norske Misjonsselskap were, however, early strained by the Synod's insistence on limiting itself to cooperation with individuals and organizations it considered sufficiently orthodox. See John Nome, *Det norske misjonsselskaps historie i norsk kirkeliv*, 2 vols. (Stavanger, 1943), 2:64–66.

21. The lectures appeared in print as "Syv Foredrag over de kirkelige Forholde blandt de Norske i Amerika," in *Lutherske Kirketidende*, 9 (1867), 1–27, 42–57, 81–102, 113–131, 145–160, 177–194, 241–263, and *Syv Foredrag over de kirkelige Forholde blandt de Norske i Amerika* (Christiania, 1867).

22. "Den lutherske Kirke i Nordamerika," in *Luthersk Kirketidende*, 11 (1869), 17–26, and "Den lutherske Kirke i Nordamerika," in *Luthersk Kirketidende*, 12 (1869), 405–416. The first of these articles, particularly important for what it reveals about Preus's attitude toward other American Lutheran synods, appears in translation in Appendix II to the present volume.

23. See, for example, some of the articles appearing in *Morgenbladet* in 1867: "Opfordring til Pastor H.A. Preus," March 6; "Svar fra Pastor H.A. Preus," March 16; "Til Hr. Pastor H.A. Preus," March 17; "Mere 'Redejørelse,' " May 6; "Er Wisconsinsynoden 'Sandheden tro i Kjærlighed'?" May 21; and "Da Presten Herman Preus," August 17.

24. Formally condemned by the Council of Orange in 529, the semi-pelagian heresy involves the doctrine that the first steps toward Christian faith are taken through the agency of human will and that the grace of God only later intervenes in the process. The Lutheran Reformation rejected the Roman Catholic teaching that the saints in heaven intercede for the living on earth.

25. "Begjæring om Skriftbevis for nye Lærdomme," in *Luthersk Kirketidende*, 9 (1867), 168–170.

26. Preus summarized the controversy in "Lærestriden mellem Pastor Domaas i Kristiania og Pastor H.A. Preus," in *Kirkelig Maanedstidende*, 15 (1870), 49–56, 66–73. A brief review of the debate including a summary of the articles written by the contestants appears in "Herman Amberg Preus," in *Livsbilleder*, 67–70.

27. "Lærestriden mellem Pastor Domaas i Kristiania og Pastor H.A. Preus," 72.

28. On Thistedahl and his influence on Norwegian-American Lutheran lead-

ers, see Oluf Kolsrud, *Bibeloversætteren Christian Thistedahl, 1813–1876* (Christiania, 1913). On Thistedahl's extreme literalism, see Molland, *Norges kirkehistorie i det 19. aarhundre*, 1:112. A tribute to Thistedahl appears in "Ole Christian Thistedahl," in *Evangelisk Lutherske Kirketidende*, 4 (1877), 484–485.

For a brief survey of the development of Norwegian Lutheran views of Scripture in the nineteenth century, see Ludvig Selmer, "Skriftprinsippet i norsk Teologi i det 19de Aarhundrede," in *Norvegia Sacra*, 4 (1924), 125–140.

29. See H.G. Stub, *To taler ved luther festen den 11te novb. 1883, holdt i vor Frelsers menigheds kirke i Minneapolis* (n.p., n.d.), 13.

30. See Appendix I, 182.

31. For comments on the evolution of this liturgical tradition, see Todd Nichol, "Liturgical Civility, Upward Mobility, and American Modernity," in *Word & World*, 3 (1983), 168–177.

32. For a brief summary of the attitudes that produced this development, see Muus, "Fra Nordamerika."

33. See H.A. Preus, "Indianerne i Nordamerika," in *Kirkelig Maanedstidende*, 2 (1857), 326 (1900 reprint).

34. Cultural and sociological factors certainly played a role in the work of the founders of the Norwegian Synod. See, for example, Nicholas Tavuchis, *Pastors and Immigrants: the Role of a Religious Elite in the Absorption of Norwegian Immigrants* (The Hague, 1963) and Peter A. Munch, "Social Class and Acculturation," in Caja Munch and Johan Storm Munch, *The Strange American Way: Letters of Caja Munch from Wiota, Wisconsin, 1855–1859 with An American Adventure, Excerpts from "Vita Mea," an Autobiography Written in 1903 for His Children by Johan Storm Munch*, trans. by Helene Munch and Peter A. Munch (Carbondale, Illinois, 1970).

Leigh D. Jordahl, in "The Gentry Tradition — Men and Women of a Leadership Class," in Charles P. Lutz, ed., *Church Roots: Stories of Nine Immigrant Groups That Became The American Lutheran Church* (Minneapolis, 1985), 101–116, has emphasized the status of the founders of the Norwegian Synod as members of the gentry class before leaving Norway and their commitment to humane studies at Luther College. Yet it should be noted that while the contrast between H.A. Preus and Elling Eielsen is, for example, striking, the leaders of several other Norwegian-American Lutheran bodies shared the cultural and social background of the founders of the Norwegian Synod and evidenced the same commitment to humane studies. Georg Sverdrup of the Lutheran Free Church was as obviously a member of the Norwegian gentry and an inheritor of its parsonage traditions as any of the founders of the Norwegian Synod. That he differed with the founders of the Norwegian Synod over the nature of humane studies and proper preparation of ministers is a matter of divergent emphasis rather than of neglect of liberal studies. It might also be noted that a common social background, university training, and the parsonage ethos did not prevent several clergymen, including, for example, Bernt Julius Muus and Marcus Olaus Bøckmann, from breaking fellowship with the Norwegian Synod over a matter of doctrine and forming what was in effect a separate synod, the Anti-Missourian Brotherhood, in 1887. While Preus, Sverdrup, Muus, and Bøckmann were united by a common cultural and sociological background, they found themselves deeply divided over theological and intellectual matters. It was, finally, this considered division of theological opinion which prompted them to sponsor profoundly different visions of church life in America. While Tavuchis, Munch, and Jordahl rightly emphasize important and consequential factors in the life of the Norwegian Synod, the "Seven Lectures" seems to reinforce an interpretation which argues that commitment to doctrinal purity was for its leaders the essential factor in the determination of the Norwegian Synod's identity.

For a clear statement of the priority self-consciously attached by its founders to doctrine as opposed to cultural factors in the life of the Norwegian Synod, see Jacob Aall Ottesen, "Blik i General Synoden," in *Kirkelig Maanedstidende*, 4 (1859), 122. For a late reiteration of these priorities by a pastor of the Norwegian Synod who became vice-president of the Norwegian Lutheran Church of America and president of Luther Theological Seminary in St. Paul, Minnesota, see T.F. Gullixson, "Our English Work, the Problem," in *Teologisk Tidsskrift*, 3 (1920), 301–314.

The question of what prompted their various constituencies to align themselves with these leaders is, of course, another matter that requires separate consideration. For an illuminating study of denominational loyalties in the Norwegian-American Lutheran constituency, see Arvid Gerald Dyste, "Causes of Religious Conflicts Among Immigrants in America: A Case Study of the Norwegian Lutherans in the Christiania Settlement in Minnesota From 1854–1904." (M.A. thesis, University of Minnesota, 1989).

35. On Elling Eielsen and his synod, see Christian O. Brohaug and J. Eistensen, *Kortfattet beretning om Elling Eielsens liv og virksomhed*, foreword by A. Weenaas (Chicago, 1883); Clarence J. Carlsen, "Elling Eielsen: Pioneer Lay Preacher and First Norwegian Lutheran Preacher in America" (M.A. thesis, University of Minnesota, 1932); E.O. Mørstad, *Elling Eielsen og den "Evangelisk-lutherske Kirke" i Amerika* (Minneapolis, 1917); Kjell Nese et al., eds., *Elling Eielsen Sundve, 1804–1883: Foredrag holdne paa Eielsen-seminariet paa Voss, 3.-5. August, 1979* (Voss, 1980); Olaf Morgan Norlie, *Eielsen Was First: A Bibliography* (Northfield, Minnesota, 1942); Norlie, *Elling Eielsen: A Brief History* (n.p., 1940); O.H. Oace, *Hauge's Synod (Revsede men ikke ihelslagene): Samt et foredrag af H.H. Bergsland om forsoningen* (St. Paul, 1932); O. Olafsen, "Legpredikanten og presten Elling Eielsen," in *Norvegia Sacra*, 9 (1929), 202–211; Ansgar E. Sovik, "Elling Eielsen and Some Elements of the Church Strife among Norwegian-American Lutherans in the 1840's and 1850's" (M.Th. thesis, Princeton Theological Seminary, 1946). See also S.S. Gjerde and P. Ljostveit, eds., *The Hauge Movement in America* (n.p., 1941).

36. Pontoppidan's catechism, *Sandhed til gudfrygtighed*, was published in several revisions and a multitude of editions after it first appeared in 1737. For an abridged English translation, see *An Epitome of Rev. Dr. Erik Pontoppidan's Explanation of Martin Luther's Small Catechism*, trans. Edmund Balfour (Chicago, 1878). For brief comments on Eielsen's devotion to the Norwegian Lutheran catechetical tradition, see Nelson and Fevold, *The Lutheran Church Among Norwegian-Americans*, 1:77–78.

37. On this history see Nelson and Fevold, *The Lutheran Church Among Norwegian-Americans*, 1:126–150.

38. On the early history of this body, see G. Everett Arden, *Augustana Heritage: A History of the Augustana Lutheran Church* (Rock Island, Illinois, 1963); Erik Norelius, *De svenska lutherska församlingarnas och svenskarnes historia*, 2 vols. (Rock Island, Illinois, 1910); Norelius, *The Pioneer Swedish Settlements and Swedish Lutheran Churches in America*, trans. by Conrad Bergendoff (Rock Island, Illinois, 1984); Oscar N. Olson, *The Augustana Lutheran Church in America, 1846–1860* (Rock Island, 1950); Oscar N. Olson, *The Augustana Lutheran Church in America, 1860–1910: The Formative Period* (Davenport, Iowa, 1956); Hugo Söderström, *Confession and Cooperation: the Policy of the Augustana Synod in Confessional Matters and the Synod's Relations with Other Churches Up to the Beginning of the Twentieth Century*, vol. 4 of Bibliotheca Historico-Ecclesiastica Lundensis (Lund, 1973); George M. Stephenson, *The Founding of the Augustana Synod, 1850–1860* (Rock Island, Illinois, 1927).

39. The best account of these developments is in Nelson and Fevold, *The Lutheran Church Among Norwegian-Americans*, 1:191–238.

40. See the note by Herman Amberg Preus appended to Ottesen, "Blik i Generalsynoden," 125.

41. For extended discussion of this early phase in Scandinavian-American theological controversy, see Söderström, *Confession and Cooperation*, 63–66, 84–87. See also Nelson and Fevold, *The Lutheran Church Among Norwegian-Americans*, 1:243–245, and J. Magnus Rohne, *Norwegian-American Lutheranism Up to 1872* (New York, 1926), 158–179, 223–243.

42. For a brief summary of this controversy, see Rohne, *Norwegian-American Lutheranism*, 227–233.

43. There exists no full-length, critical history of the Missouri Synod. See, however, the centennial publication by Walter A. Baepler, *A Century of Grace: A History of the Missouri Synod* (St. Louis, 1947).

44. For the early history of this friendship, see Belgum, "The Old Norwegian Synod," 170–218, 340–412, and Carl S. Meyer, *Pioneers Find Friends: Luther College Lectures, February 21, 22, 1962. Decorah, Iowa* (Decorah, Iowa, 1963).

45. See Bredesen, "Pastor Herman Amberg Preus as I Knew Him," 100.

46. An excellent introduction to the labyrinthine history of this controversy is in Eugene L. Fevold, "Coming of Age, 1875–1900," in E. Clifford Nelson, ed., *The Lutherans in North America* (Philadelphia, 1980), 313–325. A complete study is Hans R. Haug, "The Predestination Controversy in the Lutheran Church in North America" (Ph.D. dissertation, Temple University, 1968).

47. See note 36 above.

48. For the formation of this body, see Nelson and Fevold, *The Lutheran Church Among Norwegian-Americans*, 1:302–335 and 2:3–37. On the history of this body, consult N.C. Brun, ed., *Fra ungdoms aar. En oversigt over den forenede norsk lutherske Kirkes historie og fremskridt i de svundne femogtyve aar* (Minneapolis, 1915), and Norlie, *Den forenede norsk lutherske Kirke i Amerika* (Minneapolis, 1914).

49. For the history of the Synodical Conference, see Carl S. Meyer, "Notes on the History of the Synodical Conference," in *The Lutheran Historical Conference: Essays and Reports of the Sixth Biennial Meeting Held at Wartburg Theological Seminary, Dubuque, Iowa on 19–21 October 1972*, 5:137–169; Meyer,

"The Synodical Conference—The Voice of Confessionalism," in *Proceedings . . . Synodical Conference . . . 1956*, 14–71; John Theodore Mueller, *A Brief History of the Origin, Development, and Work of the Evangelical Lutheran Synodical Conference of North America Prepared for Its Diamond Jubilee, 1872–1947, Upon the Request of Its President and Its Missionary Board* (St. Louis, n.d.).

For the standard account of the union of 1917, the importance of the *Opgjør*, and Missouri's reaction to it, see Nelson and Fevold, *The Lutheran Church Among Norwegian-Americans*, 2:129–225.

50. George Henry Gerberding, *Reminiscent Reflections of a Youthful Octogenarian* (Minneapolis, 1928), 154.

51. For the history of this body, see Theodore A. Aaberg, *A City Set on a Hill: A History of the Evangelical Lutheran Synod (Norwegian Synod), 1918–1968* (Mankato, Minnesota, 1968) and S.C. Ylvisaker *et al., eds., Grace for Grace: Brief History of the Norwegian Synod* (Mankato, Minnesota, 1943).

52. For an introduction to this history, antecedent developments, and its consequences see Nelson, *The Lutherans in North America*.

53. For introductions to the history of these bodies, consult Nelson, *The Lutherans in North America*. A collection of essays reflecting the history of these and other bodies eventually merging to form the American Lutheran Church in 1960–1963 is Lutz, *Church Roots*.

54. An excellent history of the formation of the "Old" American Lutheran Church is Fred W. Meuser, *The Formation of the American Lutheran Church: A Case Study in Lutheran Unity* (Columbus, Ohio, 1958).

55. On the history of the Lutheran Free Church, see A.B. Batalden, ed., *Our Fellowship*, (Minneapolis, 1947); Clarence J. Carlsen, *The Years of Our Church* (Minneapolis, 1942); Eugene L. Fevold, *The Lutheran Free Church: A Fellowship of American Lutheran Congregations, 1897–1963* (Minneapolis, 1969); Andreas Helland, *Den lutherske frikirke og dens fællesgjøremaal* (Minneapolis, 1914).

For the history of the American Lutheran Conference, see Thomas George Koelln, "The Role of the American Lutheran Conference in Lutheran Unity" (M.Th. thesis, Luther Northwestern Theological Seminary, 1986), and Todd W. Nichol, "The American Lutheran Church: An Historical Study of Its Confession of Faith According to Its Constitutional Documents" (Th.D. dissertation, Graduate Theological Union, 1988).

56. See Nichol, "The American Lutheran Church," 64–224.

57. See Nichol, "The American Lutheran Church," 275–393.

58. See Nichol, "The American Lutheran Church," 394–505.

59. *Handbook of the American Lutheran Church: Edition of 1960*, 27.

60. *Handbook*, 25.

61. For a fine evocation of the spirit of the Norwegian Synod by a contemporary theologian with personal roots in its traditions, see Gerhard O. Forde, "The 'Old Synod': A Search for Objectivity," in Warren Quanbeck *et al.*, eds., *Striving for Ministry: Centennial Essays Interpreting the Heritage of Luther Theological Seminary* (Minneapolis, 1977), 67–80.

VIVACIOUS DAUGHTER

LECTURE I

1. This is an allusion to the Acts of the Apostles 16:9–10. This passage records a vision in which a Macedonian appears to Paul the Apostle and says "Come over to Macedonia and help us." Preus's original hearers and readers would not have missed the reference. It would have indicated to them his hope that his lectures would prompt Norwegian candidates for the ministry to accept calls to congregations in the United States.

2. Preus places his estimate too high. The United States census of 1870 puts the number of Norwegian-born inhabitants of the United States at 114,243. See *The Statistics of the Population of the United States . . . From the Original Returns of the Ninth Census (June 1, 1870)*, (Washington, D.C., 1872), 1:341.

3. Preus's memory of American geography plays him false here. There is no St. Croix county in Minnesota. He may refer to St. Croix county in Wisconsin.

4. Many Norwegian settlers did establish themselves in, for example, Iowa. Large numbers also continued to move west and north as well. For a thorough study of settlement patterns, see Carlton C. Qualey, *Norwegian Settlement in the United States* (Northfield, Minnesota, 1938).

5. For an excellent study of the Norwegian-American experience in one urban setting, see Odd S. Lovoll, *A Century of Urban Life: The Norwegians in Chicago before 1930* (Northfield, Minnesota, 1988).

6. Johannes Wilhelm Christian Dietrichson (1815–1883), a pastor of the Church of Norway, was instrumental in organizing pioneer congregations and the church body eventually to become "The Synod for the Norwegian Evangelical Lutheran Church in America," popularly known as the "Norwegian Synod" or the "Old Synod."

Claus Lauritz Clausen (1820–1892), a Dane, emigrated to the United States as a schoolteacher. He was eventually ordained to serve as pastor to Norwegian settlers and took part in the organization of the church which was to become the Norwegian Synod, serving as president or "superintendent" from 1851 to 1852. Clausen was later an organizer and president of another denomination, the Conference for the Norwegian-Danish Evangelical Lutheran Church, which appeared on the Norwegian-American scene in 1870. On Clausen, see Carlton C. Qualey, trans. and ed., "Claus L. Clausen: Pioneer Pastor and Settlement Promoter," in *Norwegian-American Studies and Records*, 6 (1931), 12–29; R. Andersen, *Pastor Claus Lauritz Clausen. Banebryder for den norske og danske kirke i Amerika* (Brooklyn, 1921); A. Margareth Jorgensen, "Claus L. Clausen, Pioneer Pastor and Settlement Promoter, 1843–1868" (M.A. thesis, University of Minnesota, 1930); H. Fred Swansen, *The Founder of St. Ansgar* (Blair, Nebraska, 1949).

7. Lebrecht Friedrich Ehregott Krause (1804–1885) served as a pastor in both the Buffalo and Missouri synods. For Krause's account of the examination and ordination of Clausen, see Meyer, ed., *Moving Frontiers: Readings in the History of the Lutheran Church—Missouri Synod* (St. Louis, 1964), 130–131. See also Nelson and Fevold, *The Lutheran Church Among Norwegian-Americans*, 1:87–90.

8. See E. Clifford Nelson, ed., *A Pioneer Churchman: J.W.C. Dietrichson in Wisconsin, 1844–1850* (New York, 1973), for documentation and a complete

account of Dietrichson's career in America. For the role of Peter Sørenson in inspiring and making possible Dietrichson's mission to the United States, see pp. 21, 45, 149–150, and 251, note 125.

9. Preus refers to views associated with the teaching of Danish theologian Nikolai Frederik Severin Grundtvig (1783–1872) and propagated in Norway by a number of influential theologians and pastors, including Wilhelm Andreas Wexels (1797–1866). Particularly offensive to Preus and the ministerial colleagues who joined him in charging Dietrichson with doctrinal error was the contention that the Apostles' Creed, as well as the canonical books of the Old and New Testaments, contained God's revealed word. See Nelson and Fevold, *The Lutheran Church Among Norwegian-Americans*, 1:154–157.

10. Elling Eielsen (1804–1883) was the founder and president of "The Evangelical Lutheran Church of America." Popularly known as "Eielsen's Synod," this Norwegian-American body embodied the ardent piety of the Haugean revival in Norway. On Eielsen and his synod, see "Introduction," note 35.

11. Hans Andreas Stub (1822–1907) and Adolph Carl Preus (1814–1878) were among the pastors of the Church of Norway who took part in organizing the Norwegian Synod in 1851 and 1853. Adolph Preus, a cousin of the author, served from 1853–1862 as president of the Norwegian Synod before returning permanently to Norway.

12. The text of the constitution of the Norwegian Synod as approved in 1868 appears in *Beretning . . . Synoden for den norsk-evangelisk-lutherske Kirke i Amerika . . . 1868*, 53–57. A translation of this document appears in Appendix I of the present volume.

On the constitutional history of the Norwegian Synod, see "Konstitutionsforandringer og Synodens Deling i Distrikter," in Halvorsen, *Festskrift*, 192–206, and E. Clifford Nelson, "The Making of a Constitution," in J.C.K. Preus, ed., *Norsemen Found a Church: An Old Heritage in a New Land* (Minneapolis, 1953), 191–221. The text of the original constitution of the Norwegian Synod approved in 1853 appears in translation in Nelson and Fevold, *The Lutheran Church Among Norwegian-Americans*, 1:344–350.

13. See note 12 above.

14. Preus refers to Bernt Julius Muus (1832–1900) and Thomas Johnson (1837–1906). Both, however, served in southern Minnesota. Of Muus, the editors of a directory of Norwegian-American clergy published in 1928 note that he "had for some time as many as 28 congs. in a district as large as Denmark, with now more than 150 congs." The same editors note of Johnson that he served as a "missionary in 17 counties, (his field gradually divided between 50 pastors)." See Norlie, Rasmus Malmin, and O.A. Tingelstad, *Who's Who Among Pastors in All the Norwegian Lutheran Synods of America, 1843–1927* (Minneapolis, 1928), 394 and 295.

15. The Norwegian mile is approximately 6.7 English miles.

16. *Kirkelig Maanedstidende for den norsk-evangelisk-lutherske Kirke i Amerika* was an official organ of the Norwegian Synod. For a brief account of its history and Herman Preus's editorship, see Laur. Larsen, "Vort Kirkeblad," in Halvorsen, *Festskrift*, 215–221. *Kirkelige Maanedstidende* was eventually re-

named *Evangelisk Luthersk Kirketidende*, under which name it was published until 1917.

17. In Lutheran theology and practice the "Office of the Keys" refers to the authority to bind and loose sins held to have been entrusted by Jesus Christ to the entire church.

18. This is a direct reference to 2 Corinthians 12:9.

19. This is likely a reference to 1 John 4:1. It may also refer to Luther's remark to Huldrych Zwingli at the Marburg Colloquy in 1529 during which Luther is reputed to have said to Zwingli, "You are of a different spirit."

20. Omitted in the translation is the text of the constitution then proposed for adoption by the Norwegian Synod. It appears in Preus's text on pp. 15–20. For the complete text of this document as finally adopted in 1868, see Appendix I of the present volume. See also note 12 above.

21. See Ephesians 4:3.

22. The mention of Babel is a reference to Genesis 11:1–9.

23. In the Lutheran catechetical tradition, the Fourth Commandment ("Honor your father and your mother") is interpreted as a call to respect and honor all those placed over an individual in the structures of family, church, and state. See Luther's explanation of the Fourth Commandment in the Small Catechism in Theodore G. Tappert *et al.*, trans. and ed., *The Book of Concord; The Confessions of the Evangelical Lutheran Church* (Philadelphia, 1959), 343.

24. In this context "ritual" refers not to the ceremonial aspect of common worship but to the collection of liturgical texts used in Norwegian Lutheran worship and gathered in *Danmarks og Norgis kirke-ritual* (Copenhagen, 1685), often simply called *Ritualet* (The Ritual).

25. This is a reference to a standard maxim of Protestant theology, *Scriptura sui interpres*, literally translated "Scripture interprets itself." The contention is that Scripture speaks for itself, that it is self-authenticating. This claim stands over against those characteristically associated with hierarchichal ecclesiastical traditions which contend that the church has the authority to interpret the texts of the Bible.

26. See John 10:27.

27. Omitted in the translation are several conventional proof texts from Luther's writings. These quotations appear without documentation in Preus's text on pp. 24–25.

28. For the biblical reference, see note 21 above.

LECTURE 2

1. With this provision for the office of trustee, the Norwegian Synod followed a precedent established by J.W.C. Dietrichson. The division of temporal and spiritual responsibilities between trustees and deacons is still reflected in many Lutheran congregations with roots in the Norwegian-American tradition. For commentary, see Nelson, *Pioneer Churchman*, 257, note 55. As Nelson points out, the same division of responsibility was reflected on the synodical level, establishing a pattern that has continued to influence American Lutheran church polity into the present century.

Notes

2. For the prescriptions of the *Ritual* regarding confession and absolution, see *Danmarks og Norgis kirke-ritual*, 143–159, 273–307. For further discussion of these practices, see the widely used pastoral manual by Erik Pontoppidan, *Collegium Pastorale Practicum* (Copenhagen, 1757), 529–597. An extensive history of Norwegian Lutheran practice concerning confession and absolution is Halvor Bergan, *Skriftemål og skriftestol. Skriftemålet i Den norske kirke fra reformasjonstiden til idag* (Oslo, 1982).

3. This description of congregational life is evidence of the degree to which this highly clerical Norwegian-American church body also emphasized lay participation. It also testifies to the ability of its leaders to adapt their tradition to the modern American context. The Norwegian pietist tradition of lay activity had in varying degrees prepared these young clerics and some lay members of the church for their American experience and sustained them in it.

4. Without the benefit of European ecclesiastical structures and unused to American social freedom, immigrant Lutherans of every background were forced to struggle in a new way with questions of church discipline. For purposes of comparison, see the pastoral theology of C.F.W. Walther, a theologian much admired by the leaders of the Norwegian Synod: *Amerikanisch-Lutherische Pastoraltheologie* (St. Louis, 1870), 315–355.

5. See Pontoppidan, *Collegium Pastorale Practicum*, 587–597, for a discussion of the role of the deacon in the exercise of church discipline. As in the case of congregational order, these prescriptions for church discipline reflect not only the attempt to found the practice of the Norwegian Synod on a proper scriptural and doctrinal basis, but also a strongly participatory approach to church life.

6. *Sedes doctrinae* is literally translated as "seat of doctrine," referring among Protestants to a text of Scripture identified as the fundamental basis for a given doctrine. For synodical discussion of this text of Scripture and the topic of church discipline, see, for example, *Beretning . . . den norsk-evangelisk-lutherske Kirke i Amerika . . . 1864*, 49–68, 78–95, and *Beretning . . . Synoden for den norsk-evangelisk-lutherske Kirke i Amerika . . . 1869*, 62–69.

7. In the Lutheran catechetical tradition, the Eighth Commandment ("Thou shalt not bear false witness") is interpreted not only as a summons to truthfulness in speech but also as a call to put the best construction on all that one's neighbor says and does. See Luther's explanation of the Eighth Commandment in the Small Catechism in Tappert *et al.*, *The Book of Concord*, 343.

8. "Aabenbare Skriftemaal og Afløsning" is described in *Danmarks og Norgis kirke-ritual*, 150–159.

9. The desire of the Norwegian Synod's leaders to establish religious schools occasioned an extended controversy among Norwegian-American Lutherans. An excellent introduction to this controversy remains "The Immigrant and the Common School," in Blegen, *Norwegian Migration to America: The American Transition*, 241–276. See also Arthur C. Paulson and Kenneth Bjørk, trans. and ed., "A School and Language Controversy in 1858: A Documentary Study," in *Norwegian-American Studies and Records*, 10 (1938), 76–106; Frank C. Nelsen, "The School Controversy Among Norwegian Immigrants," in *Norwegian-American Studies*, 26 (1974), 206–219; James S. Hamre, "Norwegian Immigrants

Respond to the Common School: A Case Study of American Values and the Lutheran Tradition," in *Church History*, 50 (1981), 302–315.

10. The report of the Norwegian Synod for 1866 does not explain why the remaining theses were not officially adopted. Given the extended discussion of the theses that were adopted, it is possible that lack of time precluded more discussion. See *Beretning . . . den norsk-evangelisk-lutherske Kirke i Amerika . . . 1866*, 19–40. This series of theses was prepared by a committee of pastors including Nils Olsen Brandt (1824–1921), Peter Laurentius [Laur.] Larsen (1833–1915), and Friedrich August [Augustus] Schmidt (1837–1928).

11. Sunday schools in many American denominations were often ecumenical in character.

12. "Unconditional absolution" is the announcement of the forgiveness of sins without qualification.

13. For provision regarding "Lønlig Skriftemaal og Afløsning," see *Danmarks og Norgis kirke-ritual*, 143–150. See also Bergan, *Skriftemål og skriftestol*, for an extended discussion of this practice.

14. The quotation is from Matthew 7:6.

15. For the history and practice of the celebration of the Holy Communion and associated rites in the Church of Norway, see Helge Fæhn, *Høymessen igår og idag. Liturgiens struktur og vekst; vår høymesse fra reformasjonen til idag* (2nd ed., Oslo, 1968), and Molland, *Norges kirkehistorie i det 19de århundre*, 2:85–106. For comments on the evolution of Norwegian American liturgical practice, see Nelson and Fevold, *The Lutheran Church Among Norwegian Americans*, 2:122–128, and Nichol, "Liturgical Civility, Upward Mobility, and American Modernity."

It was the custom in Norwegian-American Lutheran congregations for the pastor or an assistant to rehearse the questions and answers of the catechism with the congregation gathered for worship.

16. Luther's Small Catechism is divided into five chief parts: the Ten Commandments, the Apostles' Creed, the Lord's Prayer, Holy Baptism, and the Sacrament of the Altar. See the Small Catechism in Tappert *et al.*, *The Book of Concord*, 337–356.

17. These theses, previously numbers 4, 7, and 8 of a series of 8 theses presented to the Norwegian Synod by Laur. Larsen, but originally prepared by Theodore Julius Brohm (1808–1881) of the Missouri Synod, appear in *Beretning . . . den norsk-evangelisk-lutherske Kirke i Amerika . . . 1861*, 12–16. Only for the first four of these theses were officially accepted. See *Beretning . . . den norsk-evangelisk-lutherske Kirke i Amerika . . . 1861*, 29. Time prevented further discussion of the remaining theses. Omitted in the text is a series of undocumented proof texts from Luther and Philip Melanchthon. They appear in Preus's text on pages 39–40. For the history of the Synod's discussion of absolution see Nelson and Fevold, *The Lutheran Church Among Norwegian Americans*, 2: 243–245; J. Magnus Rohne, *Norwegian American Lutheranism Up to 1872* (New York, 1926), 226–233; Ylvisaker *et al.*, *Grace for Grace*, 156–160.

18. Omitted here in the translation of the theses are conventional proof texts cited from the works of Luther. In Preus's text they appear on pp. 39–40.

19. In the Church of Norway the festivals of Christmas, Easter, and Pentecost are each celebrated for three days.

20. The complex history and theology of the rite of confirmation in the Lutheran churches are summarized in Arthur C. Repp, *Confirmation in the Lutheran Church* (St. Louis, 1964), 13–180. Detailed accounts of catechesis and confirmation in Norway appear in Brynjar Haraldsø, *Konfirmasjonen i går og i dag; festskrift til 250-års jubileet 13, januar 1986* (Oslo, 1986). For an account of the observance of confirmation and its social significance among Norwegians, see Birgit Hertzberg Johnsen, *Den store dagen; konfirmasjon og tradisjon* (n.p., [1984]).

21. Preus refers to the obligation of an American denomination to provide instruction in religion like that provided in the schools linked to established churches in Europe.

22. Lutheran theology teaches that marriage is an estate open to all people, Christian and non-Christian alike. The ministers of marriage, according to this view, are the man and woman who exchange vows in public. Christians may if they choose, Lutherans teach, seek the prayers of the church as they enter the estate of marriage. The omission of these prayers does not render the marriage invalid. This theology of marriage made it easy for Lutheran pastors in the United States to assume the role of civil magistrates able by law to officiate at marriages.

23. Originating in the middle ages, the "banns" are a public announcement of a couple's intent to marry and an invitation to any who may object or who have knowledge of impediments to make these objections or impediments known. For liturgical provision for the announcement of the banns and the marriage rites, see *Danmarks og Norgis kirke-ritual*, 308–325.

LECTURE 3

1. For a list of the graduates of the Royal Frederik's University in Christiania who served the Norwegian Synod as pastors during its first fifty years, see "Bestræbelser for at faa Prester fra Norge," 123–124.

2. For a report of this visit by Norwegians Synod pastors N.O. Brandt (see Lecture 2, note 10) and Jacob Aall Ottesen (1825–1904), see "Indberetning fra Pastorerne Ottesen og Brandt . . . ," in *Kirkelig Maanedstidende*, 2 (1857), 481 (1900 reprint). For the history of this visit, see Nelson and Fevold, *The Lutheran Church Among Norwegian Americans*, 1:162–163.

3. The most recent full-length history of this body, now known as The Lutheran Church—Missouri Synod, is Baepler, *A Century of Grace*. A valuable supplement is Meyer, *Moving Frontiers*. For a typical illustration of the Norwegian Synod's attitude toward the Missouri Synod, see Ottesen, "Blik i Missourisynoden," in *Kirkelig Maanedstidende*, 3 (1858), 65–71, 161–165; and 4 (1859), 6–16.

4. For a scholarly history of this school, Concordia Theological Seminary of the Lutheran Church—Missouri Synod, see Carl S. Meyer, *Log Cabin to Luther Tower; Concordia Seminary During One Hundred and Twenty-five Years; Toward a More Excellent Ministry, 1839–1964* (St. Louis, 1965). On relations between the Norwegian Synod and the Missouri Synod, see particularly Meyer, *Pioneers Find Friends*.

5. For an excellent complete account of the life and career of this leader of the Norwegian Synod, see Larsen, *Laur. Larsen: Pioneer College President*.

6. See Meyer, *Log Cabin to Luther Tower*, 40–42, for the events surrounding these changes.

7. For a scholarly treatment of the early history of this school, later known as Luther College, see David T. Nelson, *Luther College, 1861–1961* (Decorah, Iowa, 1961).

8. Friedrich August Schmidt (1837–1928), a native of Thuringia, served as a pastor of the Missouri Synod before becoming a professor at Luther College in 1861. Schmidt was later Norwegian professor at Concordia Seminary in St. Louis and professor at the Norwegian Synod's seminary in Madison, Wisconsin. After breaking with the Norwegian Synod, Schmidt became professor at the "Luthersk Presteskole" of the Anti-Missourian Brotherhood in Northfield, Minnesota; professor at Augsburg Seminary of the United Norwegian Lutheran Church; and professor at the United Church Seminary in St. Paul, Minnesota.

9. Johannes Bjerk Frich (1835–1908) later served as professor and president of the Synod's Luther Seminary.

10. Lyder Siewers (1830–1907) taught at Luther College from 1863–1877.

11. N.O. Brandt (see Lecture 2, note 10) taught at Luther College from 1865 to 1881.

12. For comments on the significance of the "Latin school" model, see Nelson, *Luther College*, 90–91.

13. *The Book of Concord* contains the confessional statements of the Lutheran church. The standard English edition is Tappert *et al.*, *The Book of Concord*.

14. Carl Ferdinand Wilhelm Walther (1811–1887) was the guiding spirit of the Missouri Synod during its first four decades. From among several introductions to Walther's life and career, see Martin Günther, *Dr. C.F. W. Walther: Lebensbild* (St. Louis, 1890); W.G. Polack, *The Story of C.F. W. Walther* (rev. ed., St. Louis, 1947); D.H. Steffens, *Doctor Carl Ferdinand Wilhelm Walther* (Philadelphia, 1917). A critical biography of Walther remains a *desideratum*.

15. Johann Konrad Wilhelm Löhe (1808–1872), a Bavarian Lutheran pastor, developed in the village of Neuendettelsau a center for the training of Lutheran pastors, teachers, and other emissaries to serve the church. For the intricate story of Löhe's relations to American Lutherans, see James L. Schaaf, *Wilhelm Löhe's Relation to the American Church: A Study in the History of Lutheran Mission* (Th.D. dissertation, Ruprecht-Karl-Universität zu Heidelberg, 1961).

For the distinction between the "theoretical" and the "practical" seminaries and the institutional history, see Meyer, *Log Cabin to Luther Tower*, 1–64.

16. Friedrich August Crämer (1812–1891), orginally serving in America under the auspices of Wilhelm Löhe (see note 15 above), later affiliated with the Missouri Synod and served that synod as pastor, teacher, and missionary to native Americans.

17. The Norwegian Synod honored this pledge for the years 1866–1874. F.A. Schmidt (see note 8 above) represented the Norwegian Synod on the faculty of Concordia Seminary from 1872 to 1876, when the Norwegian Synod took steps toward the establishment of its own seminary in Madison, Wisconsin. See Meyer, *Log Cabin to Luther Tower*, 60–61.

18. See Nelson, *Luther College*, 61–74, for a description of this structure. For an account of the festive dedication of this building, see "Indvielsen af den nye

Notes

Bygning for den norske Luthercollege i Decorah," in *Kirkelig Maanedstidende*, 10 (1865), 353–371.

19. This, of course, is to note a principal difference between the establishment from which the founders of the Norwegian Synod had come and the denomination which they organized in the United States.

20. The Koshkonong congregation, eventually to divide into several congregations, originated as the "Norwegian Lutheran Congregation in Dane and Jefferson counties" in Wisconsin. For the institutional history, see Norlie, ed., *Norsk lutherske menigheter i Amerika, 1843–1916*, 1 (Minneapolis, 1918), 95–98.

21. Ernst Ottmar Clöter (1825–1897), one of Wilhelm Löhe's emissaries to the United States, eventually affiliated with the Missouri Synod. Clöter served as missionary to Ojibway people at Gabitaweegama, fourteen miles north of Brainerd, Minnesota, and west of the Mississippi. An uprising there in August of 1862 caused the destruction of the mission station. Missionary work was resumed later at Crow Wing, Minnesota, but discontinued in 1868.

22. Eduard Raimund Baierlein (1819–1901), sent to the United States by Wilhelm Löhe, undertook a mission to the Ojibway people and was later sent to India where he served until 1866 in the service of the Leipzig Evangelical Lutheran Mission.

23. Ernst Gustav Hermann Miessler (1826–1916) came from Germany to the United States in 1851 to serve as a missionary to the Ojibway, among whom he worked until 1869. He later became a teacher and then a physician.

24. In the Lutheran catechetical tradition the Sixth Commandment ("You shall not commit adultery") is understood to apply broadly to sexual morals. See Luther's explanation of the Sixth Commandment in the Small Catechism in Tappert *et al.*, *The Book of Concord.*, 343.

25. See "De nordamerikanske Indianere og Hinduerne," in *Kirkelig Maanedstidende*, 10 (1863), 334–335.

26. The leaders of the Norwegian Synod generally took a high view of the office of public ministry and discouraged the use of lay preachers. They opposed establishment of a recognized office for such preachers. See pp. 125–131.

27. Members of the Church of Norway in the nineteenth century organized a number of voluntary organizations in support of various causes. Several are mentioned in Molland, *Norges kirkehistorie i det 19. århundre*. The Norwegian Synod, on the other hand, attempted to retain sponsorship and direction of such activities under the auspices of the Synod itself.

28. Preus probably refers here to *Kraft og saftfulde kjerne af de evangeliske sandheder, af Dr. Martin Luthers Kirke- og huus-postiller, indeholdende en fuldkommen forklaring over all søn-og fest-dages evangelier* (Madison, Wisconsin, 1857).

29. *Luthers folkebibliotek; udvalgte fuldstændige skrifter af Dr. Martin Luther til nytte og gavn for det lutherskekristenfolk nøiagtig oversatte og udgivne af den norske lutherforening i Amerika til udgivelse af Luthers skrifter for folket*, 3 vols. (Madison, Wisconsin, 1862–1873).

30. *Frelsens Olje. Herrens afskedstale over nadverdbordet og ved opbruddet til Gethsemane* (Madison, 1862); *Konkordiebogen eller den evangelisk-lutherske*

Kirkes bekjendelsesskrifter (Madison, 1866); *Frikirken, eller en af staten uafhængig evangelisk-luthersk steds-menigheds rette skikkelse* (Madison, 1867).

31. On *Kirkelige Maanedstidende*, see Lecture 1, note 16. *The Lutheran Watchman* appeared in 1866–1867 under the editorship of F.A. Schmidt.

32. Preus refers here to the "Scandinavian Evangelical Lutheran Augustana Synod in North America," organized in 1860. Initially this body included Norwegians, Swedes, and Danes. The Norwegian and Danish element and the Swedish element did not divide into separate church bodies until 1870, when they amicably parted ways. In that year the Dano-Norwegian group itself divided into two church bodies: the "Norwegian Augustana Synod" and the "Conference for the Norwegian-Danish Evangelical Lutheran Church in America." It is crucial to a proper understanding of Preus's comments on the "Augustana Synod" appearing here and elsewhere before 1870 to recall that he often refers primarily to its Norwegian-American members. For this history from a Norwegian-American point of view, see Nelson and Fevold, *The Lutheran Church Among Norwegian-Americans*, 1:191–238. For a Swedish-American perspective, see Arden, *Augustana Heritage*, 75–114, 134–142. See also Olson, *The Augustana Lutheran Church in America, 1846–1860*; Olson, *The Augustana Lutheran Church, 1860–1910*; Stephenson, *The Founding of the Augustana Synod, 1850–1860*; and Söderström, *Confession and Cooperation*. Preus finally associates the Augustana Synod with the doctrinal compromise entailed by the so-called Prussian Union, a uniting of Lutheran and Reformed churches effected in 1817 by decree of the king of Prussia, Frederick William III.

33. Peter Andreas Rasmussen (1829–1898) successively belonged to several Norwegian-American Lutheran bodies. In 1856 he left the ranks of Eielsen's Synod and became an independent pastor. From 1862 to 1887 he belonged to the Norwegian Synod. Later he joined the so-called "Anti-Missourian Brotherhood" and finally joined the United Norwegian Lutheran Church of America when it was formed in 1890. For Rasmussen's "friends," see note 35 below.

34. On Eielsen and his synod, see Lecture 1, note 10.

35. Nils Amlund (1830–1902) and John N. Fjeld (1818–1888) joined P.A. Rasmussen in affiliating with the Norwegian Synod during this period.

36. On the Augustana Synod, see note 32 above.

37. Ole Olsen Estrem (1835–1910) joined the Norwegian Synod in 1867. Abraham Jacobson (1836–1910) affiliated with the Norwegian Synod in 1868.

38. Omitted in the translation is an appended personal statement by Ole Olsen Estrem and Abraham Jacobson detailing their reasons for leaving the Augustana Synod. This statement appears in Preus's text on pp. 59–63. See *Beretning . . . den norsk-evangelisk-lutherske Kirke i Amerika . . . 1866*, 107.

Lecture 4

1. The quotation is from 2 Corinthians 12:9.

2. The quotation is from 1 John 4:1.

3. The reference is to Mark 6:11; Matthew 10:14; Luke 9:5, 10:11; Acts 13:51.

4. For a brief account of the early years of this congregation, see C.S. Ever-

son, "Sjømandsmissionen i New York," in Halvorsen, *Festskrift*, 308–313. See also Ottesen, "Om den indre Mission i New York By," in *Kirkelig Maanedstidende*, 10 (1863), 88–92, and Herman Amberg Preus, "Uddrag af Reiseberetning til Kirkeraadet fra H.A. Preus."

5. A repetition of the thematic reference to Acts 16:9–10.

6. Georg Christian Sibbern (1816–1901) was appointed chargé d' affaires in Washington in 1850 and resident minister in 1854. He returned to service in Norway in 1856.

7. Paul Christian Sinding (1812–1887) briefly served Danish immigrants in New York. For mention of this work among Danes in New York see Andersen, *Pastor Claus Laurits Clausen*, 242–244.

8. See above, p. 8.

9. Tufve Nilsson Hasselquist (1816–1891) was among the founding pastors of the Augustana Synod. "Petersen" has not been further identified.

10. On Ottesen, see Lecture 3, note 2.

11. On Schmidt, see Lecture 3, note 8.

12. "Anderson" has not been further identified.

13. Olof Gustaf Hedström (1803–1877) pursued missionary work among Scandinavian immigrants in New York harbor, giving counsel, holding meetings, and conducting worship aboard the ship "Bethel."

14. Ole Helland (1824–1892) was among the founders of Norwegian-American Methodism.

15. On *Kirkelig Maanedstidende*, see Lecture 1, note 16.

16. Preus's figures exceed the official totals indicated by the United States Census of 1870 which counted 682 Danes, 372 Norwegians, and 1,558 Swedes in New York. See *The Statistics of the United States . . . From the Original Returns of the Ninth Census (June 1, 1870)*, 1:388, 391. However, David C. Mauk, historian of the Scandinavian colony in New York, estimates the Scandinavian population in the city at twice the official number. See letter of David C. Mauk to Odd S. Lovoll, November 22, 1989.

17. On Hedström, see note 13 above. On Helland, see note 14 above.

18. The quotation is from Mark 16:18.

19. Erland Carlsson (1822–1893) and Andreas Andreen (Andrén) (1827–1880) were among the founding pastors of the Augustana Synod. For an account of Swedish-American Lutheran efforts in New York, see Gustav Andreen, "The Early Missionary Work of the Augustana Synod in New York City, 1865–1866," in *Augustana Historical Society Publications*, 2 (Rock Island, Illinois, 1932), 1–26.

20. The pastors of the Augustana Synod generally used the liturgical manual the *Kyrko-handbok, hwaruti tadgas, huru gudstjensten i swenska församlingar skall behandlas* of the Church of Sweden (adopted in 1809 and published in 1811), but gradually introduced changes reflecting the altered context of their North American church. Immigrant Swedish congregations often resisted use of the officially recognized *Den swenska psalmboken* of 1819, preferring to use instead the *Psalmbok* proposed for the Church of Sweden by Bishop J.H. Thomander and Dean P. Wieselgren. The Augustana Synod officially approved the use of this hymnal in 1878. For discussion of this history see Allan Arvastson, *Den thomander-*

wieselgrenska psalmboken, vol. 21 of Acta Historico-Ecclesiastica Suecana, ed. Hilding Pleijel (Stockholm, [1949]); Evald B. Lawson, "The Ministry," in Emmer Engberg *et al.*, eds., *Centennial Essays: Augustana Lutheran Church, 1860–1960* (Rock Island, Illinois, 1960), 150–168; Söderström, *Confession and Cooperation*, 168–170.

21. Ulrik Vilhelm Koren (1826–1910) and Kristian Magelssen (1839–1921) were pastors of the Norwegian Synod. Koren, one of the Synod's most able and vigorous theological polemicists, was a devoted advocate of Luther College and succeeded Herman Amberg Preus as president of the Norwegian Synod, serving from 1894 to 1910.

22. A pastor of the Norwegian Synod, Ole Juul (1838–1903) served in New York from 1866–1876.

23. The reference is to "Foreningen til Evangeliets Forkyndelse for skandinaviske Sømænd i fremmede Havne," organized in 1864.

24. Roman Catholic missionary Pierre Jean De Smet (1801–1873) was famed for his success in the West and his abilities as a mediator between native Americans and white settlers.

25. Preus reflects here not only the antagonism traditional between Lutherans and Roman Catholics in this period, but also the nativism characteristic of the Protestants in the United States in the middle of the nineteenth century.

26. An introduction to Norwegian-Danish Methodism in the United States is Arlow W. Andersen, *The Salt of the Earth: A History of Norwegian-Danish Methodism in America* (n.p., 1962).

27. Henry Melchior Mühlenberg (1711–1787), a German-American pastor, arrived in Pennsylvania in 1742 and was instrumental in organizing colonial Lutherans into the first North American synod, the Ministerium of Pennsylvania.

28. Familiarly known as the Ministerium of Pennsylvania, this group, organized in 1748, was the first synodical body to appear on the American Lutheran scene.

29. The General Synod of the Evangelical Lutheran Church in the United States of America was a federation of regional synods organized in 1820. For an illustration of the Norwegian Synod's severely critical attitude toward the General Synod, see Ottesen, "Blik i Generalsynoden."

30. The symbolical books of the Lutheran church include the several confessional statements included in Tappert *et al.*, *The Book of Concord*: the Apostles' Creed, the Nicene Creed, the Athanasian Creed, the Augsburg Confession, the Apology of the Augsburg Confession, the Smalcald Articles, the Treatise on the Power and Primacy of the Pope, the Small Catechism, the Large Catechism, and the Formula of Concord.

31. Charles Porterfield Krauth (1823–1883) was a leader of the conservative confessional revival among American Lutherans in the nineteenth century. He was the leading member of the original faculty of the Lutheran Theological Seminary at Philadelphia, founded in 1864, and an editor of the *Lutheran and Missionary*, published from 1861 to 1881.

32. "American Lutheranism" refers to a movement among Lutherans seeking to create a variant of the confessional Lutheran tradition specifically adjusted to the

North American context. This movement was the object of concerted opposition from other conservative, confessional Lutherans.

33. Benjamin Kurtz (1795–1865) and Samuel Simon Schmucker (1799–1873) were leaders of the "American Lutheran" movement.

34. The *Definite Platform, Doctrinal and Disciplinarian, for Evangelical Lutheran District Synods; Constructed in Accordance with the Principles of the General Synod* (Philadelphia [1855]) proposed an American recension of the Augsburg Confession, omitting from this confession elements its proponents considered antiquated remnants of Roman Catholic belief and practice. The *Definite Platform* was published anonymously, although many knew at the time of publication that its author was Samuel Simon Schmucker.

35. On the General Synod, see note 29 above.

36. The German Evangelical Lutheran Synod of Missouri, Ohio, and Other States was organized in 1847.

37. The German Evangelical Lutheran Ministerium in Ohio and the Neighboring States, known in its early history under a variety of names, was organized in 1818.

38. Conservative, confessional Lutherans objected to lodges and other secret societies on the basis of their secrecy and certain doctrines propounded by these organizations.

39. On Löhe, see Lecture 3, note 15. The Evangelical Lutheran Synod of Iowa was organized in 1854.

40. Johannes August Andreas Grabau (1804–1879), a German-American Lutheran pastor, was the founder and guiding spirit of the Synod of the Lutheran Church Emigrated from Prussia, commonly known as the Buffalo Synod, organized in 1845.

41. "Chiliasm" or "millenialism" denotes the belief that the church will rule on earth for a thousand years either before or after the return of Christ.

42. For the complex history of controversy between the Buffalo Synod and the Missouri Synod, see Roy A. Suelflow, "The Relations of the Missouri Synod with the Buffalo Synod up to 1866," in *Concordia Historical Institute Quarterly*, 27 (1954), 1–19, 57–73, 97–132.

43. On Grabau, see note 40 above.

44. On the journey of Ottesen and Brandt, see Lecture 3, note 2.

45. For a thorough critical study of this history, see Walter O. Forster, *Zion on the Mississippi: The Settlement of the Saxon Lutherans in Missouri, 1839–1841* (St. Louis, 1953).

46. On Walther and Crämer, see Lecture 3, note 14 and note 16. Friedrich Conrad Dietrich Wyneken (1810–1876) was the second president of the Missouri Synod. Wilhelm Sihler (1801–1885) also played a prominent role in the organization of the Missouri Synod.

47. The Missouri Synod began a "teachers' seminary" in Milwaukee, Wisconsin, in 1855. Later it was moved to Fort Wayne, Indiana, in 1857 and to Addison, Illinois, in 1864. The Lutheran Hospital in St. Louis was founded in 1858 by Johann Friedrich Bünger (1810–1882).

48. *Lehre und Wehre* appeared from 1855 to 1929. The Missouri Synod's church newspaper, *Der Lutheraner*, was published from 1844 to 1974. A journal

for schoolteachers, *Evangelisches Lutherisches Schulblatt*, appeared from 1865 to 1920.

49. Gottlieb Christoph Adolf von Harless (1806–1879), Friedrich Adolf Philippi (1809–1882), Karl Ströbel (1806–1879), and Friedrich August Brunn (1819–1895) were prominent conservative Lutheran confessionalists of the mid-nineteenth century in Germany.

50. This is probably a reference to a free conference held at Pittsburgh, Pennsylvania, from October 29 through November 4, 1857. The free conference was a device that permitted theologians to exchange views without officially representing their synods or churches.

51. This is a quotation from William A. Passavant, "The Recent Free Conference," in *The Missionary*, November 12, 1857.

LECTURE 5

1. On Eielsen and his synod, see Lecture 1, note 10.

2. For a brief description of this episode, see Nelson and Fevold, *The Lutheran Church Among Norwegian-Americans*, 1:80–81.

3. Eielsen's account of his ordination appears in *Morgenbladet*, January 18, 1862.

4. *Aftenposten*, 1867, no. 98. No surviving copy exists of this issue.

5. Paul Andersen (1821–1891), Ole [Aasen] Andrewson (1818–1885), and Ole Jensen Hatlestad (1823–1892) all served for a period as pastors of the Augustana Synod. The Franckean Synod was organized in 1837 in Minden, New York. It was frequently the object of criticism on the part of conservative, confessional Lutherans who took issue with its doctrinal stance and abolitionist posture.

6. On this defection from Eielsen, see Lecture 3, note 33.

7. For an English version of the constitution of the Eielsen Synod, see Nelson and Fevold, *The Lutheran Church Among Norwegian-Americans*, 1:337–343. The quotation is from this version, p. 337. The earliest complete Norwegian text of this document is "Kirke-Konstitution for den evangelisk-lutherske Kirke i Nord-Amerika," in *Kirkelig Tidende*, 3 (1851), 297–305.

8. Quoted in Nelson and Fevold, *The Lutheran Church Among Norwegian-Americans*, 1:337.

9. This is a reference to the Donatist schism of the fourth century in North Africa. Donatists characteristically insisted on a rigorist interpretation of church discipline intended to winnow pure from impure ministers and members of the church.

10. Lutheran pietists often used the language of the "little flock" to distinguish between converted and unconverted members of the visible church.

11. See the constitution of the Eielsen Synod as translated in Nelson and Fevold, *The Lutheran Church Among Norwegian-Americans*, 1:338.

12. Translated in Tappert *et al.*, *The Book of Concord*, 32.

13. In Norwegian Lutheran liturgical practice the words of absolution imparting the forgiveness of sins are often pronounced with the hands of the minister placed on the penitent's head.

14. The pronouncement of a conditional absolution makes reference to the

need for true repentance and faith on the part of the penitent. On absolution before the Lord's Supper, see Lecture 2, notes 2, 12, 13.

15. Article 8 of the Augsburg Confession teaches: "The sacraments are efficacious even if the priests who administer them are wicked men, for as Christ himself indicated, 'The Pharisees sit on Moses' seat.' " See Tappert *et al.*, *The Book of Concord*, 33.

16. For a discussion of debates over the text of the Apostles' Creed and related issues, see Rohne, *Norwegian-American Lutheranism Up to 1872*, 147–157.

17. In the *Altar Book* the phrase of the Apostles' Creed in question reads "one holy, Christian church" (*en Hellig, Christelig Kirke*). See *Forordnet alterbog udi Danmark og Norge* (Copenhagen, 1688), 328.

18. Article 14 states: "It is taught among us that nobody should publicly teach or preach or administer the sacraments in the church without a regular call." See Tappert *et al.*, *The Book of Concord*, 36.

19. Since the time of the Reformation, Lutherans have frequently debated what constitutes an "emergency" making necessary a breach of conventional church order.

20. This statement was presented to the Norwegian Synod by C.F.W. Walther of the Missouri Synod (see Lecture 3, note 14). See *Beretning . . . den norsk-evangelisk–lutherske Kirke i Amerika . . . 1862*, 12–19. For discussion of this report and the debate that surrounded it, see Nelson and Fevold, *The Lutheran Church Among Norwegian-Americans*, 1:163–168; Rohne, *Norwegian-American Lutheranism Up to 1872*, 158–179; Ylvisaker *et al.*, *Grace for Grace*, 137–142.

At the end of his statement Walther refers to a sentence from one of the Lutheran confessions, the "Treatise on the Power and Primacy of the Pope." Walther's citation probably refers to J.T. Müller, ed., *Die symbolischen Bücher der evangelisch-luterischen Kirche deutsch und lateinsich* (Stuttgart, 1860), 341. For an English version, see Tappert *et al.*, *The Book of Concord*, 331.

21. The original text of this series of theses is in *Beretning . . . den norsk-evangelisk-lutherske Kirke i Amerika . . . 1862*, 20.

22. In the Lutheran catechetical tradition the Third Commandment ("Remember the Sabbath day, to keep it holy") is interpreted not so as to oblige Christians to worship on Saturday or Sunday but as a command to Christians to hear and honor the Word of God. See Luther's explanation of the Third Commandment in the Small Catechism in Tappert *et al.*, *The Book of Concord*, 342. For discussion of this controversy, see Rohne, *Norwegian-American Lutheranism Up to 1872*, 223–226; Ylvisaker *et al.*, *Grace for Grace*, 143–147.

This position on the observance of the sabbath markedly set these Lutherans off from American inheritors of Reformed traditions requiring strict observance of a Sunday sabbath.

23. For the text of Article 28 of the Augsburg Confession, see Tappert *et al.*, *The Book of Concord*, 281–285.

24. For the original text of this series of theses, see *Beretning . . . den norsk-evangelisk-lutherske Kirke i Amerika . . . 1862*, 22–23. For the final discussion and adoption of these statements, see *Beretning . . . den norsk-evangelisk-lutherske Kirke i Amerika . . . 1861*, 27–46.

25. On the Fourth Commandment, see Lecture 1, note 23.

26. Norwegian-Americans used a variety of editions of Pontoppidan's *Explanation* of Luther's Small Catechism. Eielsen preferred the longer or "doubled" (*dobbelte*) form of the *Explanation* to the shorter version used by some Synod pastors. Eielsen apparently used an edition of the longer version from which the final seven articles of the Augsburg Confession, the "Articles about Matters in Dispute, in which an Account is Given of the Abuses which Have Been Corrected," were omitted.

An oral tradition records that Eielsen carried *Sandhed til gudfrygtighed udi en eenfoldig og efter muelighed kort, dog tilstrækkelig forklaring* (Copenhagen, 1775) to New York in 1842 in order to secure an edition for use in America. This edition does not contain the text of the Augsburg Confession. The resulting edition of Pontoppidan's catechism, *Sandhed til gudfrygtighed* (New York, 1842), does, however, contain the text of the first twenty-one artlicles of the Augsburg Confession. On Eielsen's efforts toward the production of catechisms in the United States, see Nelson and Fevold, *The Lutheran Church Among Norwegian-Americans* 1:77–78.

27. On Rasmussen, see Lecture 3, note 33.

28. Andreas P. Aaserod (1823–1907) served as a pastor in Eielsen's Synod and later in the Norwegian-Danish Conference. For brief comments on this school, located at Deerfield, Wisconsin, see Rohne, *Norwegian-American Lutheranism Up to 1872*, 186–187.

29. On Rasmussen and his defection from Eielsen, see Lecture 3, notes 33 and 34.

LECTURE 6

1. On Andersen, Andrewson, and Hatlestad, see Lecture 5, note 5.

2. Lutherans regard baptism as an event in which the regeneration of the person baptized is effected.

3. The quotation is from *Constitution and Standing Ordinances of the Franckean Evangelic Lutheran Synod; Revised and Adopted June, 1847 together with a Discipline Recommended as a Guide for the Churches* (Norwich, New York, 1849), 45. The quotation is from the original English version.

4. Lars Paul Esbjörn (1808–1870) was among the founders of the Augustana Synod. He returned to a ministry in Sweden in 1863.

5. The Evangelical Lutheran Synod of Northern Illinois was organized in 1851 and affiliated with the General Synod in 1853.

6. See "Rev. P. Andersen's Address at the Anniversary of the Home Mission Society at Reading, Pa.," in *The Missionary*, June 11, 1857. See also Ottesen, "Blik i Generalsynoden," 117.

7. Sidney Levi Harkey (b. 1827) taught at Augustana College from 1868–1870. William M. Reynolds (1812–1876), previously president of Pennsylvania College and Capital University, served as president of Illinois State University from 1857 to 1860. He later became an Episcopalian.

8. For a brief report of this meeting of July 7–8, 1859, see "Den Skandinavisk–lutherske Conferents," in *Kirkelig Maanedstidende*, 4 (1859), 160. A longer

Notes

account appeared as "Forhandlinger i den skandinavisk-evangelisk-lutherske Conferents, afholdt i Chicago i vor Frelsers Kirke den 7de og 8de Juli 1859," in *Kirkelig Maanedstidende*, 5 (1860), 39–43. A continuation of this report is announced but seems not to have appeared. The Swedish account of this meeting is "Protokoll hållet wid Skandinaviska Ev. Lutherska konferentsmötet i Chicago den 7 och 8 Juli 1859 i Norska 'Waar Frelsers Kirke,'" in *Hemlandet, det Gamla och det Nya*, (August 17 and 24, 1859). See also Stephenson, *The Founding of the Augustana Synod, 1850–1860*, 84–87.

9. Olof Christian Telemak Andrén (1824–1870) served as a pastor of the Augustana Synod from 1856 to 1860, when he returned to Sweden.

10. On Article 14 of the Augsburg Confession see Lecture 5, note 18.

11. This is likely a reference to the decisions of an extraordinary meeting of the ministerium of the Augustana Synod held at Rockford, Illinois, from August 20 to August 24, 1866. The report of this meeting, "Ministerii Extra Möte i Rockford, Ill., 20–24 Augusti, 1866," is appended to the regular report of the Augustana Synod for the year 1867. See *Protokoll . . . Augustana Synodens åttonde årsmöte . . . 1866*, 36–38.

NB: This and all following references to the official reports of the Augustana Synod are to the editions reprinted in 1917.

12. For this exchange, see "Forhandlinger ved Mödet i vor Frelsers Kirke," in *Kirkelig Maanedstidende*, 5 (1860), 308–311, 321–338; "Til Hemlandet," in *Kirkelig Maanedstidende*, 5 (1860), 294; "Ny uppfinding i Theologien," in *Hemlandet, det Gamla och det Nya*, September 5, 1860.

13. The reference is uncertain.

14. See "De Svenske og Norske i Nordre Illinois Synoden," in *Kirkelig Maanedstidende*, 5 (1860), 167. For the Swedish report, see "Protokoll hållet wid de förenade Mississippi- och Minnesota-Konferensen sammanträde i Swenska Lutherska kyrkan i Chicago den 23–27 April 1860," in *Hemlandet, det Gamla och det Nya*, May 2, 1860.

15. On the founding of the Augustana Synod, see Lecture 3, note 32. An extended discussion of relations between the Norwegian Synod and the new Augustana Synod is in Söderström, *Confession and Cooperation*, 56–93.

When the Norwegians and Swedes initiated moves toward separation from the Synod of Northern Illinois, the Norwegian Synod made overtures toward union with the departing Scandinavians. These efforts were rebuffed, and the Augustana Synod emerged as an independent denomination. For accounts of these events, see "Til de Skandinavisk-lutherske Præster i Amerika," in *Kirkelig Maanedstidende*, 5 (1860), 246–247, and "Hvorfor kunde der ei blive nogen Skandinavisk Luthersk Conference den 18de Octbr?" in *Kirkelig Maanedstidende*, 5 (1860), 347–349, 357–361.

The new synod quickly became the object of sharp criticism on the part of the Norwegian Synod. The year after the formation of the Augustana Synod, Herman Amberg Preus published the most extended of these attacks. See "Augustana Synoden," in *Kirkelig Maanedstidende*, 6 (1861), 79–87, 179–186, 342–350. Side by side with one installment of this essay is an article by A.C. Preus critical of the Augustana Synod's constitution. See "Augustana Synodens Constitution," in *Kirkelig Maanedstidende*, 6 (1861), 172–179.

16. Preus's figures are in error in one instance. The Augustana Synod numbered 5,507 baptized members in 1861. See *Protokoll . . . Augustana Synoden . . . 1861*, 39.

17. For a brief discussion of this episode and its background, see Lovoll, *A Century of Urban Life*, 54–65.

18. See *Protokoll . . . Augustana Synoden . . . 1860*, 14–15.

19. Augustana Seminary, later Augustana College and Theological Seminary, was originally located in Chicago, Illinois. It was moved to Paxton, Illinois, in 1863. It was later moved to Rock Island, Illinois. Augustana Theological Seminary finally returned to Chicago as a result of the negotiations toward merger which produced the Lutheran Church in America in 1962. A scholarly history of Augustana Theological Seminary is G. Everett Arden, *The School of the Prophets: The Background and History of Augustana Theological Seminary, 1860–1960* (Rock Island, Illinois, 1960).

20. William Kopp (1820–1868) taught at Paxton from 1864 to 1867.

21. On Muus, see Lecture 1, note 14. The founder of Saint Olaf College in Northfield, Minnesota, Muus eventually returned to Norway. For the remark on Hasselquist, see, "Fra Nordamerika," 375.

22. John Olsen (1834–1911) taught at Paxton from 1866 to 1867.

23. On petitions to the king and these offerings, see Oscar N. Olson, *Olof Christian Telemak Andrén: Ambassador of Good Will*, Augustana Historical Society Publications, 14 (Rock Island, Illinois, 1954), 23–44, 78–97. In addition to permitting offerings in the congregations of the Swedish church, the King donated to the Augustana Synod several thousand volumes from his personal library.

24. The Gustavus Adolphus Society was a Swedish branch of an organization originally founded in Germany in 1834 to aid needy Protestants inside and outside Germany. The Augustana Synod received help from the Gothenburg branch of the society, founded in 1854. See *Protokoll . . . Augustana Synoden . . . 1861*, 28–30. This arrangement was particularly offensive to the Norwegian Synod because of the fact that the German society had Reformed as well as Lutheran sponsors and was to the Norwegians an example of "unionism," ecclesiastical cooperation they considered inappropriate on the basis of outstanding doctrinal differences. See Herman Amberg Preus, "Augustana Synoden," 348–349.

25. On this commercial arrangement, see Arden, *The School of the Prophets*, 129–135, 168–173.

26. For these and other figures, see *Protokoll . . . Augustana Synoden . . . 1865*, 22.

27. See *Protokoll . . . Augustana Synoden . . . 1864*, 12.

28. On Carlsson, see Lecture 4, note 19.

29. *Hemlandet, det Gamla och det Nya* appeared from 1855 to 1914. This soon became a primarily political journal. *Det Rätta Hemlandet* (later *Det Rätta Hemlandet och Missionsbladet*), a religious journal, began publication in 1855 and in 1869 combined with the church monthly, *Augustana*, to become *Det Rätta Hemlandet och Augustana*. The title was changed to *Augustana* in 1889 with publication continuing until 1956.

30. Samson Madsen Krogness (1830–1894) served as a pastor of the Augustana Synod until 1870 when he affiliated with the Norwegian Augustana Synod.

Notes

He was a pastor of the United Norwegian Lutheran Church from 1890 until his death. *Den norske Lutheraner* appeared from 1866 to 1869 and was succeeded by journals bearing a variety of titles. For the lineage of this periodical, see Louis Voigt, ed., *Lutheran Serials Checklist* (Springfield, Ohio, 1971).

31. For the complete text of the constitution of the Augustana Synod, see *Protokoll . . . Augustana Synoden . . . 1860*, 17–24. For an historical study of this document, which appears originally to have been written in English and then translated into Swedish, see Conrad Bergendoff, "The Sources of the Original Constitution of the Augustana Synod," in *Augustana Historical Society Publications*, 5 (Rock Island, Illinois, 1935), 85–106. For commentary from the Norwegian Synod on this document, see A.C. Preus, "Augustana Synodens Constitution."

32. This is a reference to Article 8 of the Augsburg Confession. See Tappert *et al.*, *The Book of Concord*, 32.

33. This is a reference to Article 5 of the Augsburg Confession. See Tappert *et al.*, *The Book of Concord*, 31.

34. *Protokoll . . . Augustana Synoden . . . 1860*, 17.

35. *Protokoll . . . Augustana Synoden . . . 1860*, 21.

36. *Protokoll . . . Augustana Synoden . . . 1860*, 24.

37. *Protokoll . . . Augustana Synoden . . . 1860*, 21.

38. This is a reference to I John 4:1.

39. Carl Johan Peter Petersen (1825–1897) served as a pastor of the Augustana Synod from 1861 to 1866. Along with a majority of his congregation in Chicago, he joined the Norwegian Synod in 1866. He served that body until he returned to Norway in 1873. See note 46 below. For Petersen's account of the events that led to his affiliation with the Norwegian Synod, see *Hvad jeg oplevede under de 6 förste aar af min virksomhed i Amerika* (Privately printed, 1867).

40. *Protokoll . . . Augustana Synod . . . 1860*, 21–22.

41. Preus does not identify the document from which he quotes. He appears, however, to refer to "Proposal for a Constitution for Ev. Luth. Congregations in North America" recommended by the United Chicago and Mississippi Conference of the Ev. Luth Church in Chicago, March 18–23, 1857. An English version of this document may be consulted in *Selected Documents Dealing with the Organization of the First Congregations and the First Conferences of the Augustana Synod and their Growth Until 1860*, 2 vols., Augustana Historical Society Publications, 10 (Rock Island, Illinois, 1944), 1:125. For the Swedish text, see "Förslag till Constitution för Evangelisk-Lutherska församlingar i Norra Amerika," in "Historiska dokument rörande de svenska ev.-luth. församlingarna i N. Amerika före Augustana-synodens organisation 1860," in *Tidskrift för Svensk Ev. Luth. Kyrkohistoria i N. Amerika och för Teologiska och Kyrkliga Frågor*, 1 (1898), 77–82.

42. "Proposal for a Constitution for Ev. Luth. Congregations," 121.

43. *Protokoll . . . Augustana Synoden . . . 1860*, 22.

44. *Protokoll . . . Augustana Synoden . . . 1860*, 14–15.

45. "Proposal for a Constitution for Ev. Luth. Congregations," 123.

46. "Proposal for a Constitution for Ev. Luth. Congregations," 123. When C.J.P. Petersen defected from the Augustana Synod to join the Norwegian Synod he persuaded a majority of the Chicago congregation to leave the Augustana Synod and to lay claim to the property of the congregation. A minority protested the right

to the property in the courts and the case made its way to the Illinois Supreme Court. The court decided in favor of the majority. See Lovoll, *A Century of Urban Life*, 64–65, for a brief description of this episode. See also note 39 above.

47. The source of this quotation has not been certainly identified. This is possibly a reference to a passage in a report to the Gustavus Adolphus Society prepared in 1862. For an English version of this document see "The Report: The Scandinavian Evangelical Lutheran Augustana Synod in North America, its conditions and activities during the first year of its existence, from June 1860 to the same date 1861," in Olson, *Olof Christian Telemak Andrén*, 93.

48. For brief comments on this matter, see Lovoll, *A Century of Urban Life*, 61–65, and Lawson, "The Ministry." See also Lecture 4, note 20, and Lecture 7, note 53. Omitted here is the statement of the Norwegian Synod on the case of C.J.P. Petersen (see notes 29 and 40 above). The omitted passage is found in Preus's text, pp. 109–113. See also "Erklæring i Anledning af de mod C.J.P. Peterson førte offentlige Klagemaal og Beskyldninger og over Augustanasynodens Dom over ham, paa Begjær Deacons for den første norsk-evangel. luth. Menighed i Chicago, afgiven af H.A. Preus," in *Kirkelig Maanedstidende*, 11 (1866), 289–301, 330–338. This case is extensively documented in the official reports of the Synod and in the archives of Luther College in Decorah, Iowa.

49. Johan Hveding (1832–1866) served in Chicago from 1865–1866. The Norwegian Synod followed the practice of admitting to ordination only candidates for the ministry with calls to congregations.

50. On Hatlestad, see Lecture 5, note 5.

51. On Hveding and Andrewson, see note 49 above and Lecture 5, note 5. Peter H. Petersen (d. 1873) served in Chicago from 1857–1858 and in Leland, Illinois, from 1859–1861. Amon (Amund) Johnson (1838–1897) served in Leland, Illinois, from 1862 to 1865.

52. On Hveding and Krogness, see notes 49 and 30 above.

53. In the Reformed tradition the words "Jesus says" are often added to the words "This is my Body . . . " and "This is my blood . . . " used at the time of the distribution of the Holy Communion. Conservative Lutherans objected to the use of this formula on the grounds that it indicated concessions to Calvinist or Zwinglian doctrine.

On conditional as opposed to unconditional absolution, see Lecture 2, note 12 and Lecture 5, note 14.

The Lutheran tradition generally calls for sponsors rather than parents to present a child for baptism. The baptismal rite requires the sponsors to renounce the Devil and all his work and ways before reciting the Apostles' Creed. For the traditional baptismal formulary, see *Forordnet alterbog udi Danmark og Norge*, 323–334. For a characteristic exchange over this matter, see Ottesen, "Forsvar for den norske Alterbog Formularer ved Sakramenternes Forvaltning," in *Kirkelig Maanedstidende*, 7 (1862), 9–13, and C.J.P. Petersen, "Noget, der kan tjene til Forsvar for den Norske Alterbogs Daabs-Formular," in *Kirkelig Maanedstidende*, 12 (1867), 81–86.

For extended commentary on these questions by Herman Amberg Preus, see "Augustana Synoden," 342–348.

Notes

LECTURE 7

1. See above, pp. 125–131.

2. See above, pp. 131–134.

3. For a brief account of this conference, held on July 17–18, 1863, in Chicago, see "Den skandinaviske Konferents i Chicago," in *Kirkelig Maanedstidende*, 8 (1863), 317–318.

4. Lutheran theology teaches that the Word of God actually effects the regeneration of the ungodly. This is reflected in the Lutheran doctrine of baptism which maintains that it is the Word of God rather than water alone which brings about the new birth of the person baptized.

5. Lutheran theology teaches that the Law of God has two uses: the ordering of the creation and the working of repentance. Some theologians teach that the Law has a third use as a guide to the Christian life.

6. See I Peter 1:23 and James 1:18.

7. For a detailed account of this meeting, held at Jefferson Prairie Lutheran Church in Rock county, Wisconsin, see "Historisk Oversigt over Striden mellem Augustanasynoden og den norske Synode om Læren om Absolutionen," in *Kirkelig Maaedstidende*, 12 (1867), 337–349. For discussion of this controversy, not finally resolved among Norwegian-American Lutherans until 1906, see Lecture 2, note 17.

8. On this series of theses, see Lecture 2, note 17. Omitted from the translation are a series of proof texts from Luther and the Lutheran confessions. They appear in Preus's text on pages 116–118.

9. Lutheran theology teaches that the spoken Word of God is an effective means of grace.

10. See "Historisk Oversigt over Striden mellem Augustanasynoden og den norske Synode om Læren om Absolutionen," 342.

11. See "Historisk Oversigt over Striden mellem Augustanasynoden og den norske Synode om Læren om Absolutionen," 339, 343. On Carlsson, see Lecture 4, note 19.

12. The actual protocol of this meeting, by mutual agreement between the representatives of the Augustana Synod and the Norwegian Synod, was not published. While, according to the Norwegian Synod, theses in the conventional form were not adopted, the two parties did agree to formulations of their different positions. Accounts vary as to wording of this statement. See "Historisk Oversigt over Striden mellem Augustanasynoden og den norske Synode om Læren om Absolutionen," 342, and J.A. Bergh, *Den norske lutherske kirkes historie i Amerika*, 174.

13. Preus here appends the text of an article on this topic by U.V. Koren (see Lecture 4, note 2). Omitted from the translation, it is found in Preus's text on pp. 122–130. The original text of Koren's article, "Et venligt Ord i en vigtig Strid," is in *Kirkelig Maanedstidende*, 12 (1867), 113–122.

14. On chiliasm, see Lecture 4, note 21.

15. Some Christian millenialists teach that in the last days the Jews will come to faith in Christ and return to their ancestral home in Palestine. The quotation is

from "Judemissionen," in *Det Rätta Hemlandet och Missionsbladet*, 11 (1861), 121.

16. See Tappert *et al.*, *The Book of Concord*, 38–39.

17. Blegen, "The Slavery Controversy and the Church," in *Norwegian Migration to America: The American Transition*, 418–453, remains an excellent introduction to the Norwegian Synod's controversy over slavery. An extensive recent monograph on the topic is Haraldsø, *Slaveridebatten i Den norske synode. En undersøkelse av slaveridebatten i Den norske synode i USA i 1860-årene med særlig vekt på debattens kirkelig-teologiske aspekter* (Oslo, 1988). See also Nelson and Fevold, *The Lutheran Church Among Norwegian-Americans*, 1:169–179, and Rohne, *Norwegian American Lutheranism Up to 1872*, 202–222; Ylvisaker *et al.*, *Grace for Grace*, 148–155.

18. See "Ministerii Extra Möte i Rockford, Ill., 20–24 Augusti 1866," 38, as appended to *Protokoll . . . Augustana Synoden . . . 1867*.

19. On Clausen, see Lecture 1, note 6. Clausen's role in the slavery debate is ably presented in Blegen, "The Slavery Controversy and the Church," and in Haraldsø, *Slaveridebatten i Den norske Synode*.

20. *Beretning . . . den norsk-evangelisk-lutherske Kirke i Amerika . . . 1861*, 37–38.

21. *Beretning . . . den norsk-evangelisk-lutherske Kirke i Amerika . . . 1861*, 38.

22. *Beretning . . . den norsk-evangelisk-lutherske Kirke i Amerika . . . 1861*, 38.

23. On A.C. Preus, see Lecture 1, note 11. The Norwegian Synod published the opinion of the Christiania theological faculty in 1866. See "Brevvexling med det theologiske Fakultet i Anledning af Skriftens Lære om Slaveri," in *Beretning . . . den norsk-evangelisk-lutherske Kirke i Amerika . . . 1866*, 40–45.

24. See "Brevvexling med det theologiske Fakultet i Anledning af Skriftens Lære om Slaveri," 45–57.

25. See "Brevvexling med det theologiske Fakultet i Anledning af Skriftens Lære om Slaveri," 61–66.

26. For a detailed study of Clausen's response, see Haraldsø, *Slaveridebatten i Den norske synode*, 116–165.

27. Gibbon estimated the population of the Roman empire at 120 million and suggested that 60 million of this population were slaves. See Edward Gibbon, *The Decline and Fall of the Roman Empire* (Modern Library edition, New York, 1932), 37–38.

28. The "Weimar Bible," which appeared in a number of editions, was a widely read annotated version of the Scripture. Knud Gislesen's *Dr. Martin Luthers liden catechismus* was published in several editions after it first appeared in 1844 and was widely used in Norway.

29. Both H.A. Preus and C.L. Clausen visited Norway in 1867 and spent an evening discussing slavery with Gisle Johnson (1822–1894) of the Christiania theological faculty. See "Professor Johnsons Erklæring," in *Beretning . . . den norsk-evangelisk-lutherske Kirke i Amerika . . . 1867*, 86; *Historisk fremstilling af den strid, som i aarene 1861 til 1868 indenfor den norske Synode i*

Amerika har været ført i anledning af skriftens lære om slaveri (Madison, 1868), 47; Clausen, *Gjenmæle mod kirkeraadet for den norske synode i anledning af dets skrift kaldet "Historisk fremstilling af den strid som i aarene 1861 til 1868 indenfor den norske synode i Amerika har været ført i anledning af skriftens lære om slaveri"* (Chicago, 1869), 76–80. The latter two works are summary statements on the part of the church council of the Norwegian Synod and C.L. Clausen respectively.

30. See "Beretning om det sjette ordentlige Synodemøde for den norsk-evangelisk lutherske Kirke i Amerika afholdt i Rock River Kirke fra 10de til 17de June 1863," in *Kirkelig Maanedstidende*, 8 (1863), 301–302, 311.

31. Ole Olsen Estrem and Abraham Jacobson (see Lecture 3, note 28) and C.J.P. Petersen (see Lecture 6, note 39) all left the Augustana Synod in 1866 and eventually affiliated with the Norwegian Synod.

32. Preus refers to John Olsen (see Lecture 6, note 22), Samson Madsen Krogness (see Lecture 6, note 30) and Johannes Møller Eggen (1841–1913).

33. It was common in Norway for theological candidates waiting for calls to the parish ministry to serve for a time as schoolmasters, as had Herman Amberg Preus before coming to the United States.

APPENDIX I

1. See above, p. 41. See also Lecture 1, note 12.

2. See *Beretning . . . den norsk-evangelisk-lutherske Kirke i Amerika . . . 1861*, 41, 44–48.

3. See *Beretning . . . den norsk-evangelisk-lutherske Kirke i Amerika . . . 1863*, 46–47. On Koren, see Lecture 4, note 21. On Schmidt see Lecture 3, note 8. On Larsen, see Lecture 2, note 10.

4. For this draft and the spirited discussion that followed its presentation, see *Beretning . . . den norsk-evangelisk-lutherske Kirke i Amerika . . . 1865*, 33–36, 16–32.

5. See *Beretning . . . den norsk-evangelisk-lutherske Kirke i Amerika*, 26–32.

6. See *Beretning . . . den norsk-evangelisk-lutherske Kirke i Amerika . . . 1867*, 11–17.

7. See *Beretning . . . Synoden for den norsk-evangelisk-lutherske Kirke i Amerika . . . 1868*, 54.

8. See *Beretning . . . Synoden for den norsk-evangelisk-lutherske Kirke i Amerika . . . 1868*, 53–57.

9. "Constitution of the Synod for the Norwegian Evangelical Lutheran Church in America," in *The Lutheran Watchman*, 2 (1867), 115–117.

APPENDIX II

1. H.A. Preus, "Den lutherske Kirke i Nordamerika," in *Luthersk Kirketidende*, 11 (1868), 17–26.

2. On the Missouri Synod, see Lecture 3, note 3.

3. For a brief introduction to the history of the Buffalo Synod, see Paul H. Buehring, "The Buffalo Synod," in *The Spirit of the American Lutheran Church*

(Columbus, Ohio, 1940), 15–33. A study of Buffalo's early history by a participant is Heinrich von Rohr, "Der Entstehung, Auswanderung, Ansiedlung und kirchliche Entwicklung der in den Jahren 1839 und 1843 aus Preussen nach Nordamerika ausgewanderten evangelisch-lutherischen Kirchen oder Gemeinden, jetzt als Synode von Buffalo bekannt," in *Kirchliches Informatorium*, 15 (April 15, 1867) serially through 19 (April 1, 1872). A later, more complete history is Ernst Denef, "Die Geschichte der Buffalo Synode," in *Die Wachende Kirche*, 54 (June 15, 1920) serially through 63 (November, 1929).

4. For an account of this figure's stormy life, see Johann A. Grabau, "Johann Andreas August Grabau," in *Concordia Historical Institute Quarterly*, 23 (1950), 10–17, 66–74, 176–181; 24 (1951), 35–39, 74–79, 124–132; 25 (1952), 49–71. See also Alfred H. Ewald, "Buffalo (1845): From a German Jail," in Lutz, *Church Roots*, 41–59.

5. "Senior" is a technical term, similar to "president" or "bishop," used by Lutherans to designate the office of oversight and administration.

6. On the history of controversy between the Buffalo Synod and the Missouri Synod, see Suelflow, "The Relations of the Missouri Synod with the Buffalo Synod up to 1866."

7. For the record of this colloquy, see *Das Buffaloer Colloquium, abgehalten vom 20. November bis 5. Dezember 1866, das ist, die schliesslichen Erklärungen der die Synode von Buffalo und die von Missouri, Ohio u.a. Staaten vertretenden Colloquenten über die bisher zwischen beiden Synoden streitigen und besprochenen Lehren* (St. Louis, 1866). For an historical account of this conference by a participant, see Chr. Hochstetter, *Die Geschichte der Evangelisch-lutherischen Missouri-Synode in Nord-Amerika und ihrer Lehrkämpfe von der sächsischen Auswanderung im Jahre 1838 an bis zum Jahre 1884* (Dresden, 1885), 256–278.

The leaders of the Norwegian Synod followed this and succeeding events in the Buffalo Synod with intense interest. See "The Colloquium at Buffalo," in *The Lutheran Watchman*, 2 (1867), 9–10; "Elucidation of the Final Declarations arrived at in the Buffalo Colloquy," in *The Lutheran Watchman*, 2 (1867), 33–35, 49–53, 81–83, 97–100; "Pastor Grabau og Buffalo Synoden," in *Kirkelig Maanedstidende*, 12 (1867), 257–264.

8. On Walther and Wyneken, see Lecture 3, note 14 and Lecture 4, note 46. Heinrich Christian Schwann (1819–1905), pastor of the Missouri Synod, served as its president from 1878 to 1899. Heinrich Karl Georg von Rohr (1797–1874) and Christian Hochstetter (1828–1905) were among the earliest pastors of the Buffalo Synod.

9. *Das Buffaloer Colloquium*, 31–32.

10. Heinrich Karl Georg von Rohr and Friedrich G. Maschhopp organized the von Rohr Synod in 1866. This small body continued to exist until 1877.

11. For the invitation to this meeting, see "Aufforderung," in *Kirchliches Informatorium*, 15 (1867), 13. The record of this meeting is "Zehnter Synodalbrief der lutherischen Synode von Buffalo, versammel zu Buffalo, N.Y. vom 26 Febr. zum 1 März 1867," in "Beilage zum Informatorium No. 3," appended to *Kirchliches Informatorium*, 15 (March 1, 1867).

12. For the original text of these resolutions, see "Zehnter Synodalbrief," 3.

13. On the "Office of the Keys," see Lecture 1, note 17.

14. For the original text of these resolutions, see "Zehnter Synodalbrief," 3–4.

15. The Buffalo Synod formally severed all relations with the Missouri Synod in 1859. On this episode, see Suelflow, "The Relations of the Missouri Synod with the Buffalo Synod up to 1866," 125.

16. The Buffalo Synod published its official acts in *Synodalbriefe* or "synodical letters."

17. Grabau and his colleagues, of course, maintained that they constituted the original Buffalo Synod.

18. See above, pp. 114–115.

19. This is probably a reference to Ludwig W. Habel, originally a pastor of the Missouri Synod.

20. On the General Synod, see Lecture 4, note 29. A "union" church refers to a body to which Protestants of both the Lutheran and Reformed confessions belong.

21. On "American Lutheranism," see Lecture 4, note 32.

22. For a brief introduction to the complex institutional history that follows, see August R. Suelflow and E. Clifford Nelson, "Following the Frontier, 1840–1875," in Nelson, *The Lutherans in North America*, 210–251.

23. On the formation and history of this body, see William Alexander Good, "A History of the General Council of the Evangelical Lutheran Church in North America," (Ph.D. dissertation, Yale University, 1967). A valuable narrative and collection of documentary material is S.E. Ochsenford, *Documentary History of the General Council of the Evangelical Lutheran Church in North America* (Philadelphia, 1912).

24. On Schmidt and Koren, see Lecture 3, note 8 and Lecture 4, note 21. For an editorial assessment of this meeting from the press of the Norwegian Synod, see "The Recent Convention at Reading, Pa.," in *The Lutheran Watchman*, 2 (1867), 3–5.

25. These statements are quoted from the original English text conveniently accessible in Ochsenford, *A Documentary History of the General Council*, 136–139.

26. The texts of the constitution and bylaws are conveniently accessible in Ochsenford, *Documentary History of the General Council*, 178–187. For observations on this meeting from the perspective of the Norwegian Synod, see "Det förste Möde af 'the General Council,' " in *Kirkelig Maanedstidende*, 13 (1868), 33–44.

27. Preus's figures are in error in one instance. The English Synod of Ohio numbered 30 rather than 11 congregations. See Ochsenford, *Documentary History of the General Council*, 172.

28. The following is a paraphrase of the Ohio Synod's questions. For the original text and the response of the General Council, see Ochsenford, *Documentary History of the General Council,* 154–156.

29. A thorough study of the ensuing debate over the so-called "Four Points" is Donald Lester Huber, "The Controversy Over Pulpit and Altar Fellowship in the General Council of the Evangelical Lutheran Church, 1866–1889" (Th.D. dissertation, Duke University, 1971). See also Dorris Aldo Flesner, "The Galesburg Rule: A Study of Lutheran Exclusivism" (M.A. thesis, University of Chicago, 1953).

30. For the documents from the Missouri and Iowa synods along with the Council's responses, see Ochsenford, *Documentary History of the General Council*, 155–163.

31. This is a paraphrase of the official response of the General Council. See Ochsenford, *Documentary History of the General Council*, 155–156.

32. The source of this quotation has not been identified.

33. Preus translates here a quotation from "The General Council, the Joint Synod of Ohio, and the Synod of Iowa," in *The Lutheran and Missionary*, December 12, 1867. Quotation from the English original.

Index

231